Oracle Warehouse Builder 11gR2: Getting Started 2011

Extract, Transform, and Load data to build a dynamic, operational data warehouse

Bob Griesemer

PUBLISHING

BIRMINGHAM - MUMBAI

Oracle Warehouse Builder 11gR2: Getting Started 2011

First published: April 2011

Production Reference: 2100511

Published by Packt Publishing Ltd.
32 Lincoln Road
Olton
Birmingham, B27 6PA, UK.

ISBN 978-1-849683-44-9

www.packtpub.com

Cover Image by Natasha (natashapnini@gmail.com)

Credits

Author
Bob Griesemer

Reviewers
Ehsun Behravesh
David Allan

Acquisition Editor
Amey Kanse

Development Editor
Susmita Panda

Technical Editor
Neha Damle

Indexer
Monica Ajmera Mehta

Editorial Team Leader
Vinodhan Nair

Project Team Leader
Priya Mukherji

Project Coordinator
Srimoyee Ghoshal

Proofreader
Aaron Nash

Graphics
Geetanjali Sawant

Production Coordinator
Alwin Roy

Cover Work
Alwin Roy

About the Author

Bob Griesemer has over 27 years of software and database engineering/DBA experience in both government and industry, solving database problems, designing and loading data warehouses, developing code, leading teams of developers, and satisfying customers. He has been working in various roles involving database development and administration with the Oracle Database with every release since Version 6 of the database from 1993 to the present. He has also been performing various tasks, including data warehouse design and implementation, administration, backup and recovery, development of Perl code for web-based database access, writing Java code utilizing JDBC, migrating legacy databases to Oracle, and developing Developer/2000 Oracle Forms applications. He is currently an Oracle Database Administrator Certified Associate , and is employed by the Northrop Grumman Corporation, where he is currently a Senior Database Analyst on a large data warehouse project.

I'd like to thank David Allan of the Oracle Warehouse Builder development team at Oracle for agreeing to review the book and for putting up with my numerous questions and requests for clarification. His input was extremely beneficial in explaining new functionality of OWB. I'd like to acknowledge my co-worker Ed Cody, whose work on his book, *The Business Analyst's Guide to Oracle Hyperion Interactive Reporting 11,* with Packt Publishing, inspired me to get started on the second edition of my book. Lastly and most importantly, of course, to my family, wife Lynn and children Robby, Melanie, Hilary, Christina, Millie and Mikey, thanks for being the inspiration and motivation behind everything I do.

About the Reviewers

Ehsun Behravesh is a 27 year old software engineer with Khorasan Newspaper (http://www.khorasannews.com) in Mashhad, Iran. He holds a Bachelors degree from London Metropolitan University (http://www.londonmet.ac.uk/). He started programming when he was in high school and has developed software systems for almost 10 years. He is a fan of open source software and one of his open source projects, MyPasswords (http://sourceforge.net/projects/mypasswords7/), won a comparison competition in *Linux Format*, Jan 2011 magazine. He loves computer programming, music, and animals.

> I want to thank my wife who has always encouraged me to work and study. I also want to thank my parents who helped me to study abroad.

David Allan has 20 years of experience in software development and over 10 years of experience in data warehouse tooling. In his current role, he is one of the architects responsible for Oracle's data integration portfolio, and as such, he takes a leading role in working with Oracle Warehouse Builder and Oracle Data Integrator. David is well-known for his blog on Oracle Warehouse Builder where he provides users with real-world examples and in-depth product knowledge.

www.PacktPub.com

Support files, eBooks, discount offers, and more

You might want to visit www.PacktPub.com for support files and downloads related to your book.

Did you know that Packt offers eBook versions of every book published, with PDF and ePub files available? You can upgrade to the eBook version at www.PacktPub.com and as a print book customer, you are entitled to a discount on the eBook copy. Get in touch with us at service@packtpub.com for more details.

At www.PacktPub.com, you can also read a collection of free technical articles, sign up for a range of free newsletters and receive exclusive discounts and offers on Packt books and eBooks.

http://PacktLib.PacktPub.com

Do you need instant solutions to your IT questions? PacktLib is Packt's online digital book library. Here, you can access, read, and search across Packt's entire library of books.

Why Subscribe?
- Fully searchable across every book published by Packt
- Copy and paste, print and bookmark content
- On demand and accessible via web browser

Free Access for Packt account holders

If you have an account with Packt at www.PacktPub.com, you can use this to access PacktLib today and view nine entirely free books. Simply use your login credentials for immediate access.

Instant Updates on New Packt Books

Get notified! Find out when new books are published by following @PacktEnterprise on Twitter, or the Packt Enterprise Facebook page.

Table of Contents

Preface

Competing in today's world requires a greater emphasis on strategy, long-range planning, and decision making, and this is why businesses are building data warehouses. Data warehouses are becoming more and more common as businesses have realized the need to mine the information that is stored in electronic form. Data warehouses provide valuable insight into the operation of a business and how best to improve it. Organizations need to monitor their processes, define policy, and at a more strategic level, define the visions and goals that will move the company forward in the future. If you are new to data warehousing in general, and to **Extract, Transform, and Load (ETL)** in particular, and need a way to get started, the Oracle Warehouse Builder is a great application to use to build your warehouse. The **Oracle Warehouse Builder (OWB)** is a tool provided by Oracle that can be used at every stage of the implementation of a data warehouse right from the initial design and creation of the table structure to ETL and data-quality auditing.

We will build a basic data warehouse using the latest release of Oracle Warehouse Builder, 11*g*R2. It has the ability to support all phases of the implementation of a data warehouse from designing the source and target information, the mappings to map data from source to target, the transformations needed on the data, and building the code to implementing the mappings to load the data. You are free to use any or all of the features in your own implementation.

What this book covers

This book is an introduction to the **Oracle Warehouse Builder (OWB)**. This is an introductory, hands-on book so we will be including in this book the features available in Oracle Warehouse Builder 11*g*R2 that we will need to build our first data warehouse.

The chapters are in chronological order to flow through the steps required to build a data warehouse with a couple of chapters at the end on special topics, including one devoted to a major new feature of OWB 11gR2, code templates. So if you are building your first data warehouse, it is a good idea to read through each chapter sequentially to gain maximum benefit from the book. Those who have already built a data warehouse and just need a refresher on some basics can skip around to whatever topic they need at that moment.

We'll use a fictional toy company, ACME Toys and Gizmos, to illustrate the concepts that will be presented throughout the book. This will provide some context to the information presented to help you apply the concepts to your own organization. We'll actually be constructing a simple data warehouse for the ACME Toys and Gizmos company. At the end of the book, we'll have all the code, scripts, and saved metadata that was used. So we can build a data warehouse for practice, or use it as a model for building another data warehouse.

Chapter 1, An Introduction to Oracle Warehouse Builder, starts off with a high-level look at the architecture of OWB and the steps for installing it. It covers the schemas created in the database that are required by OWB, and touches upon some installation topics to provide some further clarification that is not necessarily found in the Oracle documentation. Most installation tasks can be found in the Oracle **README** files and installation documents, and so they won't be covered in depth in this book.

Chapter 2, Defining and Importing Source Data Structures, covers the initial task of building a data warehouse from scratch, that is, determining what the source of the data will be. OWB needs to know the details about what the source data structures look like and where they are located in order to properly pull data from them using OWB. This chapter also covers how to define the source data structures using the Data Object Editor and how to import source structure information. It talks about three common sources of data — flat files, Oracle Databases, and Microsoft SQL Server databases — while discussing how to configure Oracle and OWB to connect to these sources.

Chapter 3, Designing the Target Structure, explains designing the data warehouse target. It covers some options for defining a data warehouse target structure using relational objects (star schemas and snowflake schemas) and dimensional objects (cubes and dimensions). Some of the pros and cons of the usage of these objects are also covered. It introduces the Warehouse Builder for design and starts with the creation of a target user and module.

Chapter 4, Creating the Target Structure in OWB, implements the design of the target using the Warehouse Builder. It has step-by-step explanations for creating cubes and dimensions using the wizards provided by OWB.

Chapter 5, Extract, Transform, and Load Basics, introduces the ETL process by explaining what it is and how to implement it in OWB. It discusses whether to use a staging table or not, and describes mappings and some of the main operators in OWB that can be used in mappings. It introduces the Warehouse Builder Mapping Editor, which is the interface for designing mappings.

Chapter 6, ETL: Putting it Together, is about creating a new mapping using the Mapping Editor. A staging table is created with the Data Object Editor, and a mapping is created to map data directly from the source tables into the staging table. This chapter explains how to add and edit operators, and how to connect them together. It also discusses operator properties and how to modify them.

Chapter 7, ETL: Transformations and Other Operators, expands on the concept of building a mapping by creating additional mappings to map data from the staging table into cube and dimensions. Additional operators are introduced for doing transformations of the data as it is loaded from source to target.

Chapter 8, Validating, Generating, Deploying, and Executing Objects, covers in great detail the validation of mappings, the generation of the code for mappings and objects, and deploying the code to the target database. This chapter introduces the Control Center Service, which is the interface with the target database for controlling this process, and explains how to start and stop it. The mappings are then executed to actually load data from source to target. It also introduces the Control Center Manager, which is the user interface for interacting with the Control Center Service for deploying and executing objects.

Chapter 9, Extra Features, covers some extra features provided in the Warehouse Builder that can be very useful for more advanced implementations as mappings get more numerous and complex. The metadata change-management features of OWB are discussed for controlling changes to mappings and objects. This includes the recycle bin, cutting/copying and pasting objects to make copies or backups, the snapshot feature, and the metadata loader facility for exporting metadata to a file. Keeping objects synchronized as changes are made is discussed, and so is the auto-binding of tables to dimensional objects. Lastly, some additional online references are provided for further study and reference.

Chapter 10, Code Template Mappings, covers a major new feature of the 11*g*R2 release of OWB—code templates, which are the knowledge module functionality brought over into OWB from Oracle Data Integrator. It includes detailed descriptions of implementing a JDBC connection to an external database and the implementation of a code template mapping to access it. It includes discussion of the main code templates provided by default with OWB 11*g*R2 and describes everything you need to know to implement your first code template mapping.

What you need for this book

The following software is required for this book:

- Oracle Warehouse Builder 11*gR2*
- Microsoft SQL Server 2008 Express with Advanced Services

Who this book is for

If you are new to data warehousing and you have to build your first data warehouse using OWB, or have implemented a data warehouse using another tool and are now using OWB for the first time, this book is for you. You can also use it as a refresher if you are a more advanced user. An ever-increasing number of businesses are implementing data warehouses and if you are reading this book, then yours too has most likely chosen to implement one.

This book is for anyone tasked with building a data warehouse and loading data into it using Oracle Warehouse Builder. It is primarily aimed at database administrators and engineers who are new to data warehousing and are building a data warehouse for the first time using OWB. This book can also be used as a refresher on basic OWB features. Think of it as a beginner's guide to OWB. It can be helpful for any IT professional looking to broaden his or her knowledge about data warehousing in general and Oracle Warehouse Builder in particular.

Conventions

In this book, you will find a number of styles of text that distinguish between different kinds of information. Here are some examples of these styles, and an explanation of their meaning.

Code words in text are shown as follows: "We can include other contexts through the use of the include directive."

A block of code is set as follows:

```
#include <stdio.h>
#include "wstr.h"
void wstr(const char* const str) {
  printf("%s\n", str);
}
```

When we wish to draw your attention to a particular part of a code block, the relevant lines or items are set in bold:

```c
#include <stdio.h>
#include "wstr.h"
void wstr(const char* const str) {
  printf("%s\n", str);
}
```

New terms and **important words** are shown in bold. Words that you see on the screen, in menus or dialog boxes for example, appear in the text like this: "clicking the **Next** button moves you to the next screen".

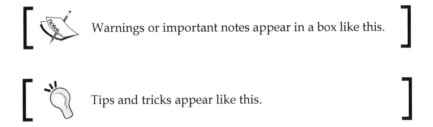

> Warnings or important notes appear in a box like this.

> Tips and tricks appear like this.

Reader feedback

Feedback from our readers is always welcome. Let us know what you think about this book—what you liked or may have disliked. Reader feedback is important for us to develop titles that you really get the most out of.

To send us general feedback, simply send an e-mail to feedback@packtpub.com, and mention the book title via the subject of your message.

If there is a book that you need and would like to see us publish, please send us a note in the **SUGGEST A TITLE** form on www.packtpub.com or e-mail suggest@packtpub.com.

If there is a topic that you have expertise in and you are interested in either writing or contributing to a book, see our author guide on www.packtpub.com/authors.

Customer support

Now that you are the proud owner of a Packt book, we have a number of things to help you to get the most from your purchase.

Downloading the example code

You can download the example code files for all Packt books you have purchased from your account at http://www.PacktPub.com. If you purchased this book elsewhere, you can visit http://www.PacktPub.com/support and register to have the files e-mailed directly to you.

Errata

Although we have taken every care to ensure the accuracy of our content, mistakes do happen. If you find a mistake in one of our books—maybe a mistake in the text or the code—we would be grateful if you would report this to us. By doing so, you can save other readers from frustration and help us improve subsequent versions of this book. If you find any errata, please report them by visiting http://www.packtpub.com/support, selecting your book, clicking on the **errata submission form** link, and entering the details of your errata. Once your errata are verified, your submission will be accepted and the errata will be uploaded on our website, or added to any list of existing errata, under the Errata section of that title. Any existing errata can be viewed by selecting your title from http://www.packtpub.com/support.

Piracy

Piracy of copyright material on the Internet is an ongoing problem across all media. At Packt, we take the protection of our copyright and licenses very seriously. If you come across any illegal copies of our works, in any form, on the Internet, please provide us with the location address or website name immediately so that we can pursue a remedy.

Please contact us at copyright@packtpub.com with a link to the suspected pirated material.

We appreciate your help in protecting our authors, and our ability to bring you valuable content.

Questions

You can contact us at questions@packtpub.com if you are having a problem with any aspect of the book, and we will do our best to address it.

1
An Introduction to Oracle Warehouse Builder

The **Oracle Warehouse Builder (OWB)** is what this book is all about, so let's start discussing it by looking at it from a high level. We'll talk about some installation topics and the various components that compose this application. Oracle provides some detailed installation documentation and user guides that give you step-by-step instructions on how to install the product and the prerequisites we need to have in place. So we will focus more on some general topics that will help us understand the installation better. We'll walk through a basic installation that can be followed along and actually performed while reading. We'll be accepting most of the defaults during the installation for simplicity. For more advanced installation requirements, dig into the Oracle installation documentation to get familiar with the options that are available. You can find this at `http://www.oracle.com/pls/db112/homepage` by clicking on the **Installing and Upgrading** link in the left hand frame.

In this chapter we're going to cover the following specific topics:

- Introduction to data warehousing and where OWB fits in
- Installing Oracle database software and OWB
    - ° Installing the database software
    - ° Configuring the Listener
    - ° Creating the database
- OWB Components and Architecture
- Configuring the repository and workspaces

Introduction to data warehousing

Although you may not be familiar with data warehousing, you have probably at least heard the term. Data warehouses are becoming increasingly common as businesses have realized the need to be able to mine the information they have stored in the electronic form in order to provide a valuable insight into the operation of their business and how best to improve it. Organizations need to monitor these processes, define policies, and — at a more strategic level — define the visions and goals that will move the company forward in the future. Operational transactional systems have greatly benefited the daily functioning of the enterprise. But now, organizations are shifting to a more decisional-based requirement from their computing platforms and are looking to build data warehouses. This is where OWB enters the picture to help organizations with the task of building that data warehouse.

Introduction to our fictional organization

The manuals that Oracle supplies with its database and applications contain a great deal of information. However, it can be hard to relate that information to the real-world ways of implementing the database and applications. Anyone who has ever tried to read a technical user guide or reference provided with a database or application will know what that means. It is a great benefit to be able to learn about a new software tool by seeing how that tool is actually used within the context of an actual organization conducting a business. This is precisely the focus of this book. We'll be building an actual data warehouse using a fictional organization as an example.

Before we talk about what a data warehouse is, let's get introduced to the fictional organization we'll be using to demonstrate the use of the Warehouse Builder to build a data warehouse. Throughout this book, we will be using examples of the concepts involved by making reference to a fictional organization named *ACME Toys and Gizmos*, which is sales oriented. It is an entirely made-up organization, and any similarity to a real company is completely coincidental. This book will provide explanations throughout on how to use the OWB tool to build a data warehouse within the context of this invented company, which is involved in storefront and online Internet sales. Thus, it will demonstrate practical ways of implementing a data warehouse that can be directly applied in the real world.

ACME Toys and Gizmos will have stores all over the United States as well as a number of other countries, and will also have an online storefront for Internet sales. The **online transactional processing** systems **(OLTP)** play a huge role in the functioning of any business today, especially in the operation of a sales-oriented business. So this makes a good example to illustrate the subject matter of data warehousing and how to take information from those OLTP systems to load our warehouse.

Although we'll be using a sales organization for our examples, the concepts we'll discuss can apply to any business and will be as generic as possible to assist in doing that.

What is a data warehouse?

We've discussed the business case for implementing a data warehouse by showing how companies these days need information to support strategic-level decision making. We've also introduced the fictional organization that we'll use to provide examples of the concepts we'll be presenting. But we've not yet explained what a data warehouse is.

We will not be dealing in detail with the concept of a data warehouse as that topic would encompass the entire contents of a book by itself. There are a number of good books already written about that topic. Therefore, we will touch upon some high-level concepts only as an introduction and to provide a context for using OWB to build a data warehouse.

Fundamentally, a data warehouse is a decisional database system. It is designed to support the decision makers in the organization in ways a transactional processing system is ill-equipped to handle, such as the strategic-level goals and visions of an organization. To think strategically, a large amount of data over long periods of time is needed. Transactional systems are concerned with the day-to-day operations such as: How many dolls did we sell today and will we need to restock the inventory? How many orders were processed today? How many balls were shipped out today? The strategic thinkers are more concerned with questions such as: How many dolls did we sell today compared to the same time period in the last year? How has our inventory level been for the last few months?

To support that level of information, we need more data than what is provided by the day-to-day transactions. We'll need much more information compiled over greater time periods and this is where the data warehouse comes in. As a data warehouse is different from a transactional database, there are some unique terms used to describe the data it contains. There are also other techniques that should be employed for designing the database for a data warehouse, which would not be a good idea for a transactional database.

The data in a data warehouse is composed of facts (actual numerical measures) and dimensions (descriptive data about those measures) that place the facts in a context that is understandable to the end-user decision maker. For instance, a customer makes a purchase of a toy with ACME Toys and Gizmos on a particular day over the Internet, which results in a dollar amount of the transaction. The dollar amount becomes the fact and the toy purchased, the customer, and the location of the purchase (the Internet in this case) become the dimensions that provide a scope of the fact measurement and give it a meaning.

The design of a data warehouse should be different from that of a transactional database. The data warehouse must handle large amounts of data, and must be simple to query and understand by the end users. While relational techniques and normalization are excellent database design methods for transactional systems to ensure data integrity, they can make understanding a data warehouse difficult for the end users. They can also bog down a data warehouse with long-running queries that have to make use of many joins (including more than one table that share a common data element to look up additional data).

A much better means of representing the data is to de-normalize the data, so that users will not have to be concerned with retrieving the data from multiple tables. The use of foreign keys (a column that references a row in another table) should be restricted in a data warehouse. The outcome is a fact table with foreign keys only to each of the dimension tables. The diagram of the database structure has a fact table in the middle surrounded by dimension tables, resulting in something that looks like a star. Thus, the term star schema is used to refer to this representation of a data warehouse. It is also possible that these dimensions may themselves have other tables surrounding them, resulting in something akin to a snowflake. Thus, the term snowflake schema is also used. This is the dimensional modeling technique of representing a data warehouse.

This design lends itself extremely well to the task of querying large amounts of data by the end users. Users do not have to be bothered with queries involving complicated joins with multiple tables to get the descriptive information they need. This is because the information is included directly in the dimension tables in a de-normalized fashion. If a manager for ACME Toys and Gizmos needs to know what products sold well in the last quarter, the query will only involve two tables—the main fact table containing the data on number of items sold and the product dimension table that contains all the information about the product. The de-normalization means the manager will not have to be concerned with looking up product information in any other tables, as all the details about the product will be included in the one dimension table.

All this is great background information on data warehouses, but you can read any number of other books for much more detailed material on the topic. Our purpose in this book is to introduce the Oracle Warehouse Builder and use it to design and build our first data warehouse. So, let's see how it fits in to this discussion of data warehousing.

Where does OWB fit in?

The Oracle Warehouse Builder is a tool provided by Oracle, which can be used at every stage of the implementation of a data warehouse, from initial design and creation of the table structure to the ETL process and data-quality management. So, the answer to the question of where it fits in is—everywhere. It is provided as a part of the Oracle Database Release 11*g* installation. For the previous Oracle Database Releases, it can be downloaded and installed from Oracle's website as a free download.

We can choose to use any or all of the features as needed for our project, so we do not need to use every feature. Simple data warehouse implementations will use a subset of the features and as the data warehouse grows in complexity, the tool provides more features that can be implemented. It is flexible enough to provide us a number of options for implementing our data warehouse as we'll see in the remainder of the book.

Installation of the database and OWB

We'll be using the latest version of the database as of this writing—*Oracle Database 11g Release 2*—and the corresponding version of OWB that (as of this release) is included with the database install. If you have that version of the database installed already, you can skip this section and move right on to the next. If not, then keep reading as we discuss the installation of the database software.

Downloading the Oracle software

We can download the Oracle database software from Oracle's website, provided we adhere to their license agreement. This agreement basically says we agree to use the database and the accompanying software either for development of a prototype of our application or for our own learning purposes. If we proceed to use this application internally or make it commercially available, then we will need to purchase a license from Oracle. For the purpose of working through the contents of this book to learn OWB, we need to install the database, which is covered under the license agreement for the free download.

We can find the database on the **Oracle Technology Network** website (`http://www.oracle.com/technology`). The main database download is usually the first download listed under **TOP DOWNLOADS** on the main page. We need to register on the site, in order to create an account, before it lets us download any files, but there is no charge for that. The download files are classified by the platform on which they can be executed, so we'll choose the one for the system we'll be hosting the database on. We'll have to accept the license agreement first before the web page will let us download the files. The download files are anywhere from 1.7 GB to 2.3 GB in size, depending on the platform we'll be hosting it on. So we do not want to attempt this download unless we have a Broadband Internet connection (that is, cable, DSL, and so on). We'll download the install files and unzip them to a folder on a drive with enough available space. The installation files are temporary and are not needed after the installation is done, so we'll be able to delete them to free up space if needed.

A word about hardware and operating systems

When installing software of this magnitude, we have to decide whether we'll have to buy additional hardware and a different operating system to run the database and OWB. OWB will run in Oracle Database 10gR2 or later Standard or Enterprise Editions.

We'll be using the most recent version of OWB throughout this book. We can download older versions of OWB that will run on older versions of the database, but we will not have the benefit of the improvements as in the latest version of the software. Much of what we'll be doing with the software throughout the course of the book can also be done on previous versions of the software. However, due to the changes made to things such as the interface, it would be easiest to follow along using the most recent version.

For this book, the platform is Windows 7 with Oracle Database 11*g* Release 2 (11.2.0.1) Enterprise Edition (which is the most recent version as of this writing), which is available from the download site. The Enterprise Edition of the database was chosen because it allows us to make full use of the features of the Warehouse Builder, especially in the area of dimensional modeling. There are some errors that will be generated by the client software when running in the Standard Edition installation due to code dependencies. These code dependencies are in libraries that are installed with the Enterprise Edition, but not the Standard Edition. We could use OWB with the Standard Edition, but then we would be limited in the type of objects we could deploy. For instance, dimensions and cubes would be problematic, and without using them we'd be missing out on a major functionality provided by the tool. If we want to develop any reasonably-sized data warehouse, the Enterprise Edition is the way to go.

Everything that we'll work through in this book was done in an Oracle VM VirtualBox virtual machine on a laptop personal computer with an Intel Core 2 processor running at 1.67 GHz and 4 GB of RAM. Oracle says 1 GB of RAM will suffice so the virtual machine was configured with 1209MB of memory. Minimum specifications usually result in underpowered systems for all but the very basic processing but for the purpose of working through the tasks described in this book it will be sufficient. In terms of hard disk space, Oracle specifies that 4.5 GB is required for the basic database installation. We'll need about 2 GB just to save the installation files, so to make sure we have plenty of space, we should plan for something between 10 GB and 15 GB of available disk space just to be safe. We don't want to install the database software and then find that we don't have any space on our hard drive. The VirtualBox machine was configured with 30GB of disk space.

Oracle supports its database installed on Windows and Unix. For Windows, it supports Windows XP Professional or Windows Vista or Windows 7 (Business Edition, Enterprise Edition, or Ultimate Edition) as well as Windows Server 2003 and 2008. The system mentioned above that was used for writing this book and working through all the examples, is running Windows Vista Home Premium Edition with Service Pack 2 and the database installed runs on the VirtualBox VM in Windows 7 Home Premium. We certainly would not want to use this configuration for large production databases, but it works fine for simple databases and learning purposes. The installation program will first do a prerequisite check of the computer and will flag any problems that it sees, such as not enough memory or an incorrect version of the operating system. For working through this book on our own to learn about the Warehouse Builder, we should be OK as long as we are running XP ,Vista, or Windows 7. However, for business users who would be installing the Oracle Database and OWB for use at work using Windows, it would be a good idea to stick with the recommended configurations of Windows XP Professional, Windows Vista or 7 (Business Edition, Enterprise Edition, and Ultimate Edition), or Windows Server.

Server versus workstation

We don't have to use a computer that is configured as a server to host the Oracle database. It will get installed on a regular workstation as long as the minimum system requirements are met. However, we might encounter a minor issue. A workstation is usually configured to use **Dynamic Host Configuration Protocol (DHCP)** to obtain its IP address. This means the address is not specified as a fixed address and can change the next time the system boots up. The Oracle database requires a fixed address to be assigned, and it can install on a system with DHCP. But it will also require the Microsoft Loopback Adapter to be installed as the primary network interface to provide that fixed address. If this situation is encountered, the installer prerequisite checks will alert us to that and give us instructions on how to proceed. It will not harm our existing network configuration to install that option. That is the way the laptop mentioned above was configured for this book project.

Installing Oracle database software

So far we've decided what system we're going to host the database on, downloaded the appropriate install file for that system, and unzipped the install files into a folder to begin the installation. We'll navigate to that folder and run the `setup.exe` file located there. This will launch the **Oracle Universal Installer** program to begin the installation. Those of us with experience installing the Oracle Database from prior versions will immediately notice the installer for 11gR2 has a slightly different look. It is more like a setup program for the database than the Universal Installer we're used to from previous versions, including the first edition of this book.

We are installing the full database, which now automatically includes the Warehouse Builder client and database components. If we had an older version of the database (10g R2 for example) that did not include the Warehouse Builder software, or if we wanted to run the client on a different workstation than where the database software is installed, then there is the option to install the Warehouse Builder by itself.

A separately downloadable install for the standalone option is available at `http://www.oracle.com/technology/software/products/warehouse/index.html`. Skip ahead to the section titled *Installing the OWB standalone software* if just the Warehouse Builder software is needed.

1. The first thing the installer is going to ask us is our email address for use in being notified of critical system updates that are available. This is something new Oracle has started doing with their installs to get people thinking about critical vulnerabilities and keeping their databases properly patched. It's similar to Microsoft's Windows Update feature that keeps users notified of available patches for the Windows operating system. That's a good feature but we would need a support agreement with Oracle and a My Oracle Support login to really make use of it so we're going to skip this and move on to step 2. Be aware that it will pop up a warning dialog asking us if we really want to remain uninformed about security related issues. We'll answer yes and move along.

2. The second step asks us what installation option we'd like. We can choose from one of three, create and configure a database, install the software only, or upgrade an existing database. We'll choose the second option. The **Create and Install a Database** option will make some assumptions about the database that we don't want depending on what options are selected so its easier if we just install the database separately after the software is installed.

3. For the third step, we'll choose Single Instance for the Installation Type. The other option is for installing a database as part of a RAC installation (Real Application Cluster) of clustered databases.

4. In step 4 we'll choose the database language, or languages, we want to install.

5. Step 5 is where we choose the edition of the database to install, Enterprise, Standard, Standard Edition One, or Personal Edition. We'll choose the Enterprise Edition so we have access to all of the advanced features we need for the Warehouse Builder.

6. Step 6 will ask us for path names for **ORACLE_BASE** and for the **Software Location** (or Oracle home location). They will have suggested paths filled in for us. It is a good idea to leave the path names as they are and only change the drive designation if we'd like to install to a different hard drive. The install program will suggest a drive for the installation, but we might have a different preference. Oracle recommends a convention for naming folders and files that they call the **Optimal Flexible Architecture (OFA)**. This is described in Appendix B of the *Oracle Database Installation Guide* for Microsoft Windows, which can be found at the following URL: `http://download.oracle.com/docs/cd/E11882_01/install.112/e10843/ofa.htm#CBBEDHEB`. It is a good idea to follow their recommendations for standardization so that others who have to work with the database files will know where to find them, and to save us from problems with possible conflicts with other Oracle products we may have installed. If we keep the default folder locations intact and only change the drive letter, we will adhere to the standard.

7. Step 7 of the install is where it will conduct the prerequisite checks to ensure our system is capable of running the database. If everything succeeds we'll move right to step 8, bypassing step 7 results. We could hit the back button on Step to move back to see the results if we wanted. If anything failed, it would have displayed the results for us.

8. Step 8 is the summary screen. It will display the Global Settings as in the previous version but includes a new Inventory section which replaces the old Product Languages, Space Requirements, and New Installations sections.

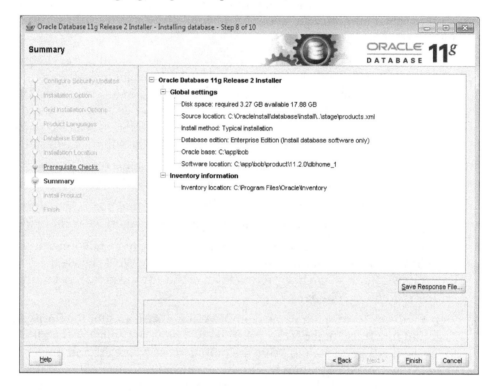

9. The actual installation happens in step 9. A progress bar proceeds to the right as the installation happens and steps for Prepare, Copy Files, and Setup Files are checked off as they are done.

10. Step 10 is the conclusion and finishes up with a success message:

    Your database configuration files have been installed in C:\app\bob while other components selected for installation have been installed in C:\app\bob\product\11.2.0\dbhome_1. Be cautious not to accidentally delete these configuration files.

The "bob" in the above paths will be whatever username was used to install as. Also, this message will probably be on one long line requiring the scroll bar to read it all.

1. We will click **Close** to end the installation.

Basic versus advance install

The installation method we're following here is the quickest and easiest, but makes many decisions for us that more advanced options will ask us about like creating a database and Desktop vs Server installs. For the purpose of working through the examples in this book, we will be OK with the basic installation. But if we were installing for a production environment, we would want to read through the *Oracle Database Installation Guide* (http://www.oracle.com/technology/documentation/database.html; click on **View Library** to view the documentation online or click on **Download** to download the documentation) to familiarize ourselves with the various situations that would require us to use the more advanced installation options. This would ensure that we don't end up with a database installation that will not support our needs.

Location of install results

A good idea is to pay particular attention to the inventory location on the Step 8 summary screen, which tells us where we can find a log of the installation. The logs that the installer keeps are stored in the Oracle folder on the system drive in the following subfolder: C:\Program Files\Oracle\Inventory\logs. The files are named with the following convention: install ActionsYYYY-MM-DD_HH-MI-SSPM where YYYY is the year, MM the month, DD the day, HH the hour, MI the minutes, SS the seconds of the time the installation was performed, and PM is either AM or PM. The files will have a .log extension. This information may come in useful later to see just what products were installed. The folder also will contain any errors encountered during the installation in files with a file extension of .err and any output generated by the installer in files with a file extension of .out.

Now that the software is installed, it's time to proceed with creating a database. But there is one step we have to do first—we need to configure the **listener**.

Configuring the listener

The listener is the utility that runs constantly in the background on the database server, listening for client connection requests to the database and handling them. It can be installed either before or after the creation of a database, but there is one option during the database creation that requires the listener to be configured – so we'll configure it now, before we create the database.

Run **Net Configuration Assistant** to configure the listener. It is available under the **Oracle** menu on the Windows **Start** menu as shown in the following image:

The welcome screen will offer us four tasks that we can perform with this assistant. We'll select the first one to configure the listener, as shown here:

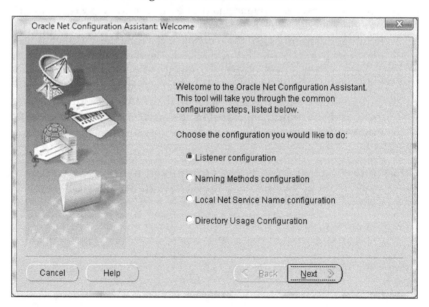

The next screen will ask you what we want to do with the listener. The four options are as follows:

- **Add**
- **Reconfigure**
- **Delete**
- **Rename**

Only the **Add** option will be available since we are installing Oracle for the first time. The remainder of the options will be grayed out and will be unavailable for selection. If they are not, then there is a listener already configured and we can proceed to the next section— *Creating the database*.

For those of us installing for the first time on our machines, we need to proceed with the configuration. The next screen will ask us what we want to name the listener. It will have **LISTENER** entered by default and that's a fine name, which states exactly what it is, so let's leave it at that and proceed.

The next screen is the protocol selection screen. It will have **TCP** already selected for us, which is what most installations will require. This is the standard communications protocol in use on the Internet and in most local networks. Leave that selected and proceed to the next screen to select the port number to use. The default port number is 1521, which is standard for communicating with Oracle databases and is the one most familiar to anyone who has ever worked with an Oracle database. So, change it only if you want to annoy the Oracle people in your organization who have all memorized the default Oracle port of 1521.

To change or not change the default listener port

Putting aside the annoyance, the Oracle people might have to suffer as there are valid security reasons why we might want to change that port number. Since it is so common, the people accustomed to working with the Oracle database aren't the only people who know that port number. Hackers looking to break into an Oracle database are going to go straight for that port number, so if we change it to something obscure, the database will be harder to find on the network for the people with malicious intent. If it does get changed, be sure to make a note of the assigned number.

There also may be firewall issues that allow only certain port numbers to be open through the firewall, which means communication on any of the other port numbers would be blocked. 1521 might be allowed by default since it is common for the Oracle database. It would be a good idea to check with the network support personnel to get their recommendation.

That is the last step. It will ask us if we want to configure another listener. Since we only need one, we'll answer "no" and finish out the screens by clicking on the **Finish** button back on the main screen.

Creating the database

So far we have the Oracle software installed and a listener configured, but we have not created a database.

We will install a new database using **Database Configuration Assistant**, which Oracle provides to walk us step-by-step through the process of creating a database. It is launched from the Windows **Start** menu as shown in the following image:

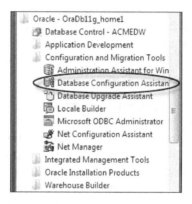

Running this application may require patience as we have to wait for the application to load after it's selected. Depending on the system it is running on, it can take over a minute to display, during which time there is no indication that anything is happening. It may be tempting to just select it again from the **Start** menu because it appears it didn't work the first time, but don't as that will just end up running two instances of the program. It will appear soon. The following are steps in the creation process:

1. The first step is to specify what action to take. Since we do not have a database created, we'll select the **Create a Database** option in step 1. If there was a database already created, the options for configuring a database or deleting a database would be selectable. Templates can be managed with the **Database Configuration Assistant** application, which are files containing preset options for various database configurations. Pre-supplied templates are provided with the application, and the application has the ability to custom-build templates.

In previous versions of the database, Automatic Storage Management could be configured as well however as of 11gR2, ASM has its own configuration assistant now, ASMCA. It is Oracle's feature for databases for automatically managing the layout and storage of database files on the system. These are both topics for a more advance book on the Oracle Database. We will be creating a database using an existing template.

2. This step will offer the following three options for a database template to select:

    ○ **General Purpose or Transaction Processing**

    ○ **Custom Database**

    ○ **Data Warehouse**

3. We are going to choose the **Data Warehouse** option for our purposes. If we already had a database installed that we wanted to use for learning OWB, but that's not configured as a data warehouse, it's not a problem. We can still run OWB hosted on it and create the data warehouse schema (database user and tables), which we'll be creating as we proceed through the book. This would be fine for learning purposes, but for production-ready data warehouses a database configured specifically as a data warehouse should be used.

4. This step of the database creation will ask for a database name. The name of the database must be one to eight characters in length. Any more than that will generate an error when trying to proceed to the next screen. This is an Oracle database limitation. The database name can also include the network domain name of the domain of the host it is running on, to further uniquely identify it. Follow the name with a period and then the domain, which itself can include additional periods.

If this database is being created for business use, a good naming scheme would reflect the purpose of the database. Since we're creating this database for the data warehouse of ACME Toys and Gizmos Company, we'll choose a name that reflects this—ACME for the company name and DW for data warehouse, resulting in a database name of ACMEDW. It is important to remember this name as it will be a part of any future connections to the database.

As the database name is typed in, the **SID** (or Oracle **System Identifier**) is automatically filled in to match it. If the domain is added to the database name, the SID will stop pre-populating after the first period is entered. The end result is that the SID becomes the same as the first part of the database name.

5. This step of the database creation process asks whether we want to configure **Enterprise Manager**. The box is checked by default and left as it is. This is a web-based utility Oracle provides for controlling a database, and as it is very useful to have, we will want to enable it. There are two options for controlling a database: registering with **Grid Control** or local management. Grid Control is Oracle's centralized feature for controlling a grid, a network of loosely coupled modular hardware and software components that can be joined and rejoined together on demand to meet business needs. That is what the "*g*" in Oracle Database 11*g* stands for. If your network is not configured in a grid architecture, or you are installing on a standalone machine, then choose the local management option. It will automatically detect a Grid Control agent that is running locally, and if it doesn't find one, the **Grid Control** option will be grayed out anyway. In that case, you will only be able to select local management.

6. New in the 11gR2 version of the DBCA is the additional tab on this screen for the Automatic Maintenance option. This step used to be all by itself as step 12 of the install process. We'll deselect that option and move on, since we don't need that additional functionality. **Automatic Maintenance Tasks** are tasks that run in predefined maintenance windows of time to perform various preconfigured maintenance operations on the database. Since the database for this book is only for learning purposes, it is not critical that these maintenance tasks be done automatically.

7. Automatic maintenance is designed to run during preset maintenance windows, which are usually in the middle of the night. So if the database system is shut down every day, there wouldn't be a good window to run the tasks on regularly anyway. If installing in a production environment with servers that will be running 24 hours a day every day, then consider setting up the automatic maintenance to occur. Oracle provides three pre-configured maintenance tasks to choose from — collecting statistics for the query optimizer (for improving performance of SQL queries), **Automatic Segment Advisor** for analyzing storage space for areas that can possibly be reclaimed for use, and the **Automatic SQL Tuning Advisor** for automatically analyzing SQL statements for performance improvements.

If an error is encountered at some point during the database creation that indicates a listener is not configured, it simply means we started the DBCA before configuring a listener. To solve that, there is no need to exit out of the database install window, just go back and perform the listener install steps and come back here where the screen will allow us to proceed.

8. On this screen (step 5) we can set the database passwords on the system accounts using a different one for each account, or by choosing one password for all four. We're going to set a single password on all four, but for added security in a production environment, it is a good idea to make a different password for each. Click on the option to **Use the Same Administrative Password for All Accounts** and enter a password. This is very important to remember as these are key system accounts used for database administrative control. Oracle has decided as of this release to attempt to make us choose better, more secure passwords by popping up a warning dialog if the password we've chosen does not meet with their standards of complexity. It is only a warning however and we can answer **Yes** and continue.

9. This step is a combination now of the old steps 6 and 7 of the installation. It is about storage and specifying the locations where database files are to be created. We'll leave it at the default of **File System** for storage management. The other two options are for more advanced installations that have greater storage needs. The locations where database files are to be created can be left at the default for simplicity (which uses the locations specified in the template and follows the OFA standard for naming folders described above). A storage screen will come up where we'll be able to change the actual file locations if we want, for all but the **Oracle-Managed Files** option.

 Te Oracle-Managed Files option is provided by the database so that we can let Oracle automatically name and locate our data files. A folder location is specified on the step 6 screen, which will become the default location for any files created using this option. This is why we won't be able to change any file locations later on during the installation if this option is chosen. However, files can still be created with explicit names and locations after the database is running.

10. The next screen is for configuring recovery options. We're up to step 8 now. If we were installing a production database, we would want to make sure to use the **Flash Recovery** option and to **Enable Archiving**. Flash Recovery is a feature Oracle has implemented in its database to provide a location that is managed by the database. It stores backups and files needed to recover a database in the event of disk failure. With **Flash Recovery Area** specified, we can recover data that would otherwise be lost in a system failure.

Enabling archiving turns on the archive log mode of the database, which causes it to archive the **redo logs** (files containing information that is used by the database to recover transactions in the event of a failure.) Having redo logs archived means you can recover your database up to the time of the failure, and not just up to the time of the last backup.

These recovery options will consume more disk space, but will provide a re-covery option in the event of a failure. Each individual will have to make the call for their particular situation whether that is needed or not.

We'll specify **Flash Recovery** and for simplicity, we will just leave the default for size and location. We will not enable archiving at this point. These options can always be modified after the database is running, so this is not the last chance to set them.

11. This step is where we can have the installation program create some sample schemas in the database for our reference, and specify any custom scripts to run. The text on the screen can be read to decide whether they are needed or not. We don't need either of these for this book, so it doesn't matter which option we choose.

12. The next screen is for **Initialization Parameters**. These are the settings that are put in place to define various options for the database such as **Memory** options. There are over 200 different parameters and to go through all of them would take much more time and space than we have here. There is no need for that at this point as there are about 28 parameters that Oracle says are basic parameters that every database installation should set. We're just going to leave the defaults set on this screen, which will set the basic parameters for us based on the amount of memory and disk space detected on our machine. We'll just move on from here. Once again, these can all be adjusted later after the database is created and running if we need to make changes.

13. The next step (step 10 of 11) is the **Database Storage** screen referred to earlier. Here the locations of the pre-built data and control files can be changed if needed. They should be left set to the default for simplicity since this won't be a production database. For a production environment, we would want to consider storing datafiles on separate partitions for performance reasons, and to minimize the impact of disk failures on the running database if something goes wrong. If all the datafiles are on one drive and it goes bad, then the whole database is down.

14. The final step has the following three options, and any or all can be selected for creating the database:

    ° Create the database directly

    ° Save the creation options as a template for later use

    ° Save database creation scripts that can be used later to create the database

    We'll leave the first checkbox checked to go ahead and create the database.

The **Next** button is grayed out since this is the last screen. So click on the **Finish** button to begin creating the database using the selections we've just chosen. It will display a summary screen showing what options it will be using to install with. We can save this as an HTML file if we'd like to keep a record of it for future reference.

All that information will be available in the database by querying system tables later, but it's nice to have it all summarized in one file. We can scroll down that window and verify the various options that will be installed, including **Oracle Warehouse Builder**, which will have a **true** in the **Selected** column as shown here:

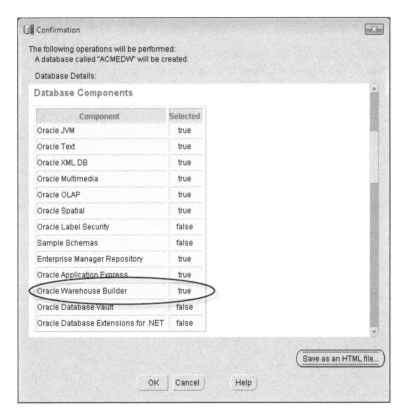

We will be presented with the progress screen next that will show us the progress as it creates the database.

When the install progress screen gets to 100% and all the items are checked off, we will be presented with a screen summarizing the database configuration details. Take a screen capture of this screen or write down the details because it's good to know information on how the database is configured. Especially, we'll need the database name in later installation steps. We may see the progress screen at 100% doing nothing with apparently no other display visible. Just look around the desktop underneath other windows for the Database Configuration Screen. It's important for the next step.

On the final Database Configuration Screen, there is a button in the lower right corner labeled **Password Management**. We need to click on this button to unlock the schema created for OWB use. Oracle configures its databases with most of the pre-installed schemas locked, and so users cannot access them. It is necessary to unlock them specifically, and assign our own passwords to them if we need to use them. Two of them are the **OWBSYS** schema and the **OWBSYS_AUDIT** schema. These are the schemas that the installation program automatically installs to support the Warehouse Builder. They are required for running the Warehouse Builder. Click on the **Password Management** button and on the resulting Password Management screen, we'll scroll down until we see the **OWBSYS and OWBSYS_AUDIT schemas.** We'll click on the check box to uncheck it on each one (indicating we want them unlocked) and then type in a password and confirm it as shown in the following image:

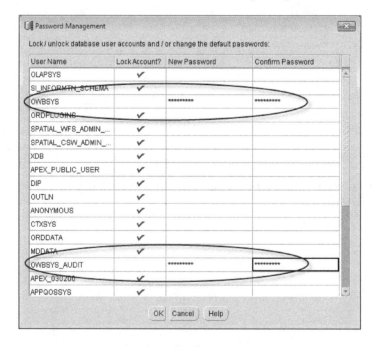

Click on the **OK** button to apply these changes and close the window. On the Database Configuration Screen, click on the **Exit** button to exit out of the Database Configuration Assistant.

That's it. We're done installing our first database and it's ready to use. Next, we'll discuss installing the OWB client if we want to run the client on another computer, or if we already have a 10*g*R2 database installed that we want to use with the Warehouse Builder.

Installing the OWB standalone software

If we are going to run the OWB client on the same computer as we just installed the Oracle database on, we don't need any more installations. That is the configuration used in this book. The OWB client software is now installed by default with the main database installation. We can verify that by checking the **Start** menu entry for Oracle. We will see a submenu entry for **Warehouse Builder** as shown in the following image:

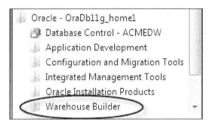

If we want to run the OWB client on another computer on the network, or if we have an older version of the database already installed (10*g* Rel 2) and want to be able to use the Warehouse Builder software with it, we'll need to continue here with the installation of the OWB client software. For all others, we can proceed to the next section on OWB—*OWB components and architecture*.

For the task of installing the standalone client, we'll need to download the OWB client install file. So we will go back to the Oracle site on the Internet. The download page is at the following URL at the time of writing: `http://www.oracle.com/technology/software/products/warehouse/index.html`. If that is not working, go to the main Oracle site and search for the **Business Intelligence | Data Warehousing** page where there is a link for the download of the OWB client.

Once again we'll have to accept the license agreement before the download links will become active. So we'll accept it and download the install file to the client computer on which we'll be installing the software. The Windows ZIP file is about 930MB in size so we need to make sure we have enough room on our hard drive to store the file. We'll need at least double that amount of space because the install files will take up that much space when unzipped.

When we have downloaded the ZIP file and unzipped it to our hard drive, run `setup.exe` in the top-level folder to run the Oracle Universal Installer. It should look familiar. Oracle is definitely correct in calling their installer "Universal". Every Oracle database product uses that installer, so we will become very familiar with it if we have to install any more Oracle products. It is universal also in the fact that it runs on every platform that Oracle supports, and so the same interface is used no matter where we install it. The installation steps are as follows:

1. The first step it goes through is asking us for the Oracle home details. It's similar to what it asked at the beginning of the database installation as shown in the following image:

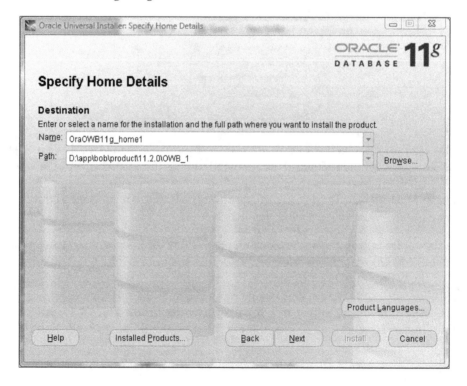

The installer will again suggest **OraDb11g_home1** or something similar, but we'll change it to **OraOWB11g_home1** since it's just the OWB installation and not the full database.

> When installing the standalone OWB software, remember that it cannot be installed into the same ORACLE home as the database. It must reside in it own Oracle home folder. So if we have a database that's already installed on the same machine, we'll have to make sure the ORACLE_ HOME we specify is different. The installer will warn us if we try to specify the same one and won't let us continue until it is different.

We need to verify the installation location for the home location also. The suggested name that it provides conforms to the OFA standard just as the database installation did, so we'll want to just change the drive letter if needed. However, the bottom-most folder name can be changed if needed without violating the OFA standard. If it has a default of **db_1**, we can change it to **OWB_1** just to be clear that it's the OWB client.

2. The second step is that email prompt again for being notified about security issues that we saw earlier in the database software install. We can just continue and answer **yes** to the popup warning.

3. The next and final step is the summary screen. The OWB client installation is not as complex as a full database installation, so it does not need all the additional information it asked for during the database installation. The summary screen should look similar to the following:

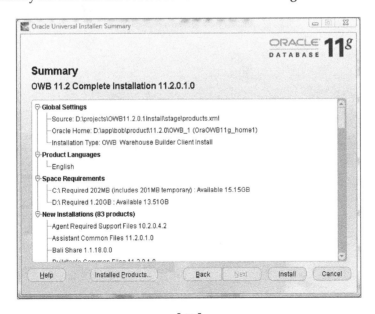

This summary gives us an idea of the disk space it will need, as well as the products that will be installed. If we scroll down the list, we'll see a number of other Oracle utilities and applications that it will install. We will also see items that are installed on the server as a part of the database install, but that will now be available to us on our client workstation. **SQL*Plus** appears there, which is the command line utility for accessing an Oracle database directly using **SQL** (**Structured Query Language**, the language used for accessing information stored in databases) among a host of other features.

Upon proceeding, the next screen will begin the installation and present us with the progress screen with a sliding bar moving to the right to indicate how far it has progressed. This is similar to what it did for the full database installation. An example of that screen is included next for reference:

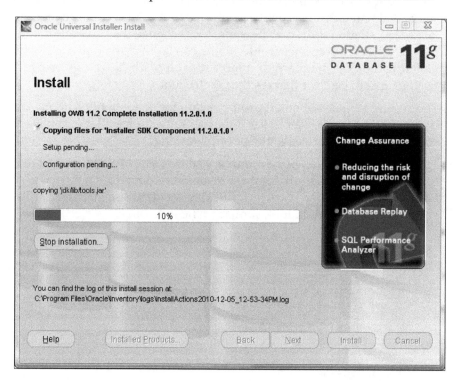

Install results

The log files with the results of the installation are stored in the same location as they are for a full database install. The universal installer will use that same folder for all its installs.

When the installation is complete, we will be presented with the final success screen and an **Exit** button. And as if to remind us about the universal nature of the installer, it will pop up a confirmation box asking if we really want to exit, even though for this installation there is nothing else that would be available to do on that final screen if we said no.

OWB components and architecture

Now that we've installed the database and OWB client, let's talk about the various components that have just been installed that are a part of the OWB and the architecture of OWB in the database. Then we'll perform one final task that is required before using OWB to create our data warehouse.

Oracle Warehouse Builder is composed on the client of the **Design Center** (including the **Control Center Manager**) and the **Repository Browser**. The server components are the **Control Center Service**, the **Repository** (including **Workspaces**), and the **Target Schema**. New for release 11gR2 is the **Control Center Agent** which is used by the new **Code Template Mappings** to communicate with a non-Oracle database. We'll be covering that in more detail in Chapter 10. A diagram illustrating the various components and their interactions follows:

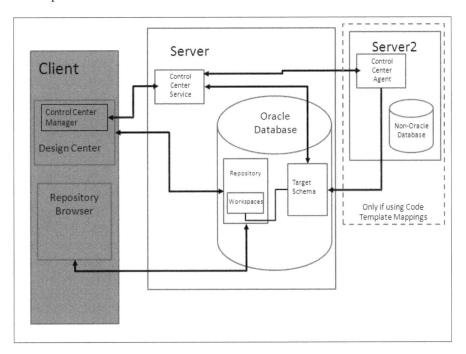

Client and server

The previous diagram depicts a client and server, but these are really just logical notions to indicate the purpose of the individual components and are not necessarily physically separate machines. The client components are installed with the database as we've seen previously and, therefore, can run on the same machine as the database. This configuration is assumed throughout the book.

The Design Center is the main client graphical interface for designing our data warehouse. This is where we will spend a good deal of time to define our sources and targets, and describe the **extract, transform, and load** (ETL) processes we use to load the target from the sources. The ETL procedures are what we will define to carry out the extraction of the data from our sources, any transformations needed on it and subsequent loading into the data warehouse. What we will create in the Design Center is a logical design only, not a physical implementation. This logical design will be stored behind the scenes in a Workspace in the Repository on the server. The user interacts with the Design Center, which stores all its work in a Repository Workspace.

We will use the Control Center Manager for managing the creation of that physical implementation by deploying the designs we've created into the Target Schema. The process of deployment is OWB's method for creating physical objects from the logical definitions created using the Design Center. We'll then use the Control Center Manager to execute the design by running the code associated with the ETL that we've designed. The Control Center Manager interacts behind the scenes with the Control Center Service, which runs on the server as shown in the previous image. The user directly interacts with the Control Center Manager and the Design Center only.

The Target Schema is where OWB will deploy the objects to, and where the execution of the ETL processes that load our data warehouse will take place. It is the actual data warehouse schema that gets built. It contains the objects that were designed in the Design Center, as well as the ETL code to load those objects. The Target Schema is not an actual Warehouse Builder software component, but is a part of the Oracle Database. However, it will contain Warehouse Builder components such as synonyms that will allow the ETL mappings to access objects in the Repository.

The Repository is the schema that hosts the design **metadata** definitions we create for our sources, targets, and ETL processes. Metadata is basically data about data. We will be defining sources, targets, and ETL processes using the Design Center and the information about what we have defined (the metadata) is stored in the Repository.

The Repository is a Warehouse Builder software component for which a separate schema is created when the database is installed—OWBSYS. This is the schema we talked about unlocking during the installation discussion previously as one of the final steps in the database creation process. This will be created automatically by the 11*g* install, but is installed separately using scripts if we want to host the Repository on an Oracle 10*g* database. The explanations in this book all assume that the Repository is hosted on an Oracle 11*g* database. The *Oracle Warehouse Builder Installation and Administration Guide* found at the following URL: `http://download.oracle.com/docs/cd/E11882_01/owb.112/e17130/toc.htm` discusses the procedure for installing the Repository schema on an Oracle 10*g* release 2 database if needed. It also contains more detailed information about the various other configurations that can be installed along with more detailed diagrams of the various options.

The Repository will contain one or more Workspaces as shown in the previous diagram. A Workspace is where we will do our work to create the data warehouse. There can be more than one workspace defined in the Repository. A common example of how multiple workspaces can be employed is to use different workspaces corresponding to sets of users working on related projects. We could have one workspace for development, one for testing, and one for production. The development team could be working in the development environment separately from the test team that would be working in the test environment. For our purposes at the ACME Toys and Gizmos Company, we will be working out of one workspace.

This concept of the workspace is new in the 11g releases of OWB. The Repository is created in the OWBSYS schema during the database installation. So setting up the Repository information and workspaces no longer requires **SYSDBA** privileges for the user to install the Repository. SYSDBA is an advanced administrative privilege that is assigned to a user in an Oracle database. This allows the user to perform tasks affecting the database and other database users that ordinary user accounts cannot do (or for that matter, other administrative accounts without SYSDBA). For security reasons, we want to restrict user accounts with SYSDBA privilege to a minimum. So it is good that we don't have to use that privilege when we install the Repository.

One final OWB component to consider is the Repository Browser on the client. It is a web browser interface for retrieving information from the Repository. It will allow us to view the metadata, create reports, and audit runtime operations. It is the only other component besides the Design Center and the Control Center Manager that the user interacts with directly.

We will have a chance to visit each one of these areas in much more detail as we progress through the design and build of our data warehouse. However, first there is one more installation step we have to take before we can begin using the Warehouse Builder. The Repository must be configured for use and a workspace must be defined.

Configuring the repository and workspaces

We have talked about the OWBSYS schema that is created for us automatically during the Oracle 11g installation, and we have also looked at unlocking it and assigning a password to it. However, if we were to connect to the database right now as that user, we would find that as yet only a couple of objects exist in that schema. Filling out that schema is what will be done during this final installation step. We are going to use the **Repository Assistant** application to configure the repository, create a workspace, and create the objects in the repository that are needed for OWB to run. The OWBSYS schema is where the Warehouse Builder will store those objects. The **Repository Assistant** application is available from the **Start** Menu under the **Warehouse Builder | Administration** submenu of the Oracle program group as shown here:

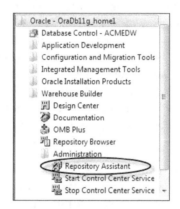

These menu options will appear locally on a client if we've installed the standalone Warehouse Builder client, as well as on the server. So where should we run the **Repository Assistant** if we have both? The most common configuration is to run this application on the same machine where the repository is located and the Control Center Service is going to run, which is all on one machine. There are other less common options for where to run the Control Center Service and where the Repository is located in relation to the target schema. These options are documented in *Oracle Warehouse Builder Installation and Administration Guide,* Chapter 1 – Overview of Installation and Configuration Architecture. The URL for the chapter in the guide is the following: `http://download.oracle.com/docs/cd/E11882_01/` `owb.112/e17130/overview.htm#CEGEBHBI`.

We want the runtime implemented on the server, which is the most common and simplest configuration. The Repository Assistant pops up an extra screen if it is running remotely from the client, which we will see next. We would see it during the installation if we were on a remote computer.

The steps for configuration are as follows:

1. We'll launch the **Repository Assistant** application on the server (the only machine we've installed it on) and the first step it is going to ask us for is the database connection information — **Host Name**, **Port Number**, and **Oracle Service Name** — or a **Net Service Name** for a **SQL*Net connection**. SQL*Net is Oracle's networking capability for communicating with databases in a distributed networked environment. A naming method is configured so that when using a Net Service name, SQL*Net will know what connection information to use for the connection. We have not configured a naming method, since we don't really need it just to connect locally, so we'll use the **Host Name**, **Port Number**, and **Oracle Service** name option as follows:

   ○ The **Host Name** is the name assigned to the computer on which we've installed the database, and we can just leave it at **LOCALHOST** since we're running it on the computer that has the database installed.

   ○ The **Port Number** is the one we assigned to the listener back when we installed it. It defaults to the standard 1521. This is an example of why the issue of changing or not changing that default port number was mentioned. If we changed it but can't remember what we changed it to, then the following tip will help out.

Determining what port your listener is listening on

There are a couple of options we have for this. One is to perform the following steps.

Open a command prompt window and type in the following command:

```
C:\>lsnrctl
```

This will launch the **Listener Control** program, which is the command line utility Oracle provides for controlling the listener. Then enter the following command at the listener control prompt:

```
LSNRCTL> status
```

Look for the line that says:

```
Listening Endpoints Summary...
```

The next line will have the port number listed along with the protocol and host name such as the following:

```
(DESCRIPTION=(ADDRESS=(PROTOCOL=tcp)(HOST=computer)
(PORT=1521)))
```

We can find information about the second option for determining the port number in the listener configuration file, listener.ora, in the Oracle home NETWORK\ADMIN directory. Open that file with Notepad and look for the above line.

- ○ For the **Service Name,** we will enter the name we assigned to our database during step 3 of the database creation process. The name we used is ACMEDW. At the end of the database configuration assistant process, a detail screen was displayed. It was suggested that it would be a good thing to take a screen capture of it because it contained details about the database configuration, which would be useful later. One of the items on that screen was the database name that was assigned. If that is not available, then here's another tip to find the database name.

Finding your database instance name

There are a number of places where the database name appears on the database server without us having to log in to the database. One is in the listener control program. Open a command prompt window and type in the following command:

`C:\>lsnrctl`

This will launch the Listener Control program. Then enter the following command at the listener control prompt:

`LSNRCTL> service`

Look for the instance name in the list of services that appears.

Another option is to check the name of the Windows service that is started for the database. The database service name is a part of that name. Open **Control Panel | Administrative Tools | Services**. The Windows service names for the Oracle processes all start with Oracle. The service that runs the actual database is named OracleService<dbname>, where <dbname> is the name of the database instance that you are looking for. The name says OracleServiceACMEDW for a database name of ACMEDW.

We can also check the Oracle base folder, which is the folder where the Oracle software was installed. The Admin folder contains a folder named for the database instance if we followed the default naming conventions for folder names during the installation. That is one reason to stick with the OFA standard when installing Oracle products.

2. Now that we've determined the connection information for our database, we'll move along to step 2 of **Repository Assistant**. It asks us what option we'd like to perform of the following:

    - ○ **Manage Warehouse Builder workspaces**
    - ○ **Manage Warehouse Builder workspace users**
    - ○ **Add display languages to repository**
    - ○ **Upgrade Repository to current release of Warehouse Builder**
    - ○ **Manage J2EE User account**

○   **Manage Optional Features**

We're going to select the first option to manage workspaces and move along to the next step.

3. This step asks us what we'd like to do with workspaces: create a new workspace or drop an existing one. We'll select the first option to create a new workspace.

4. This brings us to step 4 of the process, which is to specify an owner for the workspace. We are presented with two options: to create a new user or to use an existing user as the owner. To perform the first option, we will need to specify a database user who has DBA privileges that are required to be able to create a new user in the database. The second option is to specify an existing database user to become the owner of the workspace. This user must have the **OWB_USER** role assigned to be able to successfully designate it as a workspace owner. That is a database role required of any user who is to use the Warehouse Builder. If the existing user who is selected does not have that role, then it must be assigned to the user. An additional step will be required to specify another user who has the ability to do that assignment (grant that roll) or has DBA privileges. This second user must have the **Admin Option** specified for the OWB_USER role to be able to grant it if he or she does not have DBA privileges.

    The user specified here, whether new or existing, will become a deployment target for the Warehouse Builder. This means that the user will be able to access the Design Center for building the ETL processes and the Control Center Manager for deploying and auditing. We'll specify a new user for the ACME Toys and Gizmo's warehouse, since we've just installed this database and no other users are created yet.

5. This step will depend on which option we specified in step 4. If we are creating a new user, it will ask us for an existing user with DBA privileges in the database. The SYSTEM account is the default provided there, but if we have a different account that is a DBA in the database, we can use that. If we have specified an existing user in step 4, then step 5 will ask us for the username and password for that user, as well as the name of the new workspace to create.

    Since we're specifying a new user, we will put in the password for the system user and proceed to the next step. The password used here is the one we previously defined for the system accounts when we created our database.

6. Step 6 is new with release 11gR2 of the Warehouse Builder. It is for selecting optional features of OWB. For the purposes of this book, only the first option is required, the Data Integrator Enterprise Edition, since it includes the Code Templates that we'll be discussing in Chapter 10. This feature was named **Warehouse Builder Enterprise ETL** in previous releases. We'll uncheck the rest. These are separately licensed options also, and we now have the ability to enable or restrict them for users depending on whether we've licensed them or not.

7. In this step, we specify the new username, password, and workspace name. We'll use **acmeowb** for the username and **acme_ws** for the workspace name.

8. This step will ask for the password for the OWBSYS user. This schema was installed for OWB to use for the repository. The password it's looking for is the one we set up back on the final database configuration screen at the end of running **Database Configuration Assistant** to configure the database. This step will only be required upon first running **Repository Assistant** to create a new workspace since it also has to perform the process of initializing the repository in the OWBSYS schema first. That is a one-time process, which is why subsequent runs of **Repository Assistant** to manage workspaces will not require this step.

    After putting in that password, if we were running the **Repository Assistant** on a different machine than the database was installed on, then we would encounter the following screen. We referred to it earlier when talking about running the **Repository Assistant** remotely.

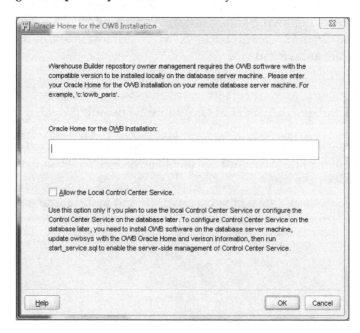

It doesn't know the location of the Oracle Home on the server, and so must prompt for it. It also provides the option for a **Local Control Center Service** that is for the remote runtime option discussed in the installation guide. Since we're running our database on the same machine as our client, we won't see this screen.

9. This step asks for **tablespace** names for the OWBSYS schema. A tablespace is a logical entity in an Oracle database for storing data. All objects created are assigned to a tablespace, which stores the data physically in a datafile or datafiles assigned to the tablespace. The administration of tablespaces in an Oracle database is more than we have room for here, so we won't be creating any new tablespaces to hold the OWBSYS data. We'll just leave the defaults selected — the **USER** tablespace for data indexes and snapshots, and the **TEMP** tablespace for temporary data. For advanced production databases, it would be a good idea (at a minimum) to specify a separate tablespace for OWBSYS, and actually think about using three new tablespaces for those three that have the USER tablespace assigned.

10. This step is to select a base language for the repository, so we'll make the appropriate selection. Once the repository is created, we cannot change the base language and there can only be one base language assigned to the repository. Physical names of repository objects are assumed to be in the base language. The **Repository Assistant** will automatically assign the base language depending on the locale that is assigned to the computer we're installing on. We also have the option of selecting one or more display languages that will allow users to assign a business name to physical objects in their own language. Unlike the base language, we can assign display languages after the repository is created. Select any of those that apply.

11. We're almost finished. The final step is the optional step 10 to specify any workspace users from existing database users. We specified the workspace owner as a new user earlier in the install process, and now it's asking for any additional users who we might want to have access to the workspace. The workspace owner is allowed to add and remove database users from the workspace.

 Removing a database user from the workspace does not delete that user account from Oracle. It only removes him or her as a valid user of the workspace.

After selecting any user, the **Repository Assistant** will present us with a summary screen of the actions it will take and the information we entered, as shown in the following image:

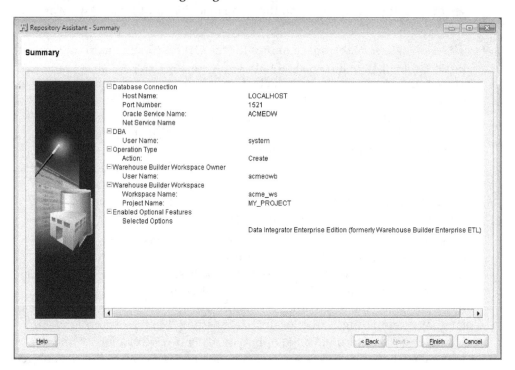

Notice the name of the project toward the end. There was no option to specify that project name, so it's just using a default name. It always sets up a default project in a new workspace by that name, but we can change it later when we actually start designing our data warehouse and working with the workspace in the Design Center.

Click on the **Finish** button and it will begin the installation, presenting us with a scroll bar moving to the right as it progresses through the installation. The very first time it runs, it will take around 5 to 10 minutes to run before reporting the success pop up, as it has to initialize the repository in the OWB-SYS schema. Creating new workspaces after the first time will be very quick, taking no more than a few seconds to complete.

Summary

That's it. We've gone through the install process of the Oracle 11*g* database. It automatically installs the Warehouse Builder components as well as the OWBSYS database user. We've also gone through a standalone installation of the OWB client on a separate workstation and have run **Repository Assistant** to configure our first workspace. We've also discussed the architecture of the Warehouse Builder components as they are now installed on our system. OWB is now installed and ready to use, so we can begin our project of designing and installing a data warehouse.

The general process we're going to follow throughout the rest of the book to actually build our data warehouse is to start by defining our data sources—where we will import the data from. We will import or define definitions of those sources, so that the Warehouse Builder knows about them. Then we will define our target data structures—where we will be loading data into during ETL and validate those structures. They will have to be generated and deployed to the target schema, which is the process of building the target. After that comes the process of designing and implementing our ETL to load the target from the sources.

Now that we have the software and database loaded, it's time to begin defining our sources of data.

2
Defining and Importing Source Data Structures

The Warehouse Builder software and Oracle database have been installed, and we're ready to begin building our data warehouse. The first thing we have to do is define what our sources of data will be. If we are going to build a useful data warehouse, we have to know what kinds of information our users are going to need out of the warehouse. To know that, we have to know the following:

- The format in which the data is currently stored and where it is stored.

- Whether there is a **transactional database** currently in use or not, which supports day-to-day operations and from which we'll be pulling the data.

  A transactional database is different from a data warehouse database in that it is designed to support the day-to-day transactions that keep an organization running.

- Whether the database is an Oracle database or another vendor's database such as Microsoft SQL Server.

- Whether there are any **flat files** of information saved from database tables or other files that users keep, which might be a source of information.

  A flat file is a file in text format that stores data in some kind of delimited format. The most common example of this kind of file is a **CSV** file, or a comma-separated file, that can be saved from a spreadsheet or extracted from a database table. It is called a flat file because it is in a text-only format and doesn't need to be interpreted by another program or application to read it.

The Warehouse Builder can help us with importing data from any (or all) of these formats into our data warehouse, and we're going to see how to do that in this chapter by covering the following major topics:

- Analysis of the source systems for the data warehouse we'll be building
- The Point of Sale transactional database
- A website orders database
- An overview of the Warehouse Builder Design Center
- Importing and defining source database object metadata
- Creating projects and modules in OWB, including Oracle and SQL Server modules
- Creating a SQL Server database connection using an ODBC gateway
- Configuring Oracle Heterogeneous Services for the ODBC gateway
- Defining source metadata manually with table editor
- Importing source metadata from a file

Preliminary analysis

In any data warehouse project, we are going to need to do some up-front analysis to determine what data will need to be captured into our warehouse. The analysis will tell us where the data is located, and in what format, so that we can begin to define our source data structures in the **Warehouse Builder**. In our case, we will presume that we have interviewed the management at the ACME Toys and Gizmos company and they have indicated the following:

- The high-priority information that they would like to see from this data warehouse project is *sales-related data* for all their stores
- They don't have an idea about the comparative sales in the various stores, so they need some way to view all that data together to do an analysis that shows how well, or poorly, the stores are doing
- In the future, they would also like to be able to compare store sales with their website sales, but that will not be required for this first data warehouse we build

We are doing a very simple analysis of our data warehouse project because the focus of the book is primarily on OWB. This book is all about using the Warehouse Builder and that begins *after* the initial analysis, and so we will cover just enough information to lay the groundwork for what follows. For more coverage of the design and analysis phase from a very practical standpoint, a very good book you should look up is *"The Data Warehouse Toolkit: The Complete Guide to Dimensional Modeling"*, *Ralph Kimball and Margy Ross, John Wiley and Sons, Inc.* This book covers in detail the analysis and design considerations you should take into account when designing a data warehouse and uses practical examples from a number of industries.

ACME Toys and Gizmos source data

Talking to users, administrators, and database administrators in ACME has helped us discover that there is a transactional system in use (called a **Point-of-Sale** or **POS** system). This system supports the stores that ACME has located in various cities throughout the country, and in other countries in Europe and Asia.

This system maintains data in a Microsoft SQL Server database named ACME_POS, and tracks individual sales transactions that occur for all of ACME's toys and gizmos. This database contains tables that store information about each sale along with all associated sales information such as the item sold, its price, the store in which it is sold, the register that processes the sale, and the employee who made the sale. Right away, we recognize that this would be a good source of data to help satisfy the management objective of analyzing their sales data better.

We have also found that the IT department that runs the website for ACME Toys and Gizmos has its own database that supports the website order management process. It is implemented in Oracle and handles the processing of all orders taken for products through the website. It contains tables that store information about:

- The orders taken
- Information about the customer who placed the order
- Information about the individual products that were ordered

This is an example of the **source data** that might not be needed in the initial stages of a data warehouse project, but that could be requested by users at a later stage. Then we can expand the data warehouse implementation to include website sales data. We will also take a look at importing source metadata for it later in this chapter.

> Scripts have been provided on the Packt website at http://www.
> packtpub.com/files/code/3449_Code.zip. These scripts can
> be used to build the Oracle website orders database referred to in this
> chapter. We also have a CSV file in this code bundle that will be required
> to import metadata. We have a script to install the SQL Server database.
> Instructions to use these files can be found with the code bundle.

However, working on it beyond that is not in the scope of this book.

The POS transactional source database

The **DBA** (**Database Administrator** — the person responsible for the maintenance
and administration of the database) is in charge of the POS transactional database.
The DBA has provided an **Entity-Relationship** (**ER**) **diagram** of the database to help
us understand the database and the relationships between the various tables. The
diagram is in the **UML** (**Universal Modeling Language**) notation. The following
image depicts a simplified version of the diagram containing the main tables
of interest and the relationships between them, including the cardinalities. The
cardinality indicates how the records in one table relate to records in the other. The
cardinality can be expressed as many-to-many, one-to-many, many-to-one, or one-to-
one, and is indicated in the diagram with counts composed of the following:

- 0..N — zero or more
- 1..N — one or more
- 1 — one only

The details about the columns in each table will be covered when we define
the metadata for them. If you are familiar with ER diagrams, the process of
implementing a database based on the diagram, and the concept of **normalization**,
you can skip the following section and move on to the *The website order management
database* section.

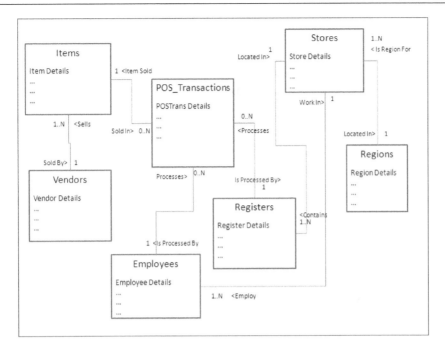

The main table in the `ACME_POS` database is the `POS_Transactions` table. It holds information about each transaction that takes place in a store, including the cash register that processed the transaction, the employee who worked the register, the item sold, the quantity sold, and the date. However, not all of that information is stored directly in the `POS_Transactions` table; only the date and quantity are stored directly. If all the details about the item were included in every record in the `POS_Transactions` table, there would be a large amount of duplicated information. After all, the store is not going to sell an item only one time because if it did, it wouldn't be in business for long. There will be potentially hundreds to thousands of sales of the same item each day, depending on how busy a particular store is. With each of those sales, a row gets placed in the `POS_Transactions` table.

We can see from the diagram that a separate table was created to hold item information and a link made from the main `POS_Transactions` table to the `Items` table. That link is created via a **foreign key** stored in the `POS_Transactions` table for the `Items` table. Instead of storing all the information about the item in the `POS_Transactions` table, a single column called the foreign key is placed there. This foreign key has a value corresponding to a value in the **primary key** column of the `Items` table. A primary key is a value that uniquely identifies a row in the table and, therefore, is not duplicated. We can then look up in the `Items` table for the information about the item for sale by using the value in the foreign key column for the item.

This concept of storing an item's information in a separate table results in a much greater accuracy of data, as we don't have to duplicate the item information. It is only entered *once* in the Item table. If it has to be updated, there is only one record in the Item table to update, and not thousands of records in the POS_Transactions table. This is known as database normalization. A transactional database is usually normalized due to this need for data accuracy.

The **attributes** of the POS_Transactions table are the individual pieces of information stored in it. Each of the attributes corresponds to one of the lines originating from the POS_Transactions table in the diagram, all except the quantity attribute. We can see that information about the employee who worked the register for the sale is stored in a separate table, the Employees table. This is similar to how the items sold are handled and stored in the Items table, as well as how the information about the register on which the sale was processed is stored in the Registers table.

In addition to these tables, we can also notice that a few other tables in the diagram are linked in various ways to these tables. They provide us with even more information about the attributes of a transaction and, therefore, about the transaction itself. We can see a table hanging off the Items table called Vendors. This table stores the information about each vendor who supplies toys and gizmos to the ACME company. A table called Stores is linked to the Registers table. This table tells us information about the store in which the register is located and, therefore, about the store that made the sale. Linked to the Stores table is the Regions table, which provides a location breakdown by region for the stores. ACME Toys and Gizmos is a worldwide operation and likes to track sales by breaking the world up into regions such as Europe and Asia, and for the US it's Northeast, Southwest, and so on.

At this point we can begin to understand why the management found it so difficult to compare sales data from all their stores and website, and why they would like to implement a data warehouse for their data explorations. Let's look at what kind of SQL query would be required to determine the number of flying discs sold today in Europe that were supplied by a particular vendor. Let's just consider the number of tables involved. We need the POS_Transactions, Items, Vendors, Registers, Stores, and Regions tables. The only table we don't need is the Employees table. But, why do we need the Registers and Stores tables when they wanted to know only the amount sold in the region? Well, the answer is that it's very tough for management to get the data they need. You see there is no direct connection from the POS_Transactions table to the Regions table.

The only way to get the region for a given transaction is to look up the register that processed the transaction, and then look up the store in which the register is located and that store record will give you the region. All of this is done with one massive **join SQL query** to join all these tables together. A join query is one that pulls data from more than one table at a time. As the database has a normalized structure, we have to include those two additional tables in our join, which we really don't want, just to get to the information we want. If we're talking about millions of transactions, which is not at all an unreasonable situation for any large sales operation, we would end up with highly inefficient queries that take a long time to run and make management very unhappy with the database.

So, we're going to solve this problem with our data warehouse, which will have a much better organization of tables for querying as we'll see in the next chapter.

The website order management database

The DBA in charge of the Oracle database for the website order management system has provided us with its ER diagram for our information. As with the POS transaction database, an ER diagram is provided here in a shortened version to give us an idea of the tables involved and their relationships with each other. Later in this book, we will have examples dealing with the POS transactional database as it contains the sales data for the stores. This database is presented here because of the possible future requirements to include this data. We'll use it to provide an example of importing from a database, and as an example of some minor issues that can be encountered when trying to analyze multiple sources of data.

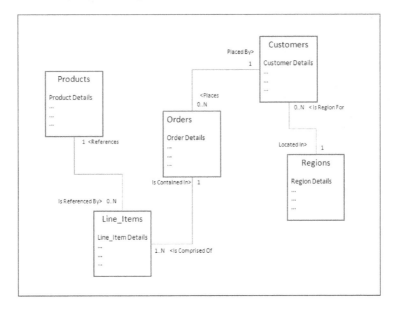

This database holds the sales information for the website, and we have to understand it before importing the database. We can see that it has some tables that are similar to the tables in the previous ER diagram that we just saw. The `Orders` table is the main table in this database instead of the `POS_Transactions` table. It holds information about customers who placed an order and a list of ordered items. The customer information includes the region in which the customer is located, and this is identical to the information in the `Regions` table in the POS Transactions database. The customer information is stored in a `Customers` table, which is linked to the `Orders` table, and we can see that the `Regions` table is linked to the `Orders` table through the `Customers` table. The list of ordered items is stored in the `Line_Items` table, which also has product information that identifies which product was ordered. The product information is stored in the `Products` table (which is similar to the `Items` table in the POS database). We can see that it has a link to the `Line_Items` table in our diagram.

Now we may get confused because this database has a `Line_Items` table and the other database has an `Items` table. But we're told that the `Products` table actually corresponds to the `Items` table, and not the `Line_Items` table. While this company is entirely fictional, this kind of issue of multiple departments, each with their own database and convention for naming tables and columns, is all too common in the real world for data warehouse projects. It's up to us to make sense out of it all and pull all that data into a single data warehouse where it can be queried at once. And this is what makes our job so interesting.

Let's look at one more issue with this order management database before we move on. This issue is the relationship between the `Orders` table and the `Line_Items` table. Each order is composed of a variable number of line items of ordered products. One person may place an order on the website for a doll and a fire truck, whereas another may order a game, a deck of cards, and a baseball bat. We've seen that this relationship between tables is accomplished in the database by storing a foreign key to the other table to indicate the relationship, but there could be any number of line items in an order. This would mean you will need any number of line item foreign keys stored in the `Orders` table, but that is not possible. The reason is that the foreign key in this situation is going the other way. The `Line_Items` table stores a foreign key to the order of which it is a part of, as a line item can be associated with only one order.

This was a brief overview of the source data structures we're going to be working with and also a very brief introduction to some database design issues. Without further ado, let's turn our attention to the Warehouse Builder, which is the real subject of this book.

An overview of Warehouse Builder Design Center

The **Design Center** is the main graphical interface that we will be using to design our data warehouse, but we also use it to define our data sources. So let's take some time at this point to go over the user interface and familiarize ourselves with it. Release 11gR2 of the Warehouse Builder has a completely updated interface, using the Fusion Client Platform style and presents an Integrated Development Environment (IDE) that is the same core IDE prevalent in other Oracle applications such as Oracle JDeveloper and SQL Developer. Anyone who has used either of those Oracle products, will immediately recognize the overall design. It is a much improved, more intuitive interface than the previous one from release 10gR2 and 11gR1 and provides such improvements as automatic layout, dockable panels, and zoom capabilities in editors within the IDE. The screenshots throughout the book have all been updated to reflect the new interface. We launch **Design Center** from the **Start** menu under the **Oracle** menu entry, as shown in the following image:

The **Design Center** must connect to a workspace in our repository. To review briefly, we discussed the architecture of the Warehouse Builder in Chapter 1. This included the repository in which we created a workspace and a user, who would be the owner of the workspace. We used the Repository Assistant application to configure our repository and create that user. The repository is located in the OWBSYS schema that was the pre-installed schema the database installation provided for us. The user name chosen was **acmeowb** and the workspace name was **acme_ws**. Now it's time to make use of this user and workspace.

The first screen we'll be presented with is the **Logon** screen, which will appear in front of the main interface screen as the first task to perform when launching the **Design Center**:

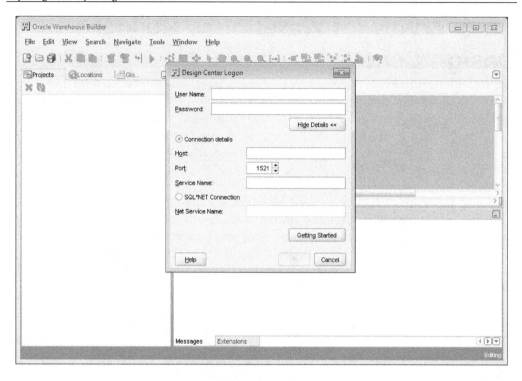

The first time we use this application, the **Logon** dialog box comes up all blank. But after we fill in our information for the first time, it will remember the **User Name** and **Connection details** on subsequent executions of the Design Center. Also, it will present us with a smaller version of the dialog box with just **User Name** and **Password**, so that we can just enter the password and don't have to re-enter the connection details. The button above the connection details that now displays **Hide Details <<** will display **Show Details >>**. If we need to change the connection details in that case or to just see what they are set to, click on the **Show Details >>** button and it will display the full dialog box as above.

As this is our first time, we have to enter all the details. The **User Name** and **Password** are what we specified in the Repository Assistant for the workspace owner, and the **Connection details** are the **Host**, **Port**, and **Service Name** we specified when we used the Database Configuration Assistant to create our database. We'll enter **acmeowb** as the username and **acmedw** as the service name.

The **Workspace Management** button to invoke **Repository Assistant** from the **Design Center Logon** dialog box is gone in this new version of the logon screen. In its place is the **Getting Started** button which launches a Help center window. Depending on your operating system version the help screen may be blank when it first comes up. There were a couple of bugs affecting the first released version of 11gR2 on Windows that were resolved in a subsequent patch.

The main **Design Center** window will be displayed next upon a successful log on. An example is shown in the following image, which depicts the default appearance of the **Design Center**:

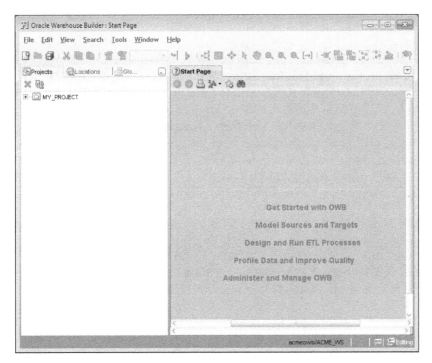

 A project called **MY_PROJECT** appears, which is the default project that the Warehouse Builder will create in every workspace.

We referred to **MY_PROJECT** back when we discussed the final results screen of the Repository Assistant, which showed this project name even though we hadn't specified one.

Before discussing the project in more detail, let's talk about the three tabs in the left window of the **Design Center** screen. They are as follows:

- **Projects**
- **Locations**
- **Globals Navigator**

The **Projects** tab is where we will work on the objects that we are going to design for our data warehouse. It was the old Project Explorer window in the previous Warehouse Builder release. It has nodes for each of the design objects we'll be able to create. It is not necessary to make use of every one of them for every data warehouse we design, but the number of options available shows the flexibility of the tool. The objects we need will depend on what we have to work with in our particular situation. In our analysis earlier, we determined that we have to retrieve data from a database where it is stored.

So, we will need to design an object under the **Databases** node to model that source database. If we expand the **Databases** node in the tree, we will notice that it includes both **Oracle** and **Non-Oracle** databases. We are not restricted to interacting with just Oracle in Warehouse Builder, which is one of its strengths. We will also talk about pulling data from a flat file, in which case we would define an object under the **Files** node. If our organization was running one of the applications listed under the **Applications** node (which includes **Oracle E-Business Suite**, **PeopleSoft**, **Siebel**, or **SAP**) and we wanted to pull data from it, we'd design an object under the **Applications** node.

The **Projects tab** isn't just for defining our source data, it also holds information about targets. Later on when we start defining our target data warehouse structure, we will revisit this topic to design our database to hold our data warehouse. So the **Projects tab** defines both the sources of our data and the targets, but we also need to define how to connect to them. This is what the **Locations tab** is for.

The **Locations tab** is where the connections are defined to our various objects in the **Projects tab**. The workspace has to know how to connect to the various databases, files, and applications we may have defined in our **Projects tab**. As we begin creating modules in the **Projects tab**, it will ask for connection information and this information will be stored and be accessible from the **Locations tab**. Connection information can also be created explicitly from within the **Locations tab**.

 Multiple projects can be defined in **the Projects tab**, but connection information is not displayed project-wise in the **Locations tab**. Connections are applicable for the entire workspace, and not just the project we are working on.

There are some objects that are common to all projects in a workspace. The **Globals Navigator** is used to manage these objects. It includes objects such as **Public Transformations** or **Public Data Rules**. A **transformation** is a function, procedure, or package defined in the database in Oracle's procedural SQL language called PL/SQL. **Data rules** are rules that can be implemented to enforce certain formats in our data.

Importing/defining source database object metadata

Now that we've been introduced to the **Design Center**, it's time to make use of it to import or define the metadata about our source database objects. **Metadata** is data that describes our data. We are going to tell the Warehouse Builder what our source database objects look like and where they are located, so that it can build the code necessary to retrieve the data from them when we design and run mappings to populate our data warehouse. The metadata is represented in the Warehouse Builder as objects corresponding to the type of the source object. So if we're representing tables in a database, we will have tables defined in the Warehouse Builder.

We have a couple of options for defining the source database objects. We can manually input the definitions into **Design Center Projects tab** ourselves, or we can choose to have the Warehouse Builder automatically import the descriptions of our data for us. As we like having the computer do the work for us whenever possible, we will choose the second option whenever we can.

> We need to be clear about the difference between importing or defining the metadata for our sources and loading the actual data as it can be confusing. At this stage, we are just importing or defining the definitions of our objects. (Metadata, or data about data, is information that tells us what the data looks like, column names, data types, and so on.) Later when we implement our targets and actually create a mapping between the source and the target and deploy it, we will be loading the actual data.

Creating a project

The very first thing we have to do in **Design Center** is make sure we have a project defined that will hold all of our work. In the last image, we saw a depiction of the **Design Center** as it appears when we first log on. Launch the **Design Center** now if you haven't already and we'll start working with it.

We can choose to use the default **My Project** project that was created for us, or create another new one. We are just going to use this default project as the Warehouse Builder was nice enough to create it for us. But, oh, that name is so boring. Let's give it a new name that is more appropriate for our company project. So right-click on the project name in the **Projects tab** and select **Rename** from the resulting pop-up menu. Alternatively, we can select the project name, then click on the **Edit** menu entry, and then on **Rename**. In either case, the name will be highlighted and turned to italics and we'll be able to use the keyboard to type a new name. We'll name the project ACME_DW_PROJECT.

If we wanted to create a new project, we would select **New...** either from the pop-up menu or from the **Design** drop-down menu. We can have any number of projects defined, but can work on only one at a time. There's a high possibility that we might be building more than one data warehouse at a time, and we could have a separate project defined for each.

Creating a module

Creating a project is the first step. But before we can define or import a source data definition, we must create a module to hold it. A **module** is an object in the **Design Center** that acts as a storage location for the various definitions and helps us logically group them. There are **Files** modules that contain file definitions and **Databases** modules that contain the database definitions. These **Databases** modules are organized as **Oracle** modules and **Non-Oracle** modules. Those are the main modules we're going to be concerned with here. We have to create an Oracle module for the **ACME_WS_ORDERS** database for the website orders, and a non-Oracle module for the **ACME_POS** SQL Server database. We'll create the Oracle module first because it is the simplest. After that, we'll create the module for the SQL Server database, which will involve a few more steps because Oracle has to communicate with the SQL Server database.

Creating an Oracle Database module

To create an **Oracle Database** module, right-click on the **Databases | Oracle** node in the **sProjects tab** of Warehouse Builder and select **New Oracle Module...** from the pop-up menu. The first screen that will appear is the **Welcome** screen, so just click on the **Next** button to continue. Then we have the following two steps:

1. In this step we give our new module a name, a status, and a description that is optional. We do the following in this step:

   ° On the next window after the **Welcome** screen, type in a name for the module

The name should reflect the name of the source database for consistency and ease of matching the module to the source database later. We're going to name our module **ACME_WS_ORDERS**, which is the name of ACME's Website Orders Oracle database as we discovered earlier when doing our analysis of the existing systems.

- ° The module status is a way of associating our module with a particular phase of the process, and we'll leave it at **Development**

- ° For the description, just enter any text that helps describe the source

With each new release of the Warehouse Builder, support for non-Oracle sources and targets is improved. Release 11gR2 now incorporates Code Templates which continues that trend. As a result, there is no option to specify whether this module we're creating is a source or a target. Previous releases had an additional option here for Oracle database modules to specify the type of module as a Data Source or a Warehouse Target and for non-Oracle databases only Data Source.

Our screen should now look similar to the following:

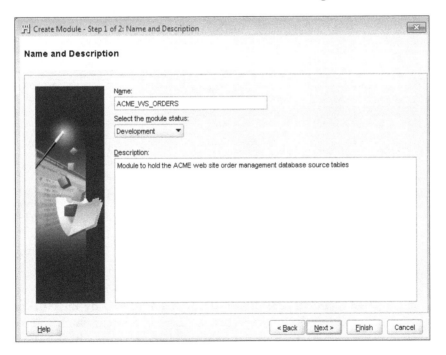

Click on the **Next** button to proceed to defining the connection.

2. In this step, we define the connection information for Warehouse Builder so that it knows how to connect to the source. We do that in the next screen using the following steps:

    ° The screen starts by suggesting a connection name based on the name we gave the module. Click on the **Edit** button beside the **Name** field to fill in the details. This will display the following screen:

    ° The name it suggested for us is **ACME_WS_ORDERS_ LOCATION1**. That's a fine name, except that 1 is on the end, so let's just remove it.

    ° For the connection details, we're going to enter **User Name**, acme_ws_ orders, and the **Password** that was given to us by the DBA for the website orders system. When we type in the username and move to the next field, the schema field will be automatically populated with the username.

If you are using the scripts downloaded from our website, the default password used is **acme1234** for the `acme_ws_orders` user.

- Enter the **Host** where the Oracle database resides and contains the `acme_ws_orders` schema, which is `localhost` as we're running everything on one system.

- The **Port** that the listener is listening on is **1521** so leave it as the default. Enter **acmedw** as the **Service Name** for the Oracle database. The schema we'll be connecting to has been automatically filled in for us

- One final step is to make sure the version of the Oracle database is set correctly. The **Version** we're working with is **11.2**, the most recent and the default.

We should now have a screen that looks similar to the following:

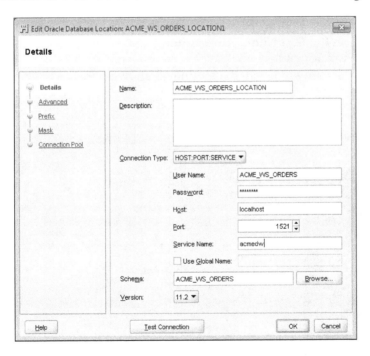

- Press the **Test Connection** button and if everything is OK, we'll see a popup with a **Successful!** message. We'll just click **OK** to close the popup. If not successful, it will display the error(s) in that popup for us so that we can debug the problem.

If we do get any errors, it's a good idea to become intimately familiar with the error manual in the Oracle documentation, which can be found at `http://download.oracle.com/docs/cd/ E11882_01/ server.112/e17766/toc.htm`. The errors will usually start with the three characters `ORA`, followed by a hyphen and then the error number. We can use all this to look up an error in the error manual to get more information. Google, Yahoo, or any Internet search engine can also be our friend here as (unfortunately) some of the errors, even after we look them up in the error manual, are not exact about the cause of the problem. Usually, searching for the error message string on the Internet can turn up others who have encountered the same issue and explanations of what to do about it.

○ The navigation window on the left on this dialog is new as of this release. The additional options are not needed for a basic Oracle connection that we're making now but are applicable to new connections like JDBC that were not available previously. We'll cover JDBC connections when we discuss Code Templates in chapter 10. For now however, we're done with this dialog so click on the **OK** button to proceed, even if an error was reported when we clicked on the **Test Connection** button. Now we will be back at the **Step 2** window where all the connection results will be filled in and it will be ready to create the module as shown here:

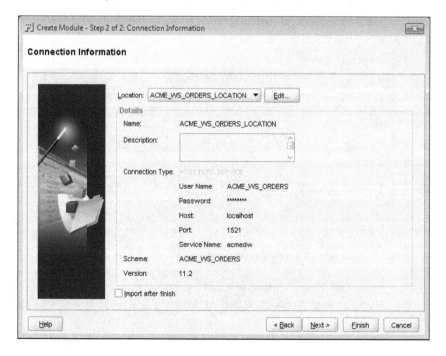

° The **Import after finish** checkbox can be used to proceed right to the import step but we're not going to check that box because we're going to move on and create a module for the SQL Server database before we import any database object metadata. So, with the box unchecked click on the **Finish** button

We are now back at the main Warehouse Builder interface and we can see that it has added our new module under the **Databases | Oracle** node in the **Projects tab** as shown below.

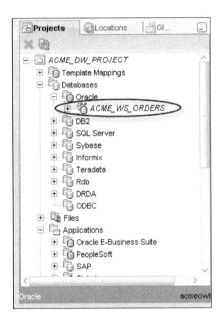

If we expand the **Locations | Databases | Oracle** module in the **Locations tab**, we'll see our location **ACME_WS_ORDERS_LOCATION** listed as shown in the following image. We just defined this location as a part of the process of creating the module.

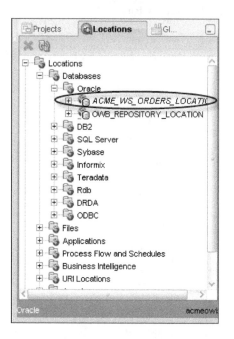

> Even if we had an error during the previous process of creating this connection, we would still see these entries created. If we could fix whatever caused the error, we'd then have a valid working connection without having to go back through the wizard to create it again.

Creating a SQL Server database module

Now that we have our module created for the Oracle database, let's create one for the SQL Server POS transactional database: **ACME_POS**. First, let's talk in brief about the external database connections in Oracle. If we expand the **Databases** node in the **Projects tab**, we'll see the list of supported databases. This is slightly different from the previous 11gR1 release of the Warehouse Builder in that all the databases are now at the same level in the tree. That is a reflection of the improved support in this release for non-Oracle databases. In the following image, a number of databases are listed, including one that says just **ODBC**:

Creating other Database Platforms

In this latest release of the Warehouse Builder, we now have the ability to create other database platforms that aren't listed above in the default set of other databases supported, such as MySQL for example. We will not need that capability for this book but if you want to read more about it, Chapter 11 of the Oracle Warehouse Builder Sources and Targets Guide has a complete write up of the new capability. You can access it online at the following URL:

```
http://download.oracle.com/docs/cd/E11882_01/owb.112/
e10582/platform_extensions.htm#CHDHEGEX
```

The POS transactional database is a Microsoft **SQL Server** database and we'll notice that it is one of the databases listed by name. We might think this is where we're going to create our source module for this import, but no.

The Warehouse Builder makes use of a couple of options for making connections to other databases. One of the options is **Oracle Heterogeneous Services.** This is a feature that makes a non-Oracle database appear as a remote Oracle database server. There are two components to make this work—the heterogeneous service that comes by default with the Oracle database and a separate agent that runs independently of the database. In addition to that option, there is now the option to use **JDBC (Java Database Connectivity)** to connect to a remote non-Oracle database.

For the Heterogeneous Services option the **agent** facilitates the communication with the external non-Oracle database and can take one of these two forms:

- An **Oracle Database Gateway agent** that is tailored specifically to the database being accessed
- A **generic connectivity agent** that is included with the Oracle Database and which can be used for any external database

The Oracle Database Gateway agents must be purchased and installed separately from the Oracle Database, and then configured to support the communication with the external database. They are provided for heavy-duty applications that do a large amount of external communication with other non-Oracle databases. The generic connectivity agent comes free with the Oracle Database. It is a low-end solution that makes use of ODBC or OLE-DB drivers for accessing the external database. **ODBC (Open Database Connectivity)** is a standard interface for accessing database systems and is platform and database independent. **OLE-DB (Object Linking** and **Embedding-Database)** is a Microsoft-provided programming interface that extends the capability provided by ODBC to add support for other types of non-relational data stores that do not implement SQL such as spreadsheets.

There is a significant difference between the Oracle Database gateways and the generic connectivity agent. The generic connectivity agent is restricted to the features of ODBC or OLE-DB and is very generic as a result. The database gateways are specifically tailored to the non-Oracle database and support a much wider range of database access features for the database being connected to. As a result, one aspect to consider is how extensive our access to the other database will be from our Oracle database and what database features we'll need to use. The generic connectivity agent is limited in some of the features it allows when accessing another non-Oracle databases compared to the gateways, and this factor may depend on whether we need these features or not. For working through the exercises in this book, the Warehouse Builder will work just fine with either option, a specific gateway or the generic connectivity option. We will use the generic option since our sample warehouse we're building is not that complicated.

Refer to the documentation to make a decision about which would be an appropriate choice of the agent in your case. The *Heterogeneous Connectivity Administrator's Guide* can be found at the following URL: http://download.oracle.com/docs/cd/E11882_01/server.112/e11050/toc.htm. The *Gateway for ODBC User's Guide* documentation can be found here: http://download.oracle.com/docs/cd/B28359_01/gateways.111/e10311/toc.htm.

There is the second option, using JDBC that we will also cover later in *Chapter 10* when we discuss the new Code Templates available now in the Warehouse Builder as of release 11gR2. If JDBC is used, the only mappings that can access the sources or targets using it are Code Template mappings, not the regular PL/Sql based original mappings in the Warehouse Builder. That is why we'll cover them separately later.

The particular method we choose will determine which of the nodes under the **Databases** node will be used to create our SQL Server database module.

> The individually named database nodes are used if we're using a transparent gateway agent tailored for that database or are using JDBC. The ODBC node is the one we use for any database connections using the generic connectivity agent.

Now that we've decided to use the generic connectivity solution, we need to create an **ODBC** module in Warehouse Builder to hold our definitions of source data for the POS transactional database. As this is a non-Oracle database we're using for the source, the module will be created under the **Databases | ODBC** node in the Warehouse Builder and not under the **Databases | Oracle** node as it is not an Oracle database. Expanding the **Databases** as shown in the previous image, we see that there is an **ODBC** node available. It is under this node that we will create our module for the source definitions for the POS transactional database.

However, there is one problem — because this is a non-Oracle database we're connecting to, we have to provide information to our Oracle database so that it knows how to connect. Warehouse Builder uses the underlying Oracle database Heterogeneous Services to make the connection. So this information must be configured before we define our module and location in the Warehouse Builder. In the following section, we will go through the steps to define our connection to the SQL Server database named ACME_POS. We're going to depart briefly from Warehouse Builder-specific topics here, but only because this is necessary for us to continue in the Warehouse Builder.

> If you are following along with each of these steps and want to create the ACME_POS database, you can run the scripts that have been provided in SQL Server to create the database and tables. They are available for download from the Packt website at http://www.packtpub.com/files/code/3449_Code.zip. Microsoft SQL Server 2008 Express was used for this book to generate the scripts because it is available free of charge. It is available from Microsoft's website at http://www.microsoft.com/express. It is available without charge and provides all the SQL Server functionality we'll need for this book.

Creating a SQL Server database connection

The first step that is required in making use of Oracle Heterogeneous Services to access a non-Oracle database using the generic connectivity agent is to create an ODBC connection. We do that by setting up a system **DSN (Data Source Name)**. A DSN is the name you give to an ODBC connection. An **ODBC connection** defines which driver to use and other physical connection details that are needed to make a connection to a database. On Microsoft Windows, we configure DSNs in the **ODBC Data Source Administrator**. The following are the steps for configuring a DSN:

1. You can access this application by navigating through the **Start | Control Panel | Administrative Tools** menu. The application is called **Data Sources (ODBC)**.

2. In **ODBC Data Source Administrator**, click on the **System DSN** tab, and then click on the **Add** button to add a new system DSN.

3. The first screen asks you to select which driver you want to use for your data source. ODBC drivers are specific to a database, so you have to use the one that is defined for accessing a SQL Server database. Scroll down the list until you see the **SQL Server** entry and click on it. Now click on the **Finish** button.

   This will take you to the screens that create an ODBC data source for connecting to SQL Server. Each ODBC driver requires a different configuration depending on the database it is connecting to.

4. For SQL Server, the first screen will ask you for a **Name, Description**, and the host on which the SQL Server database is located. For clarity, let's name our DSN **ACME_POS** after the database, enter **Data Source for connecting to the ACME POS database** for the description, and **localhost\SqlExpress** for the hostname in the **Server** field as illustrated in the following image:

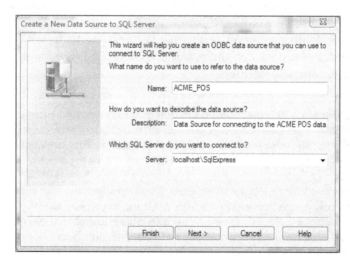

If the SQL Server instance that's being connected to is not on the same machine as the Oracle Database, then just enter the hostname where it is actually located instead of localhost. In actual business environments, the databases we are going to be using for source databases will most likely be located on other computers elsewhere on the network. We will enter the hostname for the other machine on which the SQL Server database is located in that case.

5. Click on the **Next** button to proceed.

> Notice \SqlExpress at the end of the hostname. This is required because SQL Express is installed as what is called a named instance, which basically requires that the name be included with the hostname for it to be found successfully.

6. In the next screen we will specify the authentication method to use to connect to the database. We have two options here. We can use **Windows NT Authentication using the network login ID.** (SQL Server will use the network or local machine login ID of the user connected at that time.) Alternatively, we can use **SQL Server authentication using a login ID and password** provided to us. The ACME DBA in charge of the ACME_POS database has kindly set up a username for us to access the ACME_POS database for importing definitions and data. He's given that user read permission on the tables in the database. The username is **acme_dw_user**. So we will use the second option.

> The scripts that are provided with this book are available for download and can be used to set up the SQL Server database to work through the examples in the book. This database uses the names that are provided here for the database and user.

7. There is a checkbox at the bottom of the screen to check off and have the new data source wizard connect to the SQL Server to obtain additional information. We are going to check that box if it is not checked by default, and enter the username and password provided by the ACME_POS DBA.

> An important item to note here is that this username and password are used only by the DSN creation application to access the database for some additional configuration items during the DSN setup process. This username and password will not be used by any application that subsequently uses our ODBC DSN to connect to the SQL Server. We will provide those connection details in a moment when we get to define the connection in the Warehouse Builder.

8. This is how our screen looks and we will click on **Next** to continue:

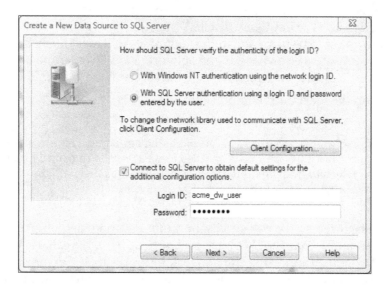

9. In the next screen, the primary item we want to verify is whether the default database is listed as **ACME_POS** so that when we use the ODBC connection it is connected to the correct database. It's quite possible for the username provided to have access to more than one database on the SQL Server instance if more than one exists. If the correct database is not showing, then check the box beside the database name and select the correct database as shown in the following screenshot:

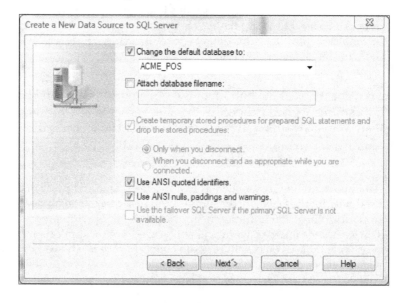

10. Leave all the other options set as they are and click on the **Next** button to continue.

11. The next screen is full of configuration options that we should just leave set to the defaults and click on the **Finish** button to complete the process. This will present us with the final summary screen of the ODBC connection details as shown in the following screenshot. The screenshot may appear with a different version number and slightly different entries depending on which version of Windows and the ODBC driver is running. These slightly different entries will not make a difference in following along in the steps in this chapter and the functionality we'll be covering.

If we want, we can test the newly created data source right here. If we click on the **Test Data Source...** button, it will make a connection to the database and return a screen indicating success or failure. Click on the **OK** button on this screen and the ODBC connection will be created. It will now appear on the **System DSN** tab of the **ODBC Data Source Administrator**.

Configuring Oracle to connect to SQL Server

Let's move on to the next step in the process of getting Oracle Heterogeneous Services to connect to our SQL Server database. We will configure Oracle now that we have our ODBC connection created. The following are the two steps involved here:

1. Create a heterogeneous service configuration file.
2. Edit the `listener.ora` file.

Creating a heterogeneous service configuration file

We will be creating a heterogeneous service configuration file in the `ORACLE_HOME\ hs\admin` folder. Just substitute your applicable `ORACLE_HOME` location. The following are the steps to create this file:

1. Open **Windows Explorer** and navigate to the `ORACLE_HOME\hs\admin` folder.

   There is a sample **init** file called `initdg4odbc.ora` that Oracle has been kind enough to supply us with. We can easily modify this file to suit our purpose. It is a plain-text file, so we can use any text editor to edit it.

   Let's open the file named `initdg4odbc.ora` in our favorite text editor, or Windows Notepad if we don't have any other text editor.

   This is the default init file for using ODBC connections. The contents will basically look like the following:

   ```
   # This is a sample agent init file that contains the HS parameters
   #that are needed for the Database Gateway for ODBC
   #
   # HS init parameters
   #
   HS_FDS_CONNECT_INFO = <odbc data_source_name>
   HS_FDS_TRACE_LEVEL = <trace_level>
   #
   # Environment variables required for the non-Oracle system
   #
   #set <envvar>=<value>
   ```

   The lines that begin with # are comment lines and will be ignored. The two lines we're interested in are the ones that are in bold in the code we just saw.

2. The `HS_FDS_CONNECT_INFO` line is where we specify the ODBC DSN that we just created in the previous section. So replace the `<odbc data_source_ name>` string with the name of the Data Source, which is (unless you changed it from what was suggested) `ACME_POS`.

3. The `HS_FDS_TRACE_LEVEL` line is for setting a trace level for the connection. The trace level determines how much detail gets logged by the service and it is OK to set the default as `0` (zero).

> To read more about what this entry's purpose is, refer to the *Oracle Database Heterogeneous Connectivity Administrator's Guide 11g Release 2* at the following URL: `http://download.oracle.com/docs/cd/ E11882_01/server.112/e11050/toc.htm`.

Having made those changes, our file should now look like the following:

```
# This is a sample agent init file that contains the HS
# parameters that are
# needed for the Database Gateway for ODBC

#
# HS init parameters
#
HS_FDS_CONNECT_INFO = ACME_POS
HS_FDS_TRACE_LEVEL = 0


#
# Environment variables required for the non-Oracle system
#
#set <envvar>=<value>
```

4. Now we will save the file with a new name and will be careful not to overwrite the default file. We'll give it a name that begins with `init` and ends with `.ora`, and contains a name in the middle that is descriptive and does not contain spaces or special characters. Let's save it as `initacmepos.ora`.

Leave out the underscore character as we're not allowed to use special characters. We might think it's just a filename and it is certainly allowed to use an underscore in the filename. However, this part of the filename must be used in the next step for a purpose that does not allow special characters to be used.

Editing the listener.ora file

Now we're going to add a SID to our `listener.ora` file. When we configured the listener back in Chapter 1, it created a `listener.ora` file in `ORACLE_HOME\network\admin`. The steps for this are:

1. Load the `listener.ora` file into a text editor (or Notepad). Add the following lines to the file:

```
SID_LIST_LISTENER=
  (SID_LIST=
    (SID_DESC=
      (SID_NAME=acmepos)
      (ORACLE_HOME=C:\app\bob\product\11.2.0\dbhome_1)
      (PROGRAM=dg4odbc)
    )
  )
```

> There is a sample `listener.ora` file called `listener.ora.sample`, which is provided for us in the `ORACLE_HOME\hs\admin` folder. It contains the above lines that can be cut and pasted into our actual `listener.ora`. We just need to correct `SID_NAME` to `acmepos`.

For `SID_NAME`, we have to specify the name we used as part of the name of our `init` file in the previous step. This is why no special characters were allowed because this name will become the SID for our database connection and SIDs cannot have special characters. However, don't include the `init` or `.ora` from the name of this file.

In the `PROGRAM` entry, we will specify the agent that will handle the connectivity for us and the name of the generic connectivity agent program supplied with the Oracle Database 11*g* is `dg4odbc`. For `ORACLE_HOME`, you will substitute your particular `ORACLE_HOME` location, which will be different unless your username is also `bob` and you installed Oracle using the default naming convention on the `C` drive.

An important tip about the PROGRAM name

Make sure you use the correct name for `PROGRAM` for your version of the database. In versions prior to 11*g*, the generic connectivity agent name was `hsodbc`. However, in Oracle Database 11*g*, it is known as `dg4odbc`. If we use the wrong name for `PROGRAM`, or misspell it, we will get a strange error message when we try to define our connection information using this external link.

There may already be a `SID_LIST_LISTENER` entry in the `listener.ora` file. If so, just add the `SID_DESC` section above the existing `SID_LIST_LISTENER` `SID_DESC` entry. By studying that entry, you can see the syntax for how the `SID_DESC` sections are listed; so just follow the same convention.

2. After we save the `listener.ora` file, we must restart the listener for the change to take effect. We can restart it by navigating to **Start** | **Control Panel** | **Administrative Tools** and then clicking on **Services**. Now, scroll down until you see the service for your database listener, which will be named starting with **Oracle** and ending in **TNSListener**. It will contain **ORACLE_ HOME—OracleOraDb11g_home1TNSListener**. Now right-click on it and select **Restart**.

Creating the Warehouse Builder ODBC module for SQL Server

Now that we have defined our source SQL Server database connection information in Oracle, we are done with our foray into non-Warehouse Builder-specific topics. We will get back to the main topic of creating the module and location in the Warehouse Builder. This process is very similar to creating a module for an Oracle database as we just did. There are some slight differences in a couple of screens, which we'll point out as we go along. The steps to create an ODBC module and location in Warehouse Builder are as follows:

1. Right-click on the **ODBC** node in the **Projects tab** of **Design Center**, and select **New ODBC Module...** from the pop-up menu. The first screen that will appear is the **Welcome** screen, so just click on the **Next** button to continue.

2. The screen with the label **Step 1** is where we provide a name as we did for the Oracle module. We're going to name this ODBC module `ACME_POS`, which is the name of ACME's POS transactional database in SQL Server as we discovered earlier when analyzing the existing systems.

3. We'll leave **module status** set to **Development**.

4. The next screen labeled **Step 2** is for the connection just as earlier. We'll click on the **Edit** button beside the name to fill in the details. This will display the following screen:

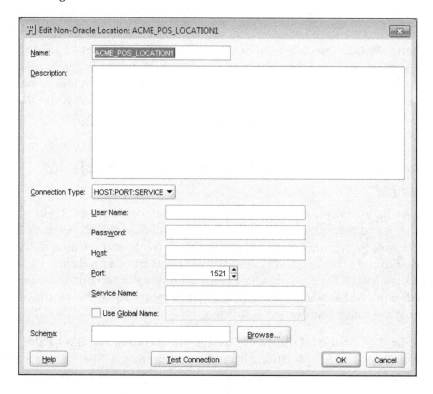

We'll remove the **1** as we did for the Oracle connection.

5. For the connection details, we will enter the **User Name** as `"acme_dw_user"`, and **Password**, which was given to us by the DBA for the transactional system.

> We have to make sure that both username and password are enclosed in double quotes. The Oracle database will automatically make them uppercase if we don't, and the SQL Server database does not like that. So, if we get a username and/or password incorrect error, we'll double-check that we enclosed them in double quotes; yes, even the password. The double quotes in the password will appear as asterisks like the rest of the password, but make sure to put them in there.

6. Enter the **Host** where the Oracle database resides and where we configured the heterogeneous services. It is **localhost** as we're running everything on the same system.

Here we might think that we have to enter the hostname of where the SQL Server database resides, as we're entering connection information to connect to it. Remember that although we're using Oracle Heterogeneous Services to make that connection for us and have already gone through the steps to configure it in the listener to connect to the ODBC DSN, where the actual connection information for the SQL Server database is specified. This means what we need to specify here is the connection information for the SID that we configured earlier as if we're connecting to an Oracle database. In reality, it will actually be connecting to the SQL Server database

7. The **Port** the listener is listening on is **1521**, so leave it as the default. Enter the **Service Name** that we configured in the previous section in the listener for the generic connectivity dg4odbc agent—**acmepos**.

8. Finally, enter the schema we'll be connecting to. For SQL Server, the owner of most databases is referred to internally as **DBO** and so this is what we're going to put here.

Just as with the username and password, we have to make sure we enclose the schema name in double quotes also or we will run into problems if we try to import data objects using this location. It is also important to make sure the schema name that is in double quotes is also all lower case letters. It will save us from having issues as we'll see in a moment when we discuss importing data objects.

9. We should now have a screen that looks similar to the following:

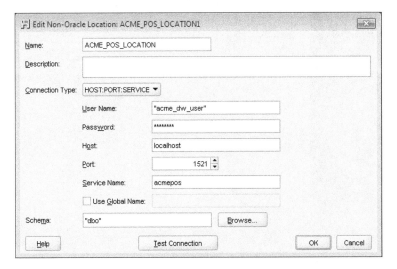

10. We can click on the **Test Connection** button to make sure everything is working properly and the results will be displayed in the **Test Results** pop-up window.

> This is where we may encounter an error if the PROGRAM name is incorrect in the listener.ora file. Here's such an example of an error and you can see how unhelpful these error messages can be: **ORA-28545: error diagnosed by Net8 when connecting to an agent Unable to retrieve text of NETWORK/NCR message 65535**. Even if we search the Internet and documentation for solutions, many suggestions will mention hsodbc, and not dg4odbc. The solution to this particular error actually refers to the PROGRAM name. In this case, the initdg4odbc.ora and the listener.ora.sample example files in the ORACLE_HOME\hs\admin folder clearly say dg4odbc and not hsodbc. Those who work a lot with Oracle 10g may (out of habit) have used hsodbc, never once thinking about double-checking whether that was correct or not. The error can also occur if we use a different service name than was actually defined in the listener.ora file. The moral of the story: Use the example files as a starting point but make sure the SID_NAME is correct!

11. Click on the **OK** button to proceed even if there was an error reported when we clicked on the **Test Connection** button. We will be back at the **Step 2** window with all the connection results now filled in and we will be ready to create the module as shown here:

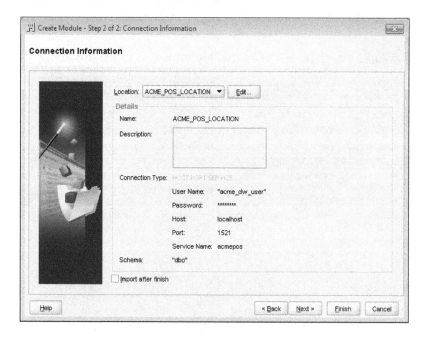

12. The **Import after finish** checkbox will not be checked by default. We'll leave it that way since we're going to import separately in the next step starting with the Oracle module. So, make sure it's unchecked and click on the **Finish** button.

We are now back at the main Warehouse Builder interface and we can see that it has added our new module (**ACME_POS**) under **Databases** in the **Projects tab** as seen below:

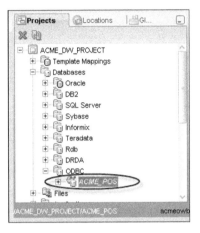

In the **Locations tab**, if we expand the **Locations | Databases| ODBC** node or module, we'll see **ACME_POS_LOCATION** listed, which is our location that we just defined as part of the process of creating the module. This is shown in the following screenshot:

> Even if we had an error during the previous process of creating this connection, we would still see these entries created. If we could fix whatever caused the error, we'd have a valid working connection without having to go back through the wizard to create it again.

Importing source database objects from a database

We are now at the point where we can finally import our source database `objects`. `source` database objects. We'll walk through the process of importing from an Oracle database, which is very similar to the process of importing from a non-Oracle database; so it will be a good exercise to walk through pointing out specific differences as we go. After that, we will walk through the process of defining the metadata for our SQL Server database tables using a data object editor for tables, which is integrated into the Warehouse Builder for working with tables. We could just as easily import the database objects from SQL Server but we'll walk through the process for one source table manually just so we can learn about the process of editing data objects. We will then leave the rest as an exercise for the reader to be done in a similar manner or to be imported automatically. Let's start by importing from the Oracle database using the following steps:

1. We are going to begin by right-clicking on the **ACME_WS_ORDERS** module name under the **Databases | Oracle** node in the **sProjects** tab and selecting **Import** and then **Database Objects...** from the pop-up menu.

> The Import submenu that appears when we right-click and choose Import on a database node has more than one choice. We might be tempted here to select the first choice, **Warehouse Builder Metadata...** for this import; however that is for a different kind of import, Metadata exports and imports that we'll look at in Chapter 9. In this new release, that option has been added to the context menus on the various objects and to differentiate that process from the task of importing data objects from source database systems, the option we want has been named **Database Objects...**.

We will then be presented with the **Import Metadata Wizard**. This is the same wizard that will be used for importing from any of the available source data options, databases, files, and so on. It will tailor its prompts for the particular type of source we selected.

We may at this point see a pop-up warning about the connection not being set and to click OK to set connection details. That's frequently just because the password didn't get saved with the connection. It will display the connection details where we can fill in the proper password before continuing.

2. Click on the **Next** button on the **Welcome** screen and we'll be presented with a screen labeled **Step 1** of the process where we choose what to import. The following image is what it looks like for an Oracle database:

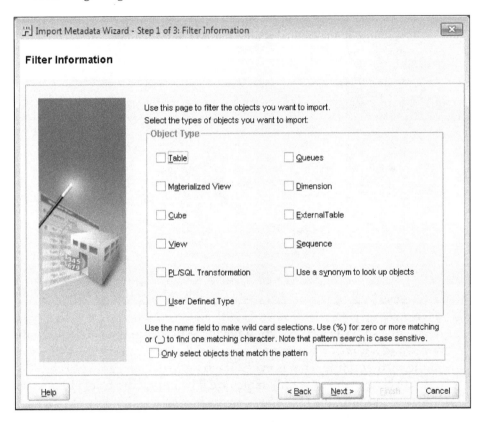

We can make selections on this screen to *filter out just what we want to import,* or we can leave everything checked to be able to import anything. This screen will appear slightly different depending on what type of source we're importing from. We will have all these options for an Oracle database, but for our ODBC connection to the SQL Server database, it will have checkboxes for just **Table** and **View** as shown next:

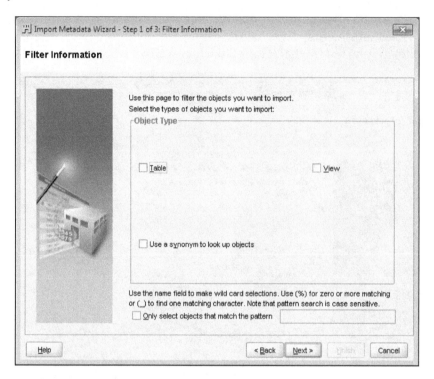

There will also be a checkbox for whether to use synonyms to look up the objects, and a text box where we can enter a search pattern to use if we want to further refine what is available to us. We're just going to check the **Table** checkbox since it is only tables we'll be importing from either source database. Checking the **Use a Synonyms** box means that if there are any synonyms defined (alternative names for database objects), then the import wizard will use those names and present them to us; otherwise it uses the underlying actual object names. As there are no synonyms being used in the **ACME_WS_ORDERS or ACME_POS** source databases, it will not make a difference whether it's checked or not.

3. Click on **Next** to move on to **Step 2**:

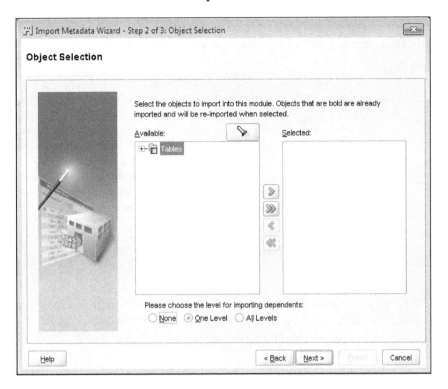

This screen is where we will choose the *specific objects that we wish to import*. There will be an entry in the left window for each of the boxes we left checked in **Step 1**. Notice (at the bottom) the buttons for choosing the level for importing dependents. The **Import Wizard** can automatically import other objects that might depend on the object we're selecting based on foreign key definitions that it detects in the source database. The number of levels means how far it goes in tracing foreign key relationships. If we say one level, which is the default, then it will import any tables that have foreign key relationships to the table selected but will not check those tables for relationships. If you say **All Levels**, then it will follow relationships until it doesn't find any further relationships. We're going to select all the tables in our ACME_WS_ORDERS schema or the ACME_POS Sql Server schema to import, so this setting will not have an effect on what gets imported. Therefore, we'll leave it set to the default.

4. Click on the plus sign beside the **Tables** entry to see the complete list of tables to choose from. We will see all of the website orders' database tables that we discussed earlier and if importing the ACME_POS Sql Server database, all of the source point of sale transaction database tables.

> If we were importing from a SQL Server database and had not enclosed the schema name in double quotes and made it lowercase, we would not see any tables show up here. There would be no error message at all. It would look like it was doing something and then the plus sign would change to a minus sign as if it had expanded and displayed all the tables but nothing would show up. In fact, no error is generated as far as the Warehouse Builder is concerned. It submits a SQL statement to the source database requesting a list of table names where the owner is the schema name we included in the location but it makes that schema name uppercase unless we use the double quotes. The schema name in MS SQL Server is lower case and therefore the SQL statement returns no results and so nothing displays. So, when setting up a SQL Server location, be sure to make the schema name lowercase and use double quotes around it.

5. Clicking on the plus sign to expand an entry on this page is the first time the wizard will actually make a connection to the source database. If we saved the connection information before and didn't test it to make sure it worked, this is where we'll find out.

   The table names will display under the tables entry. If we've already imported any of the tables previously, those will be displayed in bold. We can re-import them to pick up any changes that might have been made to them. We're going to click on all the tables, and then click on the single right arrow (**>**) in the middle of the screen to move those tables over to the right side. This will signify that we want to import them. As we want all the tables this time, we could alternatively click on the **Tables** entry itself and then on the single right arrow (**>**) to move that entry and everything in it over to the right or just click the double right arrow (**>>**) to move everything. At this point, if we had one of the options checked for importing dependents and had not already selected the dependents to import, it would display a dialog box. This dialog box would inform us of any additional objects it detected as dependents that it was going to automatically add for us.

6. We'll click on the **Next** button to proceed to the **Summary and Import** page where it will summarize the selections we've made and tell us the action it is going to take for each selection—whether to create or re-import the object. There is also an **Advanced Import Options...** button that will be available on that screen as we can see in the following image:

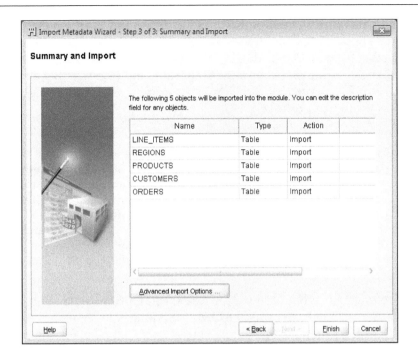

Clicking on the **Advanced Import Options...** button presents us with a dialog box similar to the following screenshot:

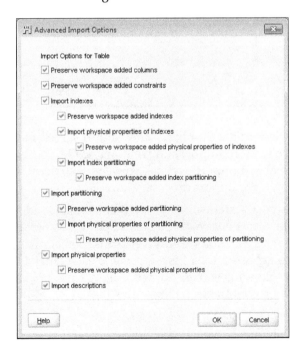

This dialog box will be slightly different, depending on the type of object and the type of source being imported. The screenshot we just saw is an example for a table from an Oracle database. It specifies whether to import certain features, such as indexes or physical properties, and also whether any possible changes we've made to the objects in the Warehouse Builder workspace after import should be preserved.

> The option for preserving changes made in the workspace would definitely be something we will need to consider if we subsequently import objects from SQL Server after defining them manually. If we don't uncheck the boxes for preserving workspace changes and we've already created all the tables manually as we're about to do, it will leave all our column definitions in place and add new columns for each of the columns in the table. In that case, we would definitely want to uncheck the preserve checkboxes so our manual edits are replaced with a clean copy.

The following is what we'll see for **Advanced Options** when importing from a SQL Server database using the ODBC module:

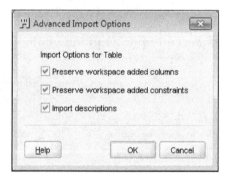

We have verified on the **Summary and Import** screen that we have included everything we want to import and we don't need to bother with unchecking any of the advanced import options. So we will click on the **Finish** button, which will begin the import process.

7. During the import, a status dialog box will be displayed showing the progress of the import as each object is imported. When it completes, we'll be presented with the final **Import Results** screen showing the status of the import. We can click on the plus sign beside each entry to see the details as shown in the following screenshot with the Customers table expanded to show each of the columns:

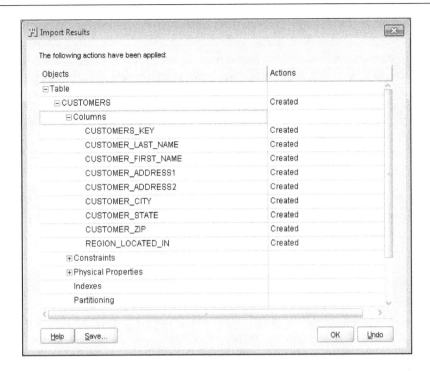

The other buttons you have on this screen are:

- ° A **Save** button which will allow us to save a **Metadata Import Result Report** log file so we can have a record of the results of our import if desired.

- ° An **Undo** button that we could click on at this point to cancel the import. The **Import Metadata Wizard** has not actually saved any information to the database yet, so clicking on the **Undo** button will just throw away what we've done so far and not make any changes to the database.

- ° The **OK** button will save the changes to the module in **Projects tab** from which we performed the import.

In this case, clicking on **OK** is going to save the imported tables in the **ACME_WS_ORDERS** module that we created under the **Databases | Oracle** node or the **ACME_POS** module under the **Databases | ODBC** node. We can verify this by going back to the **Projects tab** window and expanding the appropriate module if it's not already expanded by clicking on the plus sign, and we should see the list of tables.

Congratulations! We've imported our first set of objects into the Warehouse Builder.

Let's take a look at the **Table Editor** (a data object editor for editing tables) now as another alternative available to us for entering the metadata for our source database tables. If the import were to fail for some reason, we could always fall back to manually entering the information for our source databases. A third option would be to copy and paste table metadata across modules. We'll discuss copying and pasting metadata in Chapters 9 and 10.

We should save our work at this point. So we'll select **Design | Save All** from the toolbar menu of the **Design Center** application or press the *Ctrl + S* key combination to save our work.

Defining source metadata manually with the Table Editor

Before we can continue building our data warehouse, we must have all our source table metadata created. If the automatic import via the Metadata Import Wizard were to fail for whatever reason, we must create the source metadata manually in that case. It is not a particularly difficult task. However, attention to detail is important to make sure what we manually define in the Warehouse Builder actually matches the source tables we're defining. Warehouse Builder provides contextual data object editors for creating and editing source metadata. The **Table Editor** is a tool we can use to create database tables in the Warehouse Builder. The steps to manually define the source metadata using the **Table Editor** are:

1. To start building our source tables for the POS transactional SQL Server database, let's launch the OWB Design Center if it's not already running. Expand the **ACME_DW_PROJECT** node and take a look at where we're going to create these new tables. We created our ACME_POS module for the SQL Server source database under the **Databases | ODBC** node so that is where we'll create the tables. Navigate to the **Databases | ODBC** node, and then select the **ACME_POS** module under this node. We will create our source tables under the **Tables** node, so let's right-click on this node and select **New Table** from the pop-up menu. As no wizard is available for creating a table, we are using the Data Object Editor to do this.

2. The first screen we'll be presented with is a small popup asking us to fill in the name and a description for the new table we're creating. We're going to create the metadata for the **ITEMS** table so let's change the name to **ITEMS** and click **OK** to continue.

3. Upon selecting **OK**, we are presented with the **Table Editor**
   screen on the right hand side of the main **Design Center** interface. It's a clean
   slate that we get to fill in, and will look similar to the following screenshot:

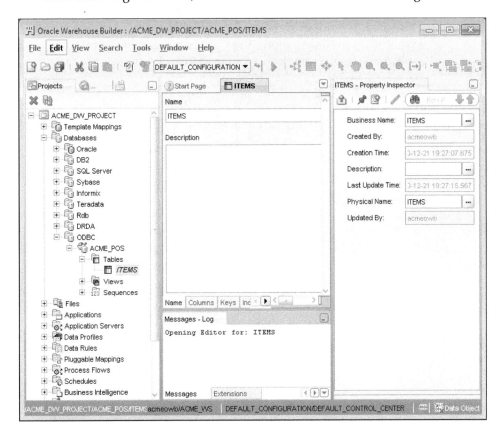

There are a number of facets to this interface but we will cover just what we need now in order to create our source tables. Later on, we'll get a chance to explore some of the other aspects of this interface for viewing and editing a data object. The interface is completely customizable also. The Sub-windows can be dragged to any position we want. For our purposes now we're going to leave the interface as it is and be working in the main Table Editor window labeled ITEMS. The fields to be edited in this **Table Editor** are as follows:

- ° The first tab it presents to us is the **Name** tab. We can see all the various tabs arrayed along the bottom of the ITEMS editor window. The Name is already filled in for us from the initial popup so we'll move on to define the columns.

- ○ Let's click on the **Columns** tab next and enter the information that describes the columns of the Items table. To make the window easier to work with we'll minimize the **Properties Inspector** to make more room for the main ITEMS editor window. Just click the minimize button in the upper right corner of the Properties Inspector and we'll see it minimize along the right hand side of the interface. Our window should now look similar to the following:

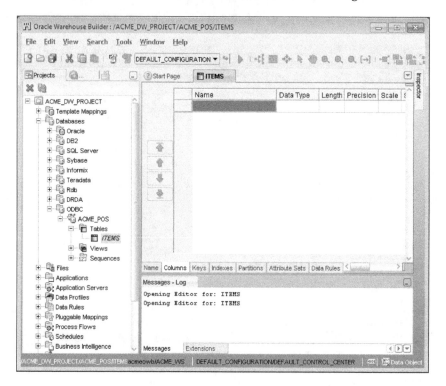

- ○ How do we know what to fill in here? Well, that is easy because the names must all match the existing names as found in the source POS transactional SQL Server database. For sizes and types, we just have to match the SQL Server types that each field is defined as, making allowances for slight differences between SQL Server data types and the corresponding Oracle data types.

The following will be the columns, types, and sizes we'll use for the Items table based on what we found in the Items source table in the POS transaction database:

```
ITEMS_KEY number(22)
ITEM_NAME varchar2(50)
ITEM_CATEGORY varchar2(50)
```

```
ITEM_VENDOR number(22)
ITEM_SKU varchar2(50)
ITEM_BRAND varchar2(50)
ITEM_LIST_PRICE number(6,2)
ITEM_DEPT varchar2(50)
```

We'll enter each of these column names on the **Columns** tab of the **Data Object Editor** for the Items table; and as we enter each name, it will suggest data types and sizes, which may or may not be adequate. It makes a best guess based on what we enter for the name, and may or may not relate to the source data type and size. For ITEMS_KEY, it suggests a number with precision 22. For ITEM_VENDOR, it actually suggested a varchar2 type. We simply change it to match the ITEMS_KEY, as we see in the SQL Server database that both these fields are defined as type INT and 22 for the precision is large enough to hold an integer from SQL Server. An integer is a four-byte number, no larger than 2,147,483,647. The other character fields in the SQL Server Items table are all of the varchar type, which is the SQL Server equivalent to a varchar2 in Oracle. So we make sure they are varchar2 with sizes that match. The ITEM_LIST_PRICE is defined with both a precision and scale because that is a decimal number in the Items table in SQL Server with that precision and scale.

Precision and scale of numbers

Properties of number data types can include a precision and scale. Oracle allows a number data type to be specified without indicating a specific precision and scale. Precision indicates the maximum number of digits the number can contain, and scale indicates the number of decimal places to the right of the decimal. If we don't specify them, Oracle Database will accept a number of any precision and scale as long as the number doesn't fall outside the range allowed, which is between 1.0 x 10-130 and 1.0 x 10126. We would specify a precision and scale to enforce greater data integrity in the database. For example, if we enter a number that has more digits than the specified precision, it will generate an error even though the number might still fall in the acceptable range.

When completed, our column list should look like the following screenshot:

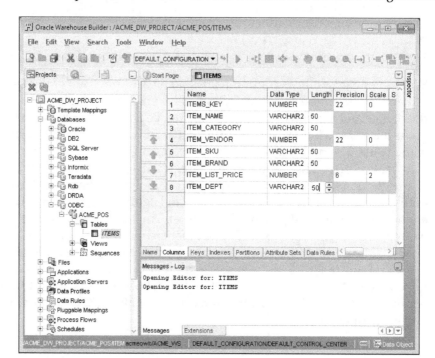

We don't have to worry about specifying information for any of the other tabs for this source table. The important details are the column names, and their types and sizes. Later in the book, we'll have a chance to revisit this editor again and discuss the remainder of the tabs.

4. We can save our work at this point and close the **Table Editor** window now before proceeding. So we'll select **File | Save All** from the main menu of the **Design Center**, or press the *Ctrl + S* key combination to save our work. We can close the Table Editor window for the ITEMS table by hovering the mouse over the ITEMS tab at the top of the window and then clicking on the **X** that appears or by selecting **File | Close** from the **Design Center**. Closing the editor window is really a matter of preference. With this new release of the Warehouse Builder, all the editors are integrated into the main interface and as new ones are opened, new tabs will be added to the canvas on the right. We can close the **Start Page** also just to clean up the work area and it will be blank until we open another tool or editor.

We now have the option to continue this process to define the metadata for the remaining SQL Server tables that we'll need or to just do the import using the Import Metadata Wizard. If continuing to enter tables manually, the process is identical; just change the names of the tables and the types and sizes of the columns to match their respective tables. We will not need all the tables defined in the ACME_POS database—only a subset is used throughout the remainder of the book to build the data warehouse. The tables needed are the POS_TRANSACTIONS, REGISTERS, STORES, and REGIONS tables. The column information for each of them is provided here for reference and help in creating the corresponding tables in the Warehouse Builder:

POS_TRANSACTIONS

```
POS_TRANS_KEY number(22)
SALES_QUANTITY number(22)
SALES_ASSOCIATE number(22)
REGISTER number(22)
ITEM_SOLD number(22)
DATE_SOLD date
AMOUNT number(10,2)
```

REGISTERS

```
REGISTERS_KEY number(22)
REGISTER_MANUFACTURER varchar2(60)
MODEL varchar2(50)
LOCATION number(22)
SERIAL_NO varchar2(50)
```

STORES

```
STORES_KEY number(22)
STORE_NAME varchar2(50)
STORE_ADDRESS1 varchar2(60)
STORE_ADDRESS2 varchar2(60)
STORE_CITY varchar2(50)
STORE_STATE varchar2(50)
STORE_ZIP varchar2(50)
REGION_LOCATED_IN number(22)
STORE_NUMBER varchar2(10)
```

REGIONS

```
REGIONS_KEY number(22)
REGION_NAME varchar2(50)
CONTINENT varchar2(50)
COUNTRY varchar2(50)
```

Case sensitivity of column names in SQL Server

We used all uppercase for the column names above because the Warehouse Builder defaults the case to upper for any column name that we enter. However, this could cause a problem later while retrieving data from the SQL Server tables using those column names if the case does not match the way they are defined in SQL Server. SQL Server will allow mixed case for column names, but the Oracle database assumes all uppercase for column names. It is possible to query a mixed-case column name in SQL Server from an Oracle database, but the name must be enclosed in double quotes. The code generated by the Warehouse Builder recognizes this and puts double quotes around any references to column name. If the import had worked, it would have created the column names with matching case and there would have been no problem. However, when the Table Editor manually enters columns, it has no option to enter a mixed-case name. We'll run into errors later if the corresponding SQL Server column names are not in all uppercase. The database scripts that can be downloaded from the Packt website (`http://www.packtpub.com/files/code/3449_Code`) to build the database contain the column names in all uppercase to avoid any problems.

To import the remainder of the tables automatically using the wizard, just follow the steps described above for importing source table metadata but start the import by right clicking on the ACME_POS database node under ODBC instead of the Oracle node. The remainder of the import steps are as documented previously.

Be sure to save each table as it is created to make sure no work gets lost. When all the tables are entered or imported, our defining and importing of source metadata is completed.

Importing source metadata from files

One final object type we need to discuss before we wrap up the source metadata importing and defining is the importing of data object metadata from a file. The Warehouse Builder can take data from a flat file and make it available in the database as if it were a table, or just load it into an existing table. The metadata that describes this file must be defined or imported in the Warehouse Builder. The file format must be delimited, usually with commas separating each column and a carriage return at the end of a record (**CSV file**). The option to use a flat file greatly expands the flexibility of the Warehouse Builder because now it allows us to draw upon data from other sources, and not just databases. That can also be of great assistance even in loading data from a database if the database is not directly network accessible to our data warehouse. In that case, the data can be exported out of the source database tables and saved to a CSV file for us to import.

For our ACME Toys and Gizmos company data warehouse, we've been provided a flat file. This file contains information for counties in the USA that the management wanted to see in the data warehouse to allow analyzing by county. For stores in the USA, the store number includes a code that identifies the county the store is located in, and the flat file we've been provided with contains the cross reference of the code to the county that we'll need.

 The file name is `counties.csv` and it is available in the download files from the Packt website at `http://www.packtpub.com/files/code/3449_Code`.

The process of creating the module and importing the metadata for a flat file is different from Oracle or non-Oracle databases because we're dealing with a file in the file system now instead of a database. The steps involved in creating the module and importing the metadata for a flat file are as follows:

1. The first task we need to perform, as we did earlier for the source databases, is to create a new module to contain our file definition. If we look in the **Projects tab** under our project, we'll see that there is a **Files** node right below the **Databases** node. We will launch the **Create Module Wizard** the same way as we did earlier, but we'll do it on the **Files** node and not the **Databases** node. We'll right-click on the **Files** node and select **New Flat File Module** from the pop-up menu to launch the wizard.

2. When we click on the **Next** button on the **Welcome** screen, we notice a slight difference already. The **Step 1** of the **Create Module** wizard only asks for a name and description. The other options we had for databases above are not applicable for file modules. We'll enter a name of **ACME_FILES** and click on the **Next** button to move to **Step 2**.

3. We need to edit the connection in **Step 2** just as we did for the database previously. So we'll click on the **Edit** button and immediately notice the other major difference in the **Create Module Wizard** for a file compared to a database. As we see in the following image, it only asks us for a name, a description, and the path to the folder where the files are:

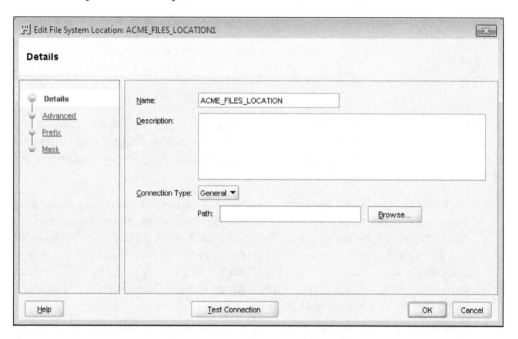

The **Name** field is prefilled with the suggested name based on the module name. As it did for the database module location names, it adds that number **1** to the end. So, we'll just edit it to remove the number and leave it set to **ACME_FILES_ LOCATION**.

1. Notice the **Type** drop-down menu. It has two entries: **General** and **FTP**. If we select **FTP (File Transfer Protocol**—used for getting a file over the network), it will ask us for slightly more information as shown in the following image:

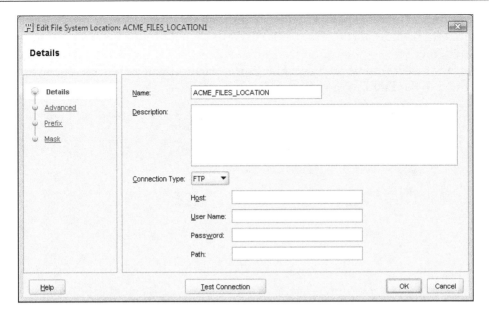

The **FTP** option can be used if the file we need is located on another computer. We will need to know the name of the computer, and have a logon username and password to access that computer. We'll also need to know the path to the location of the file. This option is used in process flows which is a more advanced option than we'll be able to cover in this book.

2. The simplest option is to store the file on the same computer on which we are running the database. This way, all we have to do is enter the path to the folder that contains the file. We should have a standard path we can use for any files we might need to import in the future. So we create a folder called GettingStartedWithOWB_files, which we'll put in the C: drive. Choose any available drive with enough space and just substitute the appropriate drive letter. We'll click on the **Browse** button on the **Edit File System Location** dialog box, choose the C:\GettingStartedWithOWB_files path, and click on the **OK** button.

3. We'll then check the box for **Import after finish** and click on the **Finish** button. We could click the **Next>** button here and it would just take us to a screen summarizing what it's going to do and then we'd hit the **Finish** button.

That's it for the **Create Module Wizard** for files. It's really very straightforward.

The **File Import** appears next. We'll work through this one in a little more detail as it is different from importing from a database. If the **File Import** window has not appeared, then just right-click on the module name under the **Files** node under our project, and select **Import** and then **Flat File...**. The following are the steps to be performed in the **File Import** screens:

1. The first screen for importing a file is shown in the following screenshot:

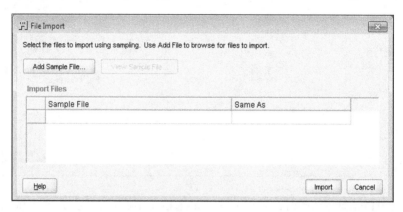

This is where we will specify the file we wish to import. We'll click **Add Sample File...** and select the counties.csv file. After selecting the file from the resulting popup, it will fill in the filename on the File Import screen. The **View Sample File...** button is now no longer grayed out so we can click on it. It will show us a view of the file we've just selected so we can verify it's the correct data as shown next:

2. If we've viewed the file we'll just click **OK** to close the dialog. We'll click the **Import** button now on the **File Import** screen to begin the import process. We are presented with an entirely new screen that we haven't seen before. This is **Flat File Sample Wizard**, which has now been started. The Flat File Sample Wizard now has two paths that we can follow through it, a standard sequence for simple files and an advanced sequence for more complex files. The previous release included all these steps into one so we had no choice but now if we have a simple CSV file to import, we can save some time. The two sets of steps are indicated on the **Welcome** screen as shown below:

3. Clicking the Next button will take us to the first step which is shown below:

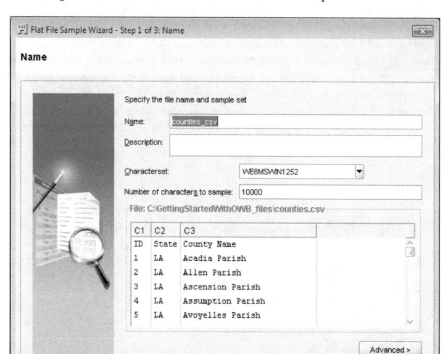

This screen displays the information the wizard pulled out of the file, displayed as columns of information. It knows what's in the columns because the file has each column separated by a comma, but doesn't know at this point what type of data or column name to use for each column—so it just displays the data. It picks a name based on the file name, which is fine. So we'll leave this and the remaining options set to the default. The following are the options on this screen:

*   More information about what those fields mean can be found by clicking on the **Help** button.

*   The **Character set** is language related. For English language, the default character set will work fine.

*   The **Number of characters to sample** determines how much of the file the wizard will read to get an idea of what's in it. If we were to import a file with multiple record types, this field might have come into play. But for our purposes, the default is enough.

4. This step 1 screen is also where we can choose to take the advanced path through the wizard which will consist of more steps, or we can just click the Next button to move on through the simple path. The simple path is for basic comma delimited files with single rows separated by a carriage return. We'll follow the simple 3 step path through the wizard and then go back and take a look at the extra steps the advanced option gives us. We're going to just click the **Next** button to move on to the simple step 2.

5. Step 2 of the simple steps includes the record and field delimiters choices as shown next:

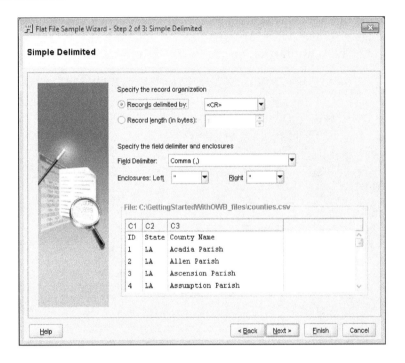

Our records are separated by a **Comma,** and that is the default, so we'll leave it at that. The **Enclosures:** selection is OWB's way of specifying the characters that surround the text values in the file. Frequently, in text-based files such as CSV files, the text is differentiated from numerical values by surrounding the text values in double quotes, single quotes, or something similar. This is where we specify the characters, if any, that surround the text-field values in this file. As our file does not use any character to surround text values and does not contain any double quotes, this setting will have no effect and we can safely ignore it. It is possible that double quotes, or any of the other characters available from the drop-down menu, might appear in text strings in the file but not as delimiters. We would need to set this to blank to indicate that there's no text delimiter in that case so that it wouldn't get confused. We'll click **Next** at this point to move on to the final step.

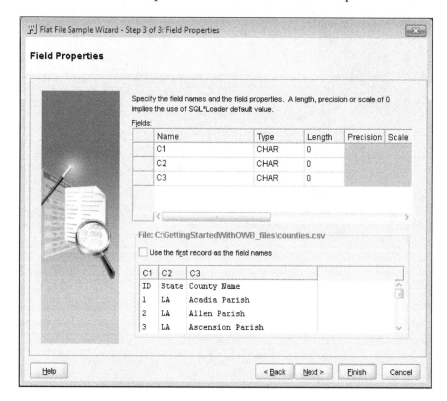

6. The final step is where we specify the details about what each field contains, and give each field a name. Check the box that says **Use the first record as the field names** and we'll see that all the column names have changed to using the values from that first row. It's not uncommon to receive a file with a large number of columns; and this can be a big time-saver. After clicking on the box, our screen now looks like the following screenshot:

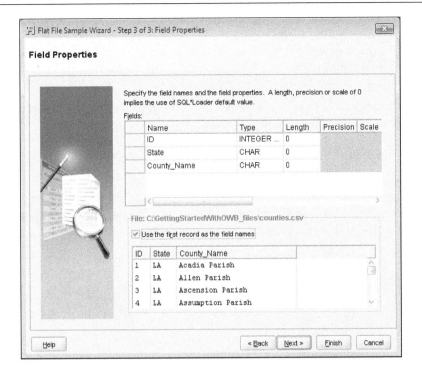

Notice that the field type for the first column has changed. The **ID** is now **INTEGER** instead of character, as it has now correctly detected that the remaining rows after that first one all contain integer data. **Length** is specified there, which defaults to **0**. If we scroll the window to the right, we'll also notice an SQL data type that is set for each field name. The reason for these extra attributes is that Warehouse Builder can directly use this file in a mapping or can use it indirectly referenced by an external table. An **external table** is a table definition within the Oracle database that actually refers to information stored in a flat file. The direct access is via the **SQL*Loader** utility. This is used to load files of information into a table in the database and when we specify the source in a mapping to be that file, it builds an SQL*Loader configuration to load it using the information provided here. More details about this can be found by clicking on the **Help** button on this screen. We do not need to worry about specifying a length here as the columns are delimited by commas. We can enter a value if we happen to know the maximum length a field could be.

7. Click on **Next** to get a summary screen of what the wizard will do, or just click on the **Finish** button to continue. After clicking **Finish** it will create our file module under the **Files** node and we will be able to access it in the **Projects tab**. We can see that the imported file is displayed as COUNTIES_CSV, which was the name it had defaulted to and which we left it set to.

What this File Sample Wizard just asked us for is a direct example of what we mean when we talk about metadata. We just entered the data that describes our data contained in an imported file.

8. We'll make sure to select **Save All** from the **Design** menu in Design Center to save the metadata we just entered.

Let's take a quick look at what the extra Advanced option steps would be:

1. The first step we saw had the **Advanced** button on it to take us down the advanced path through the wizard and if we click on that we are presented a screen where we can specify even more information about the characteristics of the file as shown in the following screenshot:

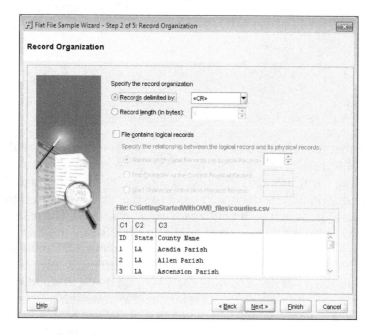

This is where we could specify detailed record information including whether the file contains logical records. It has the record delimiter we saw in the simple option step 2 above but has a different option about logical records. The commas only determine where one column ends and another begins. But where does the next row start? We can see by the display that it already seems to have figured that out because it assumes that a **carriage return** **<CR>** character will indicate the end of a row. That is the default that it uses.

This is an invisible character that gets entered into a text file when we press the *Enter* key while editing a file to move to the next line. It's possible that we might get a file with some other character indicating the end of a row, but our files use the carriage return, which is the most common. So we'll leave it set to that.

The other option here is to indicate whether or not the **file contains logical records**. Our file contains a physical record for each logical record. In other words, each row in the file is only one record. It's possible that one record's worth of information in a table might be contained in more than one physical row in the file. If this is the case, we could check that box and then specify the number of physical records that make up one complete logical record.

1. Hitting **Next** brings us to step 3 of the advanced steps and for the advanced options, this is where the field delimiter is specified that was on the simple step 2 screen or we can define the file as fixed length columns. The simple option assumed delimited fields where the advance option will allow a file that has fixed column lengths that aren't delimited.

2. Hitting the **Next** button from here takes us to step 4 of the advance options where we can specify if there are any rows to skip and what record type we have in the file, single record or multi-record as shown next:

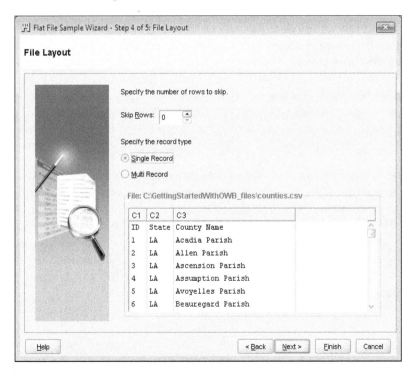

Sometimes the provided files may contain a number of rows of preliminary text information before the actual rows of data start. We can tell the wizard to skip over those rows at the start as they aren't formatted like the rows of data. All the rows in our file are formatted the same, so we will leave the default set to **0** as we want it to read all the rows. We might be tempted to skip over the first row of data by setting the number of rows to skip to 1 since that's just header information and not actual data but header rows can be used to indicate the column names as we saw above so we wouldn't want to set this to 1 or wouldn't have that option available to us.

3. The next step in the advanced install then takes us to the **Field Properties** screen the same as the final step in the simple install except this is Step 5 of 5 instead of Step 3 of 3. Finishing from here will accomplish the same task as the simple install, creating the new file node under our new files module.

This concludes all the object types we want to cover here for importing. Let's summarize what we've learned so far, and move on to the next step, which is defining our target.

Summary

That was a lot of information presented in this chapter. We began with a brief discussion about the source data for our scenario using the ACME Toys and Gizmos company. We then went through the process of importing metadata about our sources, and saw how to import metadata from an Oracle database as well as a flat file. Because we are dealing with a non-Oracle database, we were also exposed to configuring the Oracle database to communicate with a non-Oracle database using Oracle Heterogeneous Services. We also saw how to configure it for generic connectivity using the supplied ODBC agent. We worked through the process of manually creating table definitions for source tables for a SQL Server database.

At this point, you should run through these procedures to import or define the remaining tables that were identified in the source databases. For this, you can use the procedures we walked through above for practice. We'll be using the SQL Server database tables for the POS transactional database throughout the remainder of book, so be sure to have those defined at a minimum. Now that we have our sources all defined and imported, we need a target where we're going to load the data into from these sources. That's what we're going to discuss in the next chapter where we talk about designing and building our target data structures.

3
Designing the Target Structure

We have our entire source structures defined in the Warehouse Builder. But before we can do anything with them, we need to design what our target data warehouse structure is going to look like. When we have that figured out, we can start mapping data from the source to the target. So, let's design our target structure. First, we're going to take a look at some design topics related to a data warehouse that are different from what we would use if we were designing a regular relational database. We'll then discuss what our design will look like, and after that we'll be ready to move right into creating that design using the Warehouse Builder in the next chapter.

The specific topics we'll discuss in this chapter include the following:

- Data warehouse design
    - Dimensional design
    - Cube and dimensions
    - Dimensional Model Implementation
    - Relational (star schema)
    - Multidimensional (OLAP)
    - Designing the ACME data warehouse
    - Identifying dimensions
    - Designing the cube

- Data Warehouse Design in OWB
    - Creating a target user and module
    - OWB design objects

Data warehouse design

When it comes to the design of a data warehouse, there is basically one option that makes the most sense for how we will structure our database and that is the **dimensional** model. This is a way of looking at the data from a business perspective that makes the data simple, understandable, and easy to query for the business end user. It doesn't require a database administrator to be able to retrieve data from it.

When looking at the source databases in the last chapter, we saw a normalized method of modeling a database. A normalized model removes redundancies in data by storing information in discrete tables, and then referencing those tables when needed. This has an advantage for a transactional system because information needs to be entered at only one place in the database, without duplicating any information already entered. For example, in the ACME Toys and Gizmos transactional database, each time a transaction is recorded for the sale of an item at a register, a record needs to be added only to the transactions table. In the table, all details regarding the information to identify the register, the item information, and the employee who processed the transaction do not need to be entered because that information is already stored in separate tables. The main transaction record just needs to be entered with references to all that other information.

This works extremely well for a transactional type of system concerned with daily operational processing where the focus is on getting data into the system. However, it does not work well for a data warehouse whose focus is on getting data out of the system. Users do not want to navigate through the spider web of tables that compose a normalized database model to extract the information they need. Therefore, dimensional models were introduced to provide the end user with a flattened structure of easily queried tables that he or she can understand from a business perspective.

Dimensional design

A dimensional model takes the business rules of our organization and represents them in the database in a more understandable way. A business manager looking at sales data is naturally going to think more along the lines of "How many gizmos did I sell last month in all stores in the south and how does that compare to how many I sold in the same month last year?" Managers just want to know what the result is, and don't want to worry about how many tables need to be joined in a complex query to get that result. In the last chapter, we saw how many tables would have to be joined together in such a query just to be able to answer a question like the one above. A dimensional model removes the complexity and represents the data in a way that end users can relate to it more easily from a business perspective.

Users can intuitively think of the data for the above question as a cube, and the edges (or dimensions) of the cube labeled as stores, products, and time frame. So let's take a look at this concept of a cube with dimensions, and how we can use that to represent our data.

Cube and dimensions

The **dimensions** become the business characteristics about the sales, for example:

- A time dimension — users can look back in time and perform time series analysis, such as how a quarter compares to the same quarter last year
- A store dimension — information can be retrieved by store and location
- A product dimension — various products for sale can be broken out

Think of the dimensions as the edges of a cube, and the intersection of the dimensions as the measure we are interested in for that particular combination of time, store, and product. A picture is worth a thousand words, so let's look at what we're talking about in the following image:

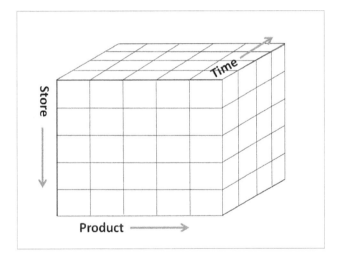

Notice what this cube looks like. How about a Rubik's Cube? We're doing a data warehouse for a toy store company, so we ought to know what a Rubik's cube is! If you have one, maybe you should go get it now because that will exactly model what we're talking about. Think of the width of the cube, or a row going across, as the product dimension. Every piece of information or measure in the same row refers to the same product, so there are as many rows in the cube as there are products. Think of the height of the cube, or a column going up and down, as the store dimension. Every piece of information in a column represents one single store, so there are as many columns as there are stores. Finally, think of the depth of the cube as the time dimension, so any piece of information in the rows and columns at the same depth represent the same point in time. The intersection of each of these three dimensions locates a single individual cube in the big cube, and that represents the measure amount we're interested in. In this case, it's dollar sales for a single product in a single store at a single point in time.

But one might wonder if we are restricted to just three dimensions with this model. After all, a cube has only three dimensions—length, width, and depth. Well, the answer is no. We can have many more dimensions than just three. In our ACME example, we might want to know the sales each employee has accomplished for the day. This would mean we would need a fourth dimension for employees. But what about our visualization above using a cube? How is this fourth dimension going to be modeled? And no, the answer is not that we're entering the Twilight Zone here with that "dimension not only of sight and sound but of mind..." We can think of additional dimensions as being cubes within a cube. If we think of an individual intersection of the three dimensions of the cube as being another cube, we can see that we've just opened up another three dimensions to use—the three for that inner cube. The Rubik's Cube example used above is good because it is literally a cube of cubes and illustrates exactly what we're talking about.

We do not need to model additional cubes. The concept of cubes within cubes was just to provide a way to visualize further dimensions. We just model our main cube, add as many dimensions as we need to describe the measures, and leave it for the implementation to handle.

This is a very intuitive way for users to look at the design of the data warehouse. When it's implemented in a database, it becomes easy for users to query the information from it.

Implementation of a dimensional model in a database

We have seen how a dimensional model is preferred over a normalized model for designing a data warehouse. Now before we finalize our model for the ACME Toys and Gizmos data warehouse, let's look at the implementation of the model to see how it gets physically represented in the database. There are two options: a **relational** implementation and a **multidimensional** implementation. The relational implementation, which is the most common for a data warehouse structure, is implemented in the database with tables and foreign keys. The multidimensional implementation requires a special feature in a database that allows defining cubes directly as objects in the database. Let's discuss a few more details of these two implementations. But we will look at the relational implementation in greater detail as that is the one we're going to use throughout the remainder of the book for our data warehouse project.

Relational implementation (star schema)

Back in Chapter 2, we saw how ACME's POS Transactional database and Order Entry databases were structured when we did our initial analysis. The diagrams presented showed all the tables interconnected, and we discussed the use of foreign keys in a table to refer to a row in another table. That is fundamentally a relational database. The term relational is used because the tables in it relate to each other in some way. We can't have a POS transaction without the corresponding register it was processed on, so those two relate to each other when represented in the database as tables.

For a relational data warehouse design, the relational characteristics are retained between tables. But a design principle is followed to keep the number of levels of foreign key relationships to a minimum. It's much faster and easier to understand if we don't have to include multiple levels of referenced tables. For this reason, a data warehouse dimensional design that is represented relationally in the database will have one main table to hold the primary facts, or **measures** we want to store, such as *count of items sold or dollar amount of sales*. It will also hold descriptive information about those measures that places them in context, contained in tables that are accessed by the main table using foreign keys. The important principle here is that these tables that are referenced by the main table contain all the information they need and do not need to go down any more levels to further reference any other tables.

The ER diagram of such an implementation would be shaped somewhat like a star, and thus the term **star schema** is used to refer to this kind of an implementation. The main table in the middle is referred to as the **fact** table because it holds the facts, or measures that we are interested in about our organization. This represents the cube that we discussed earlier. The tables surrounding the fact table are known as dimension tables. These are the dimensions of our cube. These tables contain descriptive information, which places the facts in a context that makes them understandable. We can't have a dollar amount of sales that means much to us unless we know what item it was for, or what store made the sale, or any of a number of other pieces of descriptive information that we might want to know about it.

It is the job of data warehouse design to determine what pieces of information need to be included. We'll then design dimension tables to hold the information. Using the dimensions we referred to above in our cube discussion as our dimension tables, we have the following diagram that illustrates a star schema:

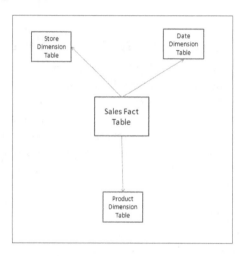

Of course our star only has three points, but with a much larger data warehouse of many more dimensions, it would be even more star-like. Keep in mind the principle that we want to follow here of not using any more than one level of foreign key referencing. As a result, we are going to end up with a **de-normalized** database structure. We discussed normalization back in Chapter 2, which involved the use of foreign key references to information in other tables to lessen the duplication and improve data accuracy. For a data warehouse, however, the query time and simplicity is of paramount importance over the duplication of data. As for the data accuracy, it's a read-only database so we can take care of that up front when we load the data. For these reasons, we will want to include all the information we need right in the dimension tables, rather than create further levels of foreign key references. This is the opposite of normalization, and thus the term de-normalized is used.

Let's look at an example of this for ACME Toys and Gizmos to get a better idea of what we're talking about with this concept of de-normalization. Every product in our stores is associated with a department. If we have a dimension for product information, one of the pieces of information about the product would be the department it is in. In a normalized database, we would consider creating a department table to store department descriptions with one row for each department, and would use a short key code to refer to the department record in the product table.

However, in our data warehouse, we would include that department information, description and all, right in the product dimension. This will result in the same information being duplicated for each product in the department. What that buys us is a simpler structure that is easier to query and more efficient for retrieving information from, which is key to data warehouse usability. The extra space we consume in repeating the information is more than paid for in the improvement in speed and ease of querying the information. That will result in a greater acceptance of the data warehouse by the user community who now find it more intuitive and easier to retrieve their data.

In general, we will want to de-normalize our data warehouse implementation in all cases, but there is the possibility that we might want to include another level—basically a dimension table referenced by another dimension table. In most cases, we will not need nor want to do this and instances should be kept to an absolute minimum; but there are some cases where it might make sense.

This is a variation of the star schema referred to as a **snowflake schema** because with this type of implementation, dimension tables are partially normalized to pull common data out into secondary dimension tables. The resulting schema diagram looks somewhat like a snowflake. The secondary dimension tables are the tips of the snowflake hanging off the main dimension tables in a star schema.

In reality, we'd want at the most only one or two of the secondary dimension tables; but it serves to illustrate the point. A snowflake dimension table is really not recommended in most cases because of ease-of-use and performance considerations, but can be used in very limited circumstances. The Kimball book on Dimensional Modeling was referred to at the beginning of Chapter 2. This book discusses some limited circumstances where it might be acceptable to implement a snowflake design, but it is highly discouraged for most cases.

Let's now talk a little bit about the multidimensional implementation of a dimensional model in the database, and then we'll design our cube and dimensions specifically for the ACME Toys and Gizmos Company data warehouse.

Multidimensional implementation (OLAP)

A multidimensional implementation or **OLAP** (**online analytic or analytical processing**) requires a database with special features that allow it to store cubes as actual objects in the database, and not just tables that are used to represent a cube and dimensions. It also provides advanced calculation and analytic content built into the database to facilitate advanced analytic querying. Oracle's Essbase product is one such database and was originally developed by Hyperion. Oracle recently acquired Hyperion, and is now promoting Essbase as a tool for custom analytics and enterprise performance management applications. The Oracle Database Enterprise Edition has an additional feature that can be licensed called **OLAP** that embeds a full-featured OLAP server directly in an Oracle database. This is an option organizations can leverage to make use of their existing database.

These kinds of analytic databases are well suited to providing the end user with increased capability to perform highly optimized analytical queries of information. Therefore, they are quite frequently utilized to build a highly specialized **data mart**, or a subset of the data warehouse, for a particular user community. The data mart then draws its data to load from the main data warehouse, which would be a relational dimensional star schema. A data warehouse implementation may contain any number of these smaller subset data marts.

We'll be designing dimensionally and implementing relationally, so let's now design our actual dimensions that we'll need for our ACME Toys and Gizmos data warehouse, and talk about some issues with the fact data (or cube) that we'll need. This will make the concepts we just discussed more concrete, and will form the basis for the work we do in the rest of the book as we implement this design. We'll then close out this chapter with a discussion on designing in the Warehouse Builder, where we'll see how it can support either of these implementations.

We have seen the word dimension used in describing both a relational implementation and a multidimensional implementation. It is even in the name of the second implementation method we discussed, so why does the relational method use it also? In the relational case, the word is used more as an adjective to describe the type of table taken from the name of the model being implemented; whereas in the multidimensional model it's more a noun, referring to the dimension itself that actually gets created in the database. In both cases, the type of information conveyed is the same—descriptive information about the facts or measures—so its use in both cases is really not contradictory. There is a strong correlation between the fact table of the relational model and the cube of the dimensional model, and between the dimension tables of the relational model and the dimensions of the dimensional model.

Designing the ACME data warehouse

We have chosen to use a dimensional model for our data warehouse, so we'll define a cube with dimensions to represent our information. Let's lay out a basic structure of information we want each to contain. We'll begin with the dimensions, since they are going to provide the context for the measure(s) we will want to store in our cube.

Identifying the dimensions

To know what dimensions to design for, we need to know what business process we're going to be supporting with our data warehouse. Is management concerned with daily inventory? How about daily sales volume? This information will guide us in selecting the correct parts of the business to model with our dimensions.

We are going to support the sales managers in managing the daily sales of the ACME Toys and Gizmos Company, and they have already given us an example of the kind of question they want answered from their data warehouse, as we saw earlier. We used that to illustrate the cube concept and to show a star schema representation of it, so the information shows us the dimensions we need. Since management is concerned with daily sales, we need some kind of date/time dimension that will provide us the context for the sales data indicating what day the sale transaction took place.

We can pretty much be guaranteed that we will need a time/date type dimension for any data warehouse we design, since one of the main features of data warehouses is to provide time-series type analytical query capabilities (as we talked about earlier).

Are we going to need both the time and the date in this dimension, or will just the date be sufficient? We can get an answer to this question by also looking back at our business process, which showed that management is concerned with daily sales volume. Also, the implementation of the time dimension in OWB does not include the time of day since it would have to include 24 hours of time values for each day represented in the dimension due to the way it implements the dimension. In the future if time is needed, there are options for creating a separate dimension just for modeling time of day values. For our initial design, we'll call our time related dimension a Date dimension just for added clarity.

Another dimension we have included is to model the product information. Each sale transaction is for a particular product, and management has indicated they are concerned about seeing how well each product is selling. So we will include a dimension that we shall call Product. At a minimum we need the product name, a description of the product, and the cost of the product as attributes of our product dimension—so we'll include those in our logical model.

So far we have a Date dimension to represent our time series and a Product dimension to represent the items that are sold. We could stop there. Management would then be able to query for sales data for each day for each product sold by ACME Toys and Gizmos, but they wouldn't be able to tell where the sale took place. Another key piece of information the management would like to be able to retrieve is how well the stores are doing compared to each other for daily sales. Unless we include some kind of a location dimension, they will not be able to tell that. That is why we have included a third dimension called Store. It is used to maintain the information about the store that processed the sales transaction. For attributes of the store dimension, we can include the store name and address at a minimum to identify each store.

These dimensions should be enough to satisfy the management's need for querying information for this particular business process—the daily sales. We could certainly include a large number of other dimensions, but we'll stop here to keep this simple for our first data warehouse. We can now consider designing the cube and what information to include in it.

Designing the cube

In the case of the ACME Toys and Gizmos Company, we have seen that the main measure the management is concerned about is daily sales. There are other numbers we could consider such as inventory numbers: How much of each item is on hand? However, the inventory is not directly related to daily sales and wouldn't make sense here. We can model an inventory system in a data warehouse that would be separate from the sales portion. But for our purposes, we're going to model the sales. Therefore, our main measure is going to be the dollar amount of sales for each item.

A very important topic to consider at this point is what will be the **grain** of the measure—the sales data—that we're going to store in our cube? The grain (or **granularity**) is the level that the sales number refers to. Since we're using sales as the measure, we'll store a sales number; and from our dimensions, we can see that it will be for a given date in a given store and for a given product. Will that number be the total of all the sales for that product for that day? Yes, so it satisfies our design criteria of providing daily sales volume for each product. That is the smallest and lowest level of sales data we want to store. This is what we mean by the grain or granularity of the data.

Levels/hierarchies

A dimensional model is naturally able to handle this concept of the different levels of data by being able to model a hierarchy within a dimension. The time/date dimension is an easy example of using of various levels. Add up the daily totals to get the totals for the month, and add up 12 monthly totals to get the yearly sales. The time/date dimension just needs to store a value to indicate the day, month, and year to be able to provide a view of the data at each of those levels. Combining various levels together then defines a hierarchy. By storing data at the lowest level, we make available the data for summing at higher levels. Likewise, from a higher level, the data is then available to drill down to view at a lower level. If we were to arbitrarily decide to store the data at a higher level, we would lose that flexibility. We'll discuss this further in the next chapter when we build our time dimension in the Warehouse Builder.

In this case, we have a source system—the POS Transactional system—that maintains the dollar amount of sales for each line item in each sales transaction that takes place. This can provide us the level of detail we will want to capture and maintain in our cube, since we can definitely capture sales for each product at each store for each day. We have found out that the POS Transactional system also maintains the count of the number of a particular item sold in the transaction. This is an additional measure we will consider storing in our cube also, since we can see that it is at the same grain as the total sales. The count of items would still pertain to that single transaction just like the sales amount, and can be captured for each product, store, and even date.

The only other pieces of information our cube is going to contain are pointers to the dimensions. In the relational model, the fact table would contain columns for the dollar amount, the quantity, the unit cost, and then foreign keys for each of the dimension tables.

There are times when it's valid in dimensional design to include more descriptive information right in the cube, rather than create a dimension for it. There may be some particularly descriptive piece of information that stands all by itself, which is not associated with anything else or whose additional descriptive information has already been included in other dimensions. In that case, it wouldn't make sense to create a whole dimension just for it; so it is included directly in the fact table or cube. This is referred to as a degenerate dimension. It is explained in more detail in the Kimball book on dimensional modeling we talked about earlier. There are many other aspects to dimensional design that we don't have the space to cover here, but are covered in the Kimball book in more detail. It would be a good idea for you to read this book or a similar one to get a better understanding of the detailed dimensional modeling concepts such as this.

Our design is drawn out in a star schema configuration showing the cube, which is surrounded by the dimensions with the individual items of information (attributes) we'll want to store for each. It looks like the following:

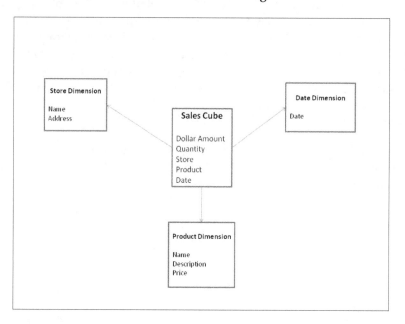

OK, we now have a design for our data warehouse. It's time to see how OWB can support us in entering that design and generating its physical implementation in the database.

Data warehouse design in OWB

The Warehouse Builder contains a number of objects, which we can use in designing our data warehouse, that are either relational or dimensional. OWB currently supports designing a target schema only in an Oracle database, and so we will find the objects all under the **Oracle** node in the **Projects tab**. Let's launch **Design Center** now and have a look at it. But before we can see any objects, we have to have an **Oracle** module defined to contain the objects. If you've been following along and working through the examples in this book, so far you should have one module already defined for the ACME website orders database—ACME_WS_ORDERS. We created this in the last chapter when we imported our metadata from that source. If that is the case, our **Projects tab** window will look similar to the following:

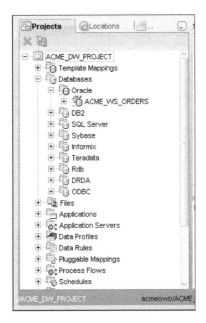

Creating a target user and module

We need a different module to create our target objects in. So before going any further, let's create a new module in the **Projects tab** for our target to hold our data warehouse design objects. However, before we can do that, we should have a target schema defined in the database that will hold our target objects when we deploy them.

So far we have discussed many different components such as the repository, workspaces, the design center, and so on. So, it can be confusing to know exactly where our main data warehouse is going to be located. The target schema is going to be the main location for the data warehouse. When we talk about our "data warehouse" after we have it all constructed and implemented, the target schema is what we will be referring to. Amid all these different components we discussed that compose the Warehouse Builder, the target is where the actual data warehouse will be built. Our design will be implemented there, and the code will be deployed to that schema by OWB to load the target structure with data from the sources.

Every target module must be mapped to a target user schema. Back in Chapter 1, when we ran the Repository Assistant to create the repository and workspace, we created the **acmeowb** user as the repository owner and mentioned that this user can be a deployment target for our data warehouse. However, it does not have to be the target user. It's a good idea to create a separate user schema to become the target so that user roles in our database can be kept separate. Using the OWB repository owner schema would mean our target data warehouse would have to be on the same database server as our repository. In large installations, that will most likely not be the case. So for maximum flexibility, we're going to create a separate user schema. In our case, that user will be created in the same database as the repository; but it can be moved to another database easily if we expand and add more servers.

Creating a target user

There are a couple of ways we can go about creating our target user — create the user directly in the database and then add to OWB, or use OWB to physically create the user. If we have to create a new user, and if it's on the same database as our repository and workspaces, it's a good idea to use OWB to create the user, especially if we are not that familiar with the SQL command to create a user. However, if our target schema were to be in another database on another server, we would have to create the user there. It's a simple matter of adding that user to OWB as a target, which we'll see in a moment. Let's begin in the **Design Center** under the **Globals tab**. We talked about that **Globals tab** back in our introduction to the **Design Center** in Chapter 2. There we said it was for various objects that pertained to the workspace as a whole.

One of those object types is a **Users** object that exists under the **Security** node as shown here:

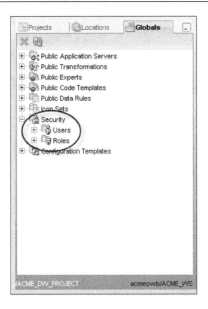

Right-click on the **Users** node and select **New User...** to launch the **Create User** dialog box as shown here:

With this wizard, we are creating a workspace user. We create a workspace user by selecting a database user that already exists or create a new one in the database. We'll just click the **Next** button to move on to step 1 as shown next:

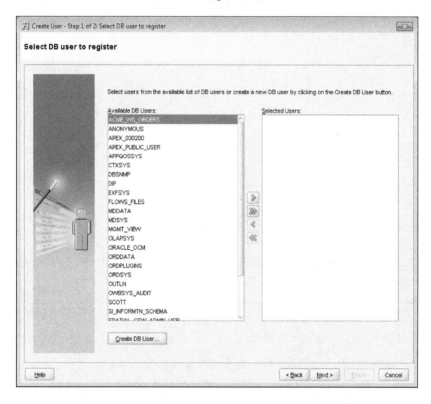

If we already had a target user created in the database, this is where we would select it. We're going to click on the **Create DB User...** button to create a new database user.

We need to enter the **system** username and password as we need a user with DBA privileges in the database to be able to create a database user. We then enter a username and password for our new user. As we like to keep things basic, we'll call our new user **ACME_DWH**, for the ACME data warehouse. We can also specify the default and temporary tablespace for our new user, which we'll leave at the defaults. The dialog will appear like the following when completely filled in:

The new user will be created when you click on the **OK** button, and will appear in the right hand window of the **Create User** dialog already selected for us. Click on the **Next** button and we'll be presented with the second step of the user creation process, whether to create a location using the user credentials or not as shown in the following image:

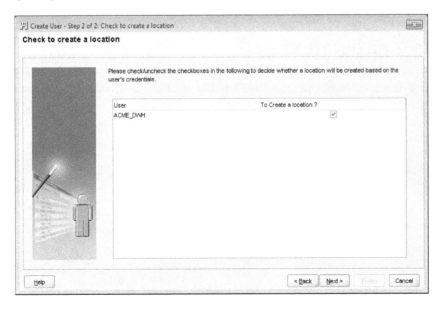

We discussed locations in the last chapter and saw how they were required for the Warehouse Builder to know where to connect to for the various tables and other database objects defined in modules we've defined in our project. Since we're going to use this new user we've just created as an eventual target for creating our data warehouse in then we will need to leave this checkbox checked so it creates a location based on this user. We could be just creating another authorized database user for accessing the workspace but not intending to use it as a target for any object creation in which case we wouldn't need a location defined for it. We'll leave the check box checked and click the **Next** button to proceed.

The final screen is just the **Summary** screen indicating the user to be created and whether a location will be created or not. We'll just click the **Finish** button and the user will be registered with the workspace, and we'll see the new username if we expand the **Users** node under **Security** in the **Globals tab**. Since we had indicated that we wanted a location created also, a location for the user will be evident on the **Locations tab** under the **Locations...Databases...Oracle** node. We can continue with creating our target module now that we have a user defined in the database to map to.

Notice that we could indicate whether we wanted a location created or not but had no way to specify the database location information. This is because it creates the user on the local database we were connected to when we logged into the **Design Center**, which is the location of our repository and workspaces. Due to this, this method can only be used to create the user if it is on the local database. In the next section where we create our target module, we'll get to specify the location and that dialog box will allow us to specify a remote database if needed.

Create a target module

We'll follow the same steps as we did in the last chapter where we created the ACME_ WS_ORDERS module. Right-click on the **Oracle** object under **Databases** and select **New Oracle Module...** from the pop-up menu to launch the **Create Module Wizard** and step through the process. We'll name this module ACME_DWH for ACME Data Warehouse.

The next step is for creating or selecting a location to use. Since we just created the user to use as the target user and had the Warehouse Builder create the location automatically for us there is a location available now on the local server we can use. We'll just click the drop down and select the location labeled **ACME_DWH_ LOCATION**. If we're creating our own test system, the source location may very well be the same as our target. But in real-world situations, it will likely be in a different database on a different server. If we had created a target user schema on a different database, this is the point at which we would be able to enter the connection information for that user in order to associate our target module with that user and make it a target. We would just create a new location by clicking the Edit button on the default **ACME_DWH_LOCATION1** to specify the connection details for that other database.

We're not going to create a new location but will be selecting an existing one and for reference, the Step 2 screen should look like the following for selecting the location of the target module:

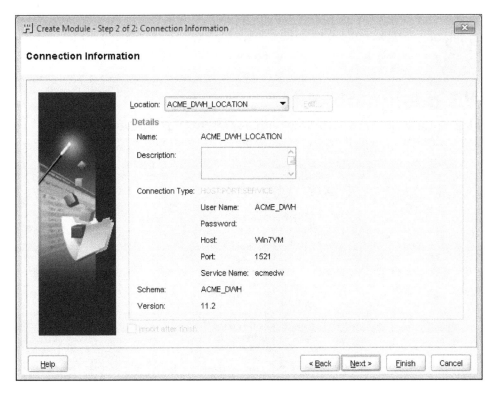

The **User Name** is the user we just created for this very purpose in the previous section. There is no password set for that user in the location yet but it will prompt us for that the first time we attempt to use it. The **Host** setting of **Win7VM** will be whatever the name is of the computer its running on so will vary. The Warehouse Builder uses the actual local computer name when creating the location for us rather than **localhost** but either will do.

> If we had specified a user on a remote database the location information (**Host**, **Port**, and **Service Name**) would specify a user in another database if needed. If our user were not in this database, we would have just entered his or her appropriate host and port for the location and the service name of that remote database.

Now that we have our target database schema and a target module defined, which is associated with a location pointing to that target schema, we will now have two Oracle modules under our Oracle object in the Projects tab. We can continue our discussion of the design objects available to us in the Warehouse Builder for designing our database. First, let's make sure we save our work so far by using the *Ctrl+S* key combination or by selecting **Design | Save All** from the main menu.

OWB design objects

Looking at our **Projects tab** window with our target Oracle module expanded, we can see a number of objects that are available to us as shown here:

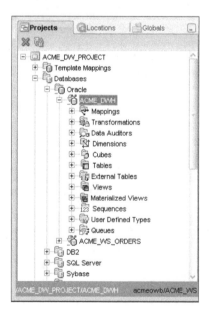

There are objects that are relational such as **Tables**, **Views**, **Materialized Views**, and **Sequences**. Also, there are dimensional objects such as **Cubes** and **Dimensions**. We just discussed relational objects versus dimensional objects. We have decided to model our database dimensionally and this will dictate the objects we create. From the standpoint of providing the best model of our business rules and representing what users want to see, the dimensional method is the way to go as we already discussed. Most data warehouse implementations we encounter will use a dimensional design. It just makes more sense for matching the business rules the users are familiar with and providing the types of information the user community will want to extract from the database.

We are thinking dimensionally in our design, but what about the underlying physical implementation? We discussed the difference between the relational and multidimensional physical implementation of a database, and now it's time to see how we will handle that here. The Warehouse Builder can help us tremendously with that because it has the ability to design the objects logically using cubes and dimensions in a dimensional design. It also has the ability to implement them physically in the underlying database as either a relational structure or a dimensional structure simply by checking a box.

In general, which option should be chosen? The relational implementation is best suited to large amounts of data that tend to change more frequently. For this reason, the relational implementation is usually chosen for the main data warehouse schema by most implementers of a data warehouse. It is much better suited to handling the large volumes of data that are imported frequently into the data warehouse. The multidimensional implementation is better suited to applications where heavy analytic processing is required, and so is a good candidate for the data marts that will be presented to users.

To be able to implement the design physically as a dimensional implementation with cubes and dimensions, we need a database that is designed specifically to support **OLAP** as we discussed previously. If that is not available, then the decision is made for us. In our case, when we installed the Oracle database in Chapter 1, we installed the Enterprise Edition with default options, and that includes the OLAP feature in the database, so we have a choice to make. Since we're installing our main data warehouse target schema, we'll choose the relational implementation.

For a relational implementation, the Warehouse Builder actually provides us two options for implementing the database: a pure relational option and the relational OLAP option. If we were to have the OLAP feature installed in our database, we could choose to still have the cubes and dimensions implemented physically in a relational format. We could have it store metadata in the database in the OLAP catalog, and so multidimensional features such as aggregations would be available to us. We could take advantage of the relational implementation of the database for handling large volumes of data, and still implement a query or reporting tool such as Oracle Discoverer or Oracle Business Intelligence Enterprise or Standard Edition (OBIEE) to access the data that made use of the OLAP features. The pure relational option just depends on whether we choose to deploy only the data objects and not the OLAP metadata. In reality, most people choose either the pure relational or the multidimensional. If they want both, they implement separate data marts. In fact, the default when creating dimensional objects and selecting relational for the implementation is to only deploy data objects. This case would allow us to use the dimensional objects to load the data warehouse without needing to deploy OLAP catalog objects representing them. Tools like OBIEE or Discoverer can still derive Business Intelligence objects for dimensional oriented models in those tools using just these relational dimensional objects in the database.

Just to be clear, does all this mean that if we haven't paid for the OLAP feature for our database, we can only design our data warehouse using the relational objects; and therefore must our decision to design dimensionally change? The answer to that would be an emphatic *no*, since we just mentioned how OWB will let us design dimensional objects, cubes and dimensions, and then implement them physically in the database as relational objects. The benefit is that the same dimensional design can be implemented at a later time in an OLAP database just by changing a single setting. There are features of the Warehouse Builder for handling dimensional features automatically for us, such as levels, surrogate keys, and slowly changing dimensions (all of which we'll talk about later) that designing dimensionally provides us. We would have to implement these manually if we designed our own tables. Most people who use the Warehouse Builder will use it in that way, so we'll definitely want to make use of that feature to maximize the usefulness of the tools to us. This provides us with flexibility and it is the way we are going to proceed with our design. We'll design dimensionally using a cube and dimensions, and then can implement it either relationally or dimensionally when we're ready.

Summary

We have now gone through the process of designing the target structure for our data warehouse. We began with a very high-level overview of data warehouse design topics, then talked about dimensional design and the relational versus multidimensional implementation, and then we discussed the differences between them. As was mentioned earlier, there are other books that are devoted solely to this topic and it would be good to read one or more of them to learn more about design than we've been able to cover here. Our design for ACME Toys and Gizmos is very rudimentary, just to give us an introduction to designing in OWB. You'll want to read in more detail about design when you tackle a real-world design because you may run into other issues we didn't have time or space to cover here.

We're going to actually implement the design in OWB in the next chapter.

4
Creating the Target Structure in OWB

Now it's time to actually start creating objects in the Warehouse Builder for our target structure. In the previous chapter, we decided what our cube and dimensions were going to be in our logical design and now we are at the point where we can implement that design in OWB. We'll create the objects using the wizards that the Warehouse Builder provides for us to simplify the task of building cubes and dimensions. We'll look at the data object editors in a little more detail than we saw in Chapter 2. Let's begin with creating the dimensions. We'll cover the following list of topics in this chapter:

- Creating dimensions in OWB
  - The Time dimension and wizard
  - The Product dimension
  - The Store dimension

- Creating a cube in OWB
  - Creating a cube with the wizard

Creating dimensions in OWB

The Warehouse Builder provides a couple of ways to create a dimension. One way is to use the wizards that it provides, which will automatically create a dimension for us. The other way is to manually create it. We have identified three dimensions that we are going to need a Date dimension, a Product dimension, and a Store dimension. The Date dimension, as we've seen, is our time/date dimension for providing a time series for our data. That kind of dimension is common to most data warehouses and the information it contains is very similar from warehouse to warehouse. So, recognizing this commonality, the Warehouse Builder provides us a special wizard to use just for time dimensions. Let's begin with that one.

 Let's talk a bit about "creating". Throughout this chapter, we'll discuss creating objects, but what we're really creating is the metadata that describes the objects. Nothing will be actually created in the database yet. We won't actually do that until Chapter 8 when we deploy our design to the target schema.

The Time dimension

Let's discuss briefly what a Time dimension is, and then we'll dive right into the Warehouse Builder Design Center and create one. A Time dimension is a key part of most data warehouses. It provides the time series information to describe our data. A key feature of data warehouses is being able to analyze data from several time periods and compare results between them. The Time dimension is what provides us the means to retrieve data by time period.

 Do not be confused by the use of the word *Time* to refer to this dimension. In this case, it does not refer to the time of day but to time in general which can span days, weeks, months, and so on. We are using it because the Warehouse Builder uses the word *Time* for this type of dimension to signify a time period. So when referring to a *Time* dimension here, we will be talking about our time period dimension that we will be using to store the date. We will give the name Date to be clear about what information it contains.

Every dimension, whether time or not, has four characteristics that have to be defined in OWB:

- **Levels**
- **Dimension Attributes**

- **Level Attributes**
- **Hierarchies**

The Levels are for defining the levels where aggregations will occur, or to which data can be summed. We must have at least two levels in our Time dimension. While reporting on data from our data warehouse, users will want to see totals summed up by certain time periods such as per day, per month, or per year. These become the levels. A multidimensional implementation includes metadata to enable aggregations automatically at those levels, if we use the OLAP feature. The relational implementation can make use of those levels in queries to sum the data. The Warehouse Builder has the following Levels available for the Time dimension when using the Time Dimension Wizard, which we'll discuss in a moment:

- Day
- Fiscal week
- Calendar week
- Fiscal month
- Calendar month
- Fiscal quarter
- Calendar quarter
- Fiscal year
- Calendar year

The Dimension Attributes are individual pieces of information we're going to store in the dimension that can be found at more than one level. Each level will have an **ID** that identifies that level, a **start and an end date** for the time period represented at that level, a **time span** that indicates the number of days in the period, and a **description** of the level.

Each level has Level Attributes associated with it that provide descriptive information about the value in that level. The dimension attributes found at that level and additional attributes specific to the level are included. For example, if we're talking about the **Month** level, we will find attributes that describe the value for the month such as the month of the year it represents, or the month in the calendar quarter. These would be numbers indicating which month of the year or which month of the quarter it is.

The Oracle Warehouse Builder Users' Guide contains a more complete list of all the attributes that are available. OWB tracks which of these attributes are applicable to which level and allows the setting of a separate description that identifies the attribute for that level. Toward the end of the chapter, when we look at the data object editor for a dimension and a cube, we'll see the feature provided by the Warehouse Builder to view details about those objects.

We must also define at least one **Hierarchy** for our Time dimension. A hierarchy is a structure in our dimension that is composed of certain levels in order; there can be one or more hierarchies in a dimension. Calendar month, calendar quarter, and calendar year can be a hierarchy. We could view our data at each of these levels, and the next level up would simply be a summation of all the lower-level data within that period. A calendar quarter sum would be the sum of all the values in the calendar month level in that quarter, and the multidimensional implementation includes the metadata to facilitate these kinds of calculations. This is one of the strengths of a multidimensional implementation.

The good news is that the Warehouse Builder contains a wizard that will do all the work for us—create our Time dimension and define the above four characteristics— just by asking us a few questions.

We could use the regular dimension wizard to create a dimension to use as a time dimension and could define our own levels but in our case, it's much simpler to make use of the special Time Dimension Wizard to create it for us.

Creating a Time dimension with the Time Dimension Wizard

Let's start creating our Time dimension by launching **Design Center** if it's not already running. In the **Project Navigator** window, we're going to expand the **Databases** node under ACME_DW_PROJECT, and then our ACME data warehouse node ACME_DWH. We will right-click on the **Dimensions** node, and select **New** to display a dialog that will show the list of options for creating a new dimension. An example of that screen is shown next since it is a new feature of this release:

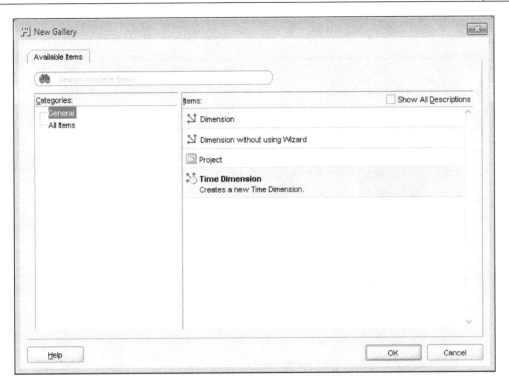

We'll select the **Time Dimension** and click **OK** to launch the **Create Time Dimension Wizard**.

The **New Gallery** window that we just saw is actually available from the pop-up menu on any of the nodes by selecting the **New...** menu entry. Most of the nodes, such as tables and dimensions, also contain a **New** menu entry (New Table, New Dimension, and so on.) that launches right into the wizard as if the New Gallery were displayed and the first option selected. Up until now we've been able to use that default **New** option to create our objects. In the previous release of the Warehouse Builder, if there were multiple options for the **New** menu option they appeared as sub-menus. This release combines those options into a list in this New Gallery window.

The **Time Dimension Wizard** will walk us through a six-step process to define the characteristics of our Time dimension. The first screen will describe these steps for us, which is shown here so we can see what it will be asking us:

1. The first step of the wizard will ask us for a name for our Time dimension. We're going to call it DATE_DIM. If we try to use just DATE, it will give us an error message because that is a reserved word in the Oracle Database; so it won't let us use it.

2. The next step will ask us what type of storage to use for our new dimension, shown as follows:

Here we get to designate whether we want a relational physical implementation in the database or a multidimensional implementation. This is what was referred to earlier as checking a box to switch between the two. Simply select one or the other, and this is how our design will be implemented in the database with no changes by us required at all.

New in release 11gR2 is the support for cube materialized views in the database for the ROLAP option so there are actually two ROLAP options to choose from but either one results in a relational implementation in the database. Oracle OLAP 11.1 introduced the concept of materialized views for cubes for query performance improvement and this new release of the Warehouse Builder now supports the ability to use them. See the Oracle OLAP Users Guide for more information on using cube materialized views at the following URL: http://download.oracle.com/docs/cd/E11882_01/olap.112/e17123/toc.htm.

As we discussed in the last chapter, we're going to implement our data warehouse using the pure relational option and not implement any OLAP features so we're going to select ROLAP: Relational Storage, as shown in the image above and will not select the materialized view option. Both the pure relational implementation and the relational OLAP option, which we discussed in the last chapter, are available by selecting the ROLAP option here. We can set a deployment configuration option that defaults to deploying data objects only. But this can be changed to deploy the OLAP metadata to the OLAP catalog also. In both cases, this will result in the generation of relational database objects in a star schema. However, if that option is selected, it will only store the OLAP metadata in the OLAP catalog in the database. We'll see where to set that option when we look at the data object editor and configuring a dimension.

3. Now this brings us to step 3, which asks us to specify the data generation information for our dimension. The Time Dimension Wizard will be automatically creating a mapping for us to populate our Time dimension and will use this information to load data into it. It asks us what year we want to start with, and then how many total years to include starting with that year. The numbers entered here will be determined by what range of dates we expect to load the data for, which will depend on how much historical data we will have available to us. We have checked with the DBAs for ACME Toys and Gizmos Company to get an idea of how many years' worth of data they have and have found out that there is data for 2007, 2008, and 2009 available to us. Based on this information, we're going to set the start year to 2007 with the number of years set to three to bring us up to 2009.

The other option available to us on the data generation step is the type of Time dimension to create. It can be based on a calendar year or fiscal year. This provides us with the flexibility to define our Time dimension based on what our company actually uses for its financial year. ACME Toys and Gizmos Company operates on a calendar-year basis, so we'll leave it set at calendar.

4. This step is where we choose the hierarchy and levels for our Time dimension. We have to select one of the two hierarchies. We can use the **Normal Hierarchy** of day, month, quarter, and year; or we can choose the **Week Hierarchy**, which consists of two levels only—the day and the calendar week. Notice that if we choose the **Week Hierarchy**, we won't be able to view data by month, quarter, or year as these levels are not available to us. This is seen in the following image:

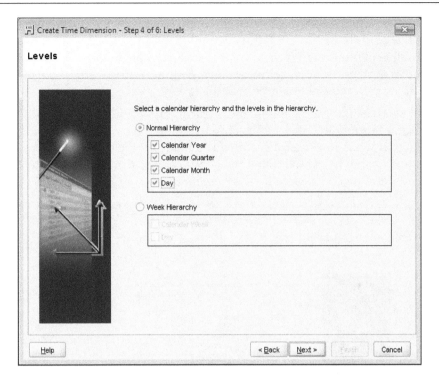

The levels are not available to us because a week does not roll up or aggregate to a month. Some months have four weeks while some have five, and that's not even exact weeks. The only month that has a month evenly divided by weeks is February, and that's only during non-leap years. So, we can see that weeks do not sum up nicely into months, or any higher level of time. How about a year? Surely, that must sum up nicely we might say, as aren't there 52 weeks in a year? Multiply 52 by 7 and we get 364 days. So, even that won't work. Thus, if we choose to model weeks as one of our levels, we get day and week and that's it.

This points out an important aspect of aggregation when deciding what our levels should be. It's very important to keep that idea of aggregation or summing in mind when choosing levels, or we will end up with data that doesn't make sense. The Time Dimension Wizard will not allow us to choose levels that don't sum up correctly because it has predefined a list of levels for us to choose from, with preset hierarchies. However, when defining any other dimension type, we'll definitely have to keep this in mind as we'll be specifying levels and hierarchies ourselves rather than choosing from the predefined ones.

We're going to select the normal hierarchy, and now we can choose which of the levels to include. It is always a good idea to include the lowest level possible in our hierarchy to provide maximum flexibility in aggregating data in this dimension. If we leave out day, then we will never be able to view our data by day, but only by month at the lowest level.

5. Let's move on to step 5 where the wizard will provide us the details about what it is going to create. An example is shown in the following image, which is what you should see if you've made all the same selections as we've moved along. In the following image we can see the dimension attributes, levels, and hierarchies that will be created:

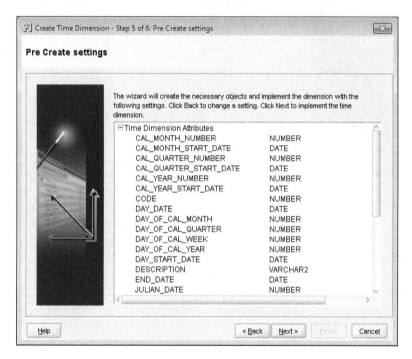

We can also see an extra item at the bottom that we haven't discussed yet, a map name, if we scroll the window down to the bottom as shown next:

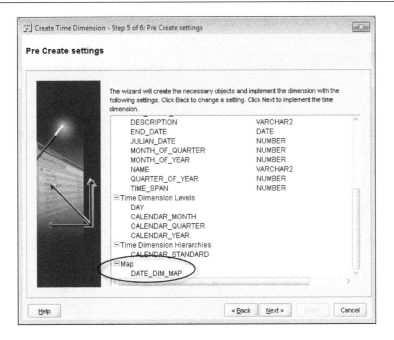

The **DATE_DIM_MAP** map entry that we can see in the previous image is a mapping for our DATE_DIM dimension, which can be run to populate the dimension. It will be created automatically for us by the wizard.

The previous version of the Warehouse Builder used to create a sequence also which was used to populate ID fields in the Time Dimension that were used as a **Surrogate Identifier**. A surrogate identifier is a value that stands in (acts as a surrogate) for the actual unique identifier. The actual identifier is called a **Business Identifier** and contains one or more attributes that are selected to uniquely identify a dimension record. We'll see these surrogate identifiers in a moment when we create the Product and Store dimensions but for Time Dimensions, it is no longer used in this new release. In its place is an actual date field for the day so there is no need for a surrogate. That date field also acts as the Business Identifier for a Time dimension, which makes it much more intuitive to use.

6. Continuing to the last step, it will display a progress bar as it performs each step and will display text in the main window indicating the step being performed. When it completes, we click on the **Next** button and it takes us to the final screen—the summary screen. This screen is a display of the objects it created and is similar to the previous display in step 5 of 6 that shows the pre-create settings. At this point, these objects have been created and we press the **Finish** button. Now we have a fully functional Time dimension for our data warehouse.

We could use a data object editor to create our Time dimension, but we would have to manually specify each attribute, level, hierarchy, and sequence to use. Then we would have to create the mapping to populate it. So we definitely saved quite a bit of time by using the wizard.

The **Time Dimension Wizard** does quite a bit for us. Not only does it create the Time dimension, but it also creates a couple of additional objects needed to support it. Take a look at the following image, which is what our Project Navigator looks like after running this wizard:

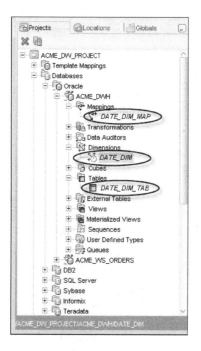

Besides the dimension that it created, we now have a mapping that appears under the **Mappings** node. This is what we will deploy and run to actually build our Time dimension. We can also see that a table was created under the **Tables** node. This is the physical table that will be created in the database to store the dimension data. We are designing dimensionally and implementing relationally in the database and this is the relational table used for the implementation.

This completes our Time dimension, so let's look at the next dimension we're going to create. It is the dimension to hold the product information.

The Product dimension

In the Product dimension, we will create the attributes that describe the products sold by ACME Toys and Gizmos. The principles of the Time dimension apply to this dimension as well. The same four characteristics need to be defined—Levels, Dimension Attributes, Level Attributes, and Hierarchies. The only difference will be that they are product-oriented instead of time/date-oriented.

Let's begin by looking at the attributes of our products, and then we'll group by levels and a hierarchy. The first thing we should consider is how each toy or gizmo sold by ACME is represented. As with any retail operation, a **Stock Keeping Unit (SKU)** is maintained that uniquely identifies each individual type of item sold. This is an individual number assigned by the main office that uniquely identifies each type of product sold by ACME, and there could be tens of thousands of different items. There could be more than one product with the same name, but they won't have the same SKU. So the SKU, together with the NAME, forms the **business identifier** we can use for the products. A business identifier contains one or more attributes that have been selected by us to uniquely represent a record to differentiate it from another. These attributes are what we think of when we think about what differentiates an individual product from another. An SKU number all by itself is not very helpful. Therefore, in our Product dimension, we will want to make available more descriptive information about each product such as the description.

Every SKU can be grouped together by brand name—the toy manufacturer who makes the product—and then by the category of product, such as game, doll, action figure, sporting goods, and so on. Each category could be grouped by department in the store. Already, a list of attributes is starting to take shape and a product hierarchy is forming in our minds. For each of those levels in the hierarchy, that is the department, category, and brand, we need to have a business identifier. For that the NAME will be sufficient as there are no departments, categories, or brands that have the same name.

Let's put this down on paper to formalize it and add some more details.

Product attributes (attribute type)

- ID (Dimension/Level)
- SKU (Level)
- Name (Dimension/Level)
- Description (Dimension/Level)
- List Price (Level)

Product levels

- Department located in
- Category of item
- Brand
- Item

Product hierarchy (highest to lowest)

- Department
- Category
- Brand
- Item

Looking at the product attributes, we see that they have been listed above with the type and that ID, Name, and Description are labeled as dimension attributes. This means they can appear on more than one level. Each level has a name (Item, Brand, Category, and Department) that identifies the level, but what about the names of the individual brands, or the different categories or departments? There has to be a place to store those names and descriptions, and that is the purpose of these dimension attributes. By labeling them as dimension attributes, they appear once for each level in the dimension. They are used to store the individual names and descriptions of the brands, categories, and departments. Likewise, each level will have a unique ID that will act as the surrogate key for that level, as well as one or more attributes defined as the business identifier. In our previous discussion about the Time dimension, we saw how a surrogate key was used as an identifier and how business identifiers were used; that same principle applies here, including the use of a surrogate key which wasn't used for a time dimension.

As we want the computer to do most of the work for us, let's use the OWB Dimension Wizard to create our Product dimension now that we've determined what will be in it.

Creating the Product dimension with the new Dimension Wizard

OWB provides a wizard that we can use to create a dimension. It is similar to the **Time Dimension Wizard** we used earlier, but is more generic for applying to other dimensions. As a result, there will be more steps involved in the wizard, just because it has to ask us more because it will not be able to make as many assumptions as it did with the Time dimension. This wizard can be used with any dimension, and therefore things such as attributes, levels, and hierarchies are going to need to be defined explicitly. Right-click on the **Dimensions** node under our ACME_DWH **Oracle** module, which is under **Databases** in the **Design Center Project Navigator**. Choose **New Dimension** to launch the **Create Dimension Wizard**. The very first screen we'll see is the **Welcome** screen that will describe for us the steps that we will be going through. We can see that it requires more steps than the Time Dimension Wizard:

We will have to provide a name for our dimension, and tell it what type of storage to use—relational or multidimensional—just as we did for the Time Dimension Wizard. It will then ask us to define our dimension attributes. We didn't have to do that for the Time dimension. That wizard had a preset number of attributes it defined for us automatically because it knew it was creating a Time dimension. We then had to define the levels where we simply chose from a preset list of levels for the Time dimension. Here we have to explicitly name the levels. This is where we'll have to pay close attention to aggregations. We will then choose our level attributes from the dimension attributes.

Then we see in the previous figure that we will have to choose the **slowly changing dimension** type, which is how we want to handle changes to values in our dimension attributes over time. This is a new concept we haven't dealt with yet that pertains to dimensional modeling, and we'll soon briefly discuss just what that involves when we see the choices we'll be able to make for it. We'll then get a last chance to review the settings, and then it will create the dimension for us showing us the progress, which is similar to the last two steps of the Time Dimension Wizard.

1. After reviewing the steps, the wizard will go to the next screen where we enter a name for the dimension that we will call `Product`.

2. We'll then proceed to step 2, which is where we will select the **ROLAP: Relational storage** option for relational, as we did for the Time dimension.

3. Proceeding to step 3, we will be able to list the attributes that we want contained in our Product dimension. We see that the wizard was nice enough to create three attributes for us already—an **ID**, a **NAME**, and a **DESCRIPTION** as shown here:

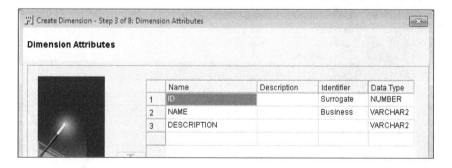

Notice that the wizard has already labeled the **ID** as the **Surrogate Identifier** and the **Name** as the **Business Identifier**, and selected data types for those attributes for us. If we scroll that window to the right, we'll see that it has chosen sizes for the character attributes also. We can change all of these options at this point, so let's modify and add to this list to suit our Product dimension.

As we enter the attributes and decide on sizes and types for them, we can look back at Chapter 2 where we defined our source data structure for the ACME_POS transactional database in SQL Server to get an idea of what types and sizes to use. We should make them at least as large as the source data so as not to lose any data when it gets loaded into the data warehouse.

We'll make the following changes:

° Enter **SKU** in the name column on line 4 and leave the data type as **VARCHAR2**, but change the length to 50. Scroll the window to the right if any columns are not visible that need to be changed. We can also expand the dialog box to show additional columns.

° Enter **LIST_PRICE** in the name column on line 5, leave the data type as **NUMBER**, and leave the precision and scale as eight and two as it suggested.

° Make **SKU** a **Business Identifier** field in addition to **Name**. (Click on the drop-down box in the identifier column for **SKU**, and select **Business**.)

° Change the length of the **NAME** column from 25 to 50.

° Change the length of the **DESCRIPTION** column from 40 to 200.

Notice how the precision and scale were entered automatically for us by the Wizard when we entered names for our attributes. Moreover, they tended to make sense for the type of attribute. The **LIST_PRICE** had a default of eight for precision and two for the scale that we did not have to modify. If we choose logical names for our measures, it is able to make very good guesses as to what the precision and scale should be. SKU is a character field created with a varchar2 type with a reasonable length. Likewise, a **LIST_PRICE** amount implies money which requires a number having two decimal places (scale 2).

Suppose we make a mistake and enter a value and then decide not to keep it. Then we can delete the row by right-clicking on the row number to the left of the row, and then selecting **Delete** from the pop-up menu.

The screen should now look like the following, expanded slightly to the right to see the additional length, precision, and scale columns:

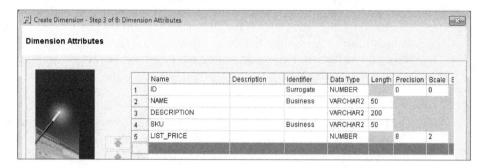

If we were to scroll that window all the way to the right, or expand it completely, we'd see even more columns such as the **Seconds Precision** and **Descriptor** column. If we press the **Help** button, it will explain what each column is. Briefly, the **Seconds Precision** is applicable to only TIMESTAMP data types, and expresses the precision of the seconds' portion of the value. The **Descriptor** is applicable to MOLAP (multidimensional) implementations and provides six standard descriptions that can be assigned to columns. It presets two columns, the Long description and the Short description. We can safely ignore them for our application.

4. The next step is where we can specify the levels in our dimension. There must be at least one level identified, but we are going to have four in our Product dimension. They are to be entered on this screen in order from top to bottom with the highest level listed first, then down to the lowest level. For our dimension, we'll enter **DEPARTMENT**, **CATEGORY**, **BRAND**, and **ITEM** in that order from top to bottom.

You might have noticed there is no step where we get to input hierarchies. The wizard will automatically create a default hierarchy called Standard that will contain the levels we enter here in this order. To create additional hierarchies, we must use the data object editor for dimensions after creating the dimension in the wizard.

The dialog box should now look like this:

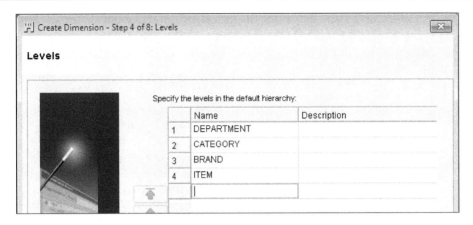

5. Moving on to the next screen, we get to specify the level attributes. At the top are the levels, and at the bottom is the list of attributes with checkboxes beside each. If we click on each level in the top portion of the dialog box, we can see in the bottom portion that the wizard has preselected attributes for us. It chooses the three default attributes it created for us to be level attributes for each level, and the other two attributes—the SKU and LIST_PRICE—that we entered as level attributes for the bottom-most level—the ITEM level. We are not going to make any changes on this screen. The wizard has chosen wisely in this case. We could edit the descriptions of each of the level attributes if we wanted to.

6. This brings us to step 6 where we get to choose the **Slowly Changing Dimension (SCD)** type. This refers to the fact that dimension values will change over time. Although this doesn't happen often, they will change and hence the "slowly" designation. For example, we might have an SKU assigned to a Super Ball made by the ACME Toy Manufacturing Company, which then gets bought out by the Big Toy Manufacturing Company. This causes the Brand that is stored in the dimension for that SKU to change. In this screen we specify how we want to handle the change. We will have the following three choices, which are related to the issue of whether or how we want to maintain a history of that change in the dimension:

    ○   **Type 1**: Do not keep a history. This means we basically do not care what the old value was and just change it.

    ○   **Type 2**: Store the complete change history. This means we definitely care about keeping that change along with any change that has ever taken place in the dimension.

    ○   **Type 3**: Store only the previous value. This means we only care about seeing what the previous value might have been, but don't care what it was before that.

The Type 2 and Type 3 options require additional licensing for our database if we want OWB to handle them automatically. We will need a license for the Warehouse Builder Enterprise ETL Option for that. As we are considering only basic functionality in this book, we'll leave this selection as Type 1 for now.

> Handling SCDs can be done manually in a relational implementation. The Type 2 option to maintain a complete history would result in needing additional attributes where we want to maintain historical information. We need attributes designated as **Triggering attributes**. If changed, these attributes will generate a historical record. We also need an **Effective Date attribute** and an **Expiration Date attribute.** The Effective Date is when the record is entered. If a triggering attribute changes, the Expiration Date is set and a new record created with the updated information.
>
> For the slowly changing Type 3 option, a new attribute in the dimension will be required to store only the most recent value.
>
> With the Enterprise ETL option, the addition of these extra attributes and describing certain attributes as triggering attributes would be handled automatically for us.
>
> *The Warehouse Builder User's Guide* documentation contains a more complete description of slowly changing dimensions. Also, there are other books available that cover dimensional modeling in depth, which give this topic much more coverage than we're able to provide here.

7. Moving on, we get our summary screen of the actions we performed. Here we can review our actions, and go back and make any changes if needed. It will look like the following, based on the selections we've made:

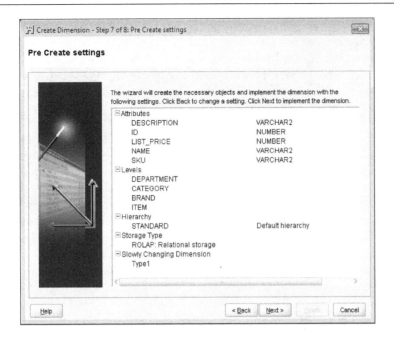

8. Everything looks fine, so we move on to step 8. This step creates the dimension, showing us a progress bar as it does its work. It will report a successful completion when it's done, and clicking on the **Next** button at this point will bring us to the summary screen where we see the above information followed by additional information that the wizard has created for us based on our responses. The extra items are as shown here:

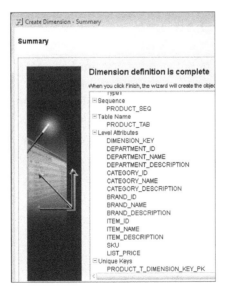

To reiterate, nothing has been physically created for us in the database yet. What the wizard has created for us are the definitions of our dimension, and the underlying table and other objects in OWB. The previous screen shows a **Sequence**, **Table Name**, and **Unique Key** that all correspond to objects that the wizard is creating for us in OWB. Later in Chapter 8, we'll deploy these objects to create the actual physical database objects in the target schema.

The sequence is an object that will be created to populate the ID values with unique numbers. It is created automatically for us by the wizard. This ID value is used as what is called the **Surrogate Identifier** for a level record which we discussed earlier as a value standing in (acting as a surrogate) for the actual unique identifier for the record. The actual identifier (a **Business Identifier** which as we discussed above) contains one or more attributes to uniquely identify a record. When we link a dimension to a cube, it will use that surrogate identifier as the key to link to, as this is easier for the database to use than a potentially multi-attribute business identifier but we'll use the business identifier to decide which actual dimension record to use since that's easier for us to understand.

We can also see the additional attribute names that were added, which will become column names in the table to support the levels we identified. When we checked these boxes (or rather left checked the ones the wizard checked) beside the attributes for each level to indicate they were level attributes for that level back in step 5, it created additional names for each based on the level name.

Our Product dimension is now created and we can see it in the **Project Navigator** window under the **Dimensions** node under our ACME_DWH Oracle module.

The Store dimension

We can create our Store dimension in a similar manner using the wizard. We will not go through it in much detail as it is very similar to how we created the Product dimension. The only difference is the type of information we're going to have in our Store dimension. This dimension provides the location information for our data warehouse, and so it will contain address information.

The creation of this dimension will be left as an exercise for the reader using the following details about the dimension.

Store attributes (attribute type), data type and size, and (Identifier)

- ID (Dimension/Level): Leave default for type and size (Surrogate ID)
- Store_Number (Level, STORE only): VARCHAR2 length 10 (Business ID)
- Name (Dimension/Level): VARCHAR2 length 50 (Business ID)
- Description (Level, COUNTRY and REGION only): VARCHAR2 length 200
- Address1 (Level, STORE only): VARCHAR2 length 60
- Address2 (Level, STORE only): VARCHAR2 length 60
- City (Level, STORE only): VARCHAR2 length 50
- State (Level, STORE only): VARCHAR2 length 50
- ZipPostalCode (Level, STORE only): VARCHAR2 length 50
- County (Level, STORE only): VARCHAR2 length 255

Store levels

- Country
- Region
- Store

Store hierarchy (highest to lowest)

- Country
- Region
- Store

Creating the Store dimension with the New Dimension Wizard

We will follow the same procedure as we had seen in the creation of the Product dimension. There are a few steps that are a little different from the previous procedure, and they are mentioned here.

In Step 3, where we put in the attributes listed previously, we need to make sure not to forget to specify the surrogate and business identifiers. The surrogate identifier can stay as the default on the ID, but we will have to change the business identifier to be the STORE_NUMBER, which is a unique number that ACME Toys and Gizmos Company assigns to each of its stores.

You may have the urge to include the region and/or country as an attribute in step 3, but resist the urge. They are being designated as levels. By specifying the level attributes to include the Name dimension attribute, we'll have our region and country included for us — as we'll see in a moment when we get to the final summary screen.

In step 5 where we specify the level attributes, (the above-listed attributes that are applicable to each level) we need to specify all the attributes except DESCRIPTION for the Store level, and then just ID, NAME, and DESCRIPTION for the Region and Country levels. This is how we will include the region and country information.

It may seem a bit redundant to include a description as well as a name for the Country and Region levels as our source data at the moment only includes one field to identify the country and region. However, this is needed to prevent an error from occurring later when we map data to this dimension. The same holds true for the Product dimension. If all we had were the ID and the NAME, those would be two key fields that cannot be changed for a record. There would be no descriptive information that could be changed, and the Warehouse Builder generates code for loading the dimension such that it requires at least one updatable field to be mapped, without which the following error would occur:

VLD-5005: No updatable inputs connected for dimension level <dimension><level>

At least one updatable input must be connected for level <dimension><level>, or the generated code will fail. Parent reference key and level natural key inputs are not updatable attributes in the target.

The New Dimension Wizard actually helps us to avoid this error by automatically including three attributes: an ID as the surrogate identifier, a NAME as the business identifier, and a DESCRIPTION as the updatable field.

In step 7, the **Pre Create settings** page, as shown next, we can see what we should have specified for the Store dimension. We can click on the **Back** button to go back to make any changes.

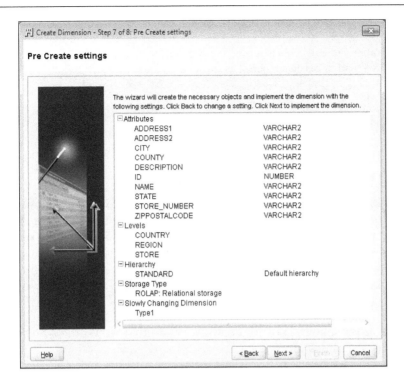

The final summary screen should look like the following when scrolled all the way to the bottom:

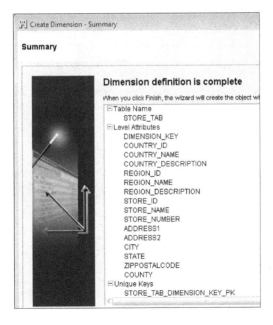

> Notice the region and country level attributes that are shown in the
> above image. This is where we see that information included as levels,
> instead of being specified as dimension attributes.

We'll make sure to save our work after creating this dimension, and then we'll move
on to creating the cube.

Creating a cube in OWB

Now that we have our dimensions defined, we have one last step to cover and our
design for our data warehouse will be complete. We need to define our cube, which
is where our measures will be stored — the facts that users will want to query. We
discussed the design of our cube and agreed that we would store two measures,
namely the sales amount and the number of items sold. We have already designed
our three dimensions, and their links and measures will go together to make up the
information stored in our cube.

There is a wizard available to us for creating a cube that we will make use of to ease
our task. So let's start designing the cube with the wizard.

Creating a cube with the wizard

We will start the wizard in a similar manner to how we started up the Dimension
wizard. Right-click on the **Cubes** node under the **ACME_DWH** module in the **Project
Navigator**, select **New Cube** to launch the cube-creation wizard. The first screen will
be the welcome screen, which will summarize the steps it will lead us through as
shown in the following image of the main part of the welcome dialog box:

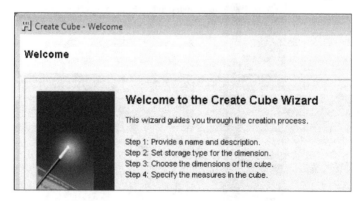

The following are the steps in the creation process:

1. We proceed right to the first step where we give our cube a name. As we will be primarily storing sales data, let's call our cube **SALES** and proceed to the next step.

2. In this step, we will select the storage type just as we did for the dimensions. We will select ROLAP: Relational Storage to match our dimension storage option, and then move to the next step.

3. In this step, we will choose the dimensions to include with our cube. We have defined three, and want them all included. So, we can click on the double arrow in the center to move all the dimensions and select them. If we had more dimensions defined than we were going to include with this cube, we would click on each, and click on the single right arrow (to move each of them over); or we could select multiple dimensions at one time by holding down the *Ctrl* key as we clicked on each dimension. Then click the single right arrow to move those selected dimensions. This step looks like the following after we've made our selections:

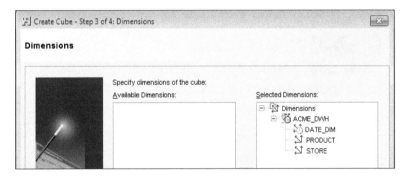

4. Moving on to the last step, we will enter the measures we would like the cube to contain. When we enter **QUANTITY** for the first measure with precision and scale set to zeros and **SALES_AMOUNT** with precision 10 and scale 2 for the second one, we end up with a screen that should look similar to this with the dialog box expanded to show all the columns:

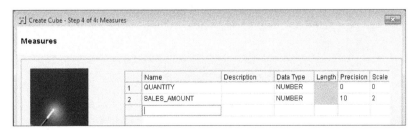

Clicking on **Next** in step 4 will bring us to the final screen where a summary of the actions it will take are listed. Selecting **Finish** on this screen will close the dialog box and place the cube in the **Project Navigator**.

The final screen looks like the following when scrolled all the way to the bottom:

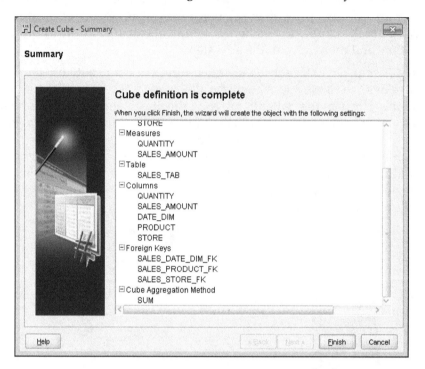

This dialog box works in a slightly different way than the dimension wizard. This final screen is the second-to-last screen when creating a dimension. The dimension wizard will present us with the progress screen as the final step. For cubes, the process is not quite as involved. That's because at this point, the cube is basically done with nothing left to do afterwards. So we may think we missed a step, but not to worry. Clicking on **Next** on this screen will exit the dialog box, and the cube will be created and will be accessible in the Project Navigator window.

Just as with the dimension wizard earlier, we get to see what the cube wizard is going to create for us in the Warehouse Builder. We gave it a name, selected the dimensions to include, and specified the measures. The rest of the information was included by the wizard on its own. The wizard shows us that it will be creating a table named SALES for us that will contain the referenced columns, which it figured out from the dimension and measures information we provided. At this point, nothing has actually been created in the database apart from the definitions of the objects in the Warehouse Builder workspace. We can verify that if we look under the **Tables** entry under our **ACME_DWH** database node. We'll see a table named SALES along with tables named PRODUCT, STORE, and DATE_DIM. These are the tables corresponding to our three dimensions and the cube.

You may have a slightly different table name. The wizard will not create a table with the same name as one already created, so it will append a unique number to the end to keep the table names from conflicting. This could happen if you've previously created a dimension with the same name, and then removed it and recreated it. It may not remove the associated table when you delete a cube or dimension object. The tables will appear in the **Project Navigator** under the **Tables** node. Expand that and you'll see the list of tables. Right-click a table and select **Delete**. The Warehouse Builder will ask if you really want to delete it, and will provide a checkbox to put the object in the recycle bin. Leave it checked just to be safe and click on **OK**, and the table will be removed.

The foreign keys we can see in the previous image are the pointers to the dimension tables. They will make the connection between our cube and our dimensions when they are deployed to the database.

There is one final item that we did not specify and that is the cube aggregation method to be used. We saw earlier in the chapter how the multidimensional implementation contains behind-the-scenes functionality that we don't have to specify. Later we also saw how important it was to be aware of the aggregation of our measures, and whether they can be summed together at different levels and within the same level. The aggregation the cube will perform for us when we view different levels is one of those behind-the-scenes capabilities we would get with the OLAP feature.

When we view the region amounts, they will automatically be summed up from the amounts of the various stores in the region without us having to do anything extra. This is a nice feature the multidimensional implementation gives us, but aggregations are not created for the pure relational storage option. As we can generate either a relational or a multidimensional implementation, this had to be specified anyway and so it defaulted to sum. If we install the OLAP option or use a separate OLAP database in the future, we can change that aggregation method. But for now, we do not need it. It is possible to use aggregations with a pure relational implementation by creating separate summing tables, and there are OLAP data mining applications that can make use of them for more advanced implementations.

We click on the **Finish** button on this final screen and our sales cube is created. We'll save our work with the *Ctrl+S* key combination or from the design main menu. Our cube and dimensions are now complete. Let's take a look next at data object editors where we can view and edit our objects.

Using the data object editors

We've mentioned the **Table Editor** previously which is the data object editor for editing tables. We used it in Chapter 2 to create our source metadata definitions for the ACME_POS transactional database, so let's take this opportunity to look a little closer at the editors for a dimension and a cube. We'll also discuss the overall Design Center interface and some of the other windows available to us in that interface as we're editing objects.

The object editors are the manual editor interfaces that the Warehouse Builder provides for us to create and edit objects. We did not have to use one to create a dimension, but more advanced implementations would definitely need to make use of it; for instance, to edit the cube to change the aggregation method that we just discussed. We'll take a brief look at editors here before moving on to get an idea of some of the features it provides.

We can get to a data object editor from the **Project Navigator** by double-clicking on an object, or by highlighting an object (by selecting it with a single click), and then right clicking and selecting **Open** from the menu. Editors in this latest release are now integrated into the main Design Center interface instead of popping open in a separate window. When editing any object now, a window appears in the Design Center containing the details to edit for the object. Let's open the DATE_DIM dimension and examine the overall interface as shown here:

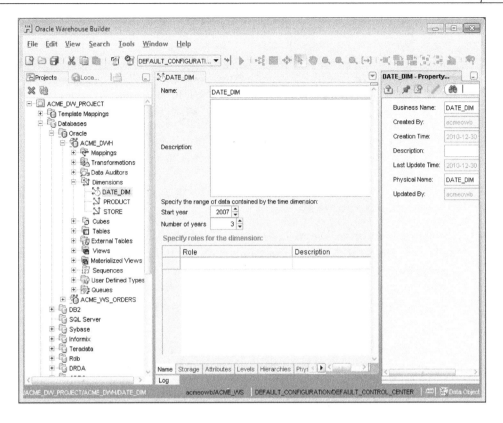

Your screen may look differently depending on what windows are open. The previous image depicts the **Navigator** window on the left which is displaying the **Project Navigator**, the main **Editor** window in the middle displaying the **DATE_DIM** dimension we just opened and the **Property Inspector** window on the right displaying properties for the **DATE_DIM** dimension. Any of these windows can be opened, closed, minimized, or relocated offering tremendous flexibility in laying out our working area. If a window is taking up space and we don't need it at the moment, just minimize it by clicking the minimize icon in the upper right corner of the window if that option is available. We can also close any window we want by hovering the mouse over the window title and clicking the X that appears or by right clicking over the window title and selecting **Close** from the popup. The main Editor window cannot be minimized but can be closed.

A complete discussion of all the windows available is in the Warehouse Builder Concepts Guide available at `http://download.oracle.com/docs/cd/E11882_01/owb.112/e10581/toc.htm`

There is a complete chapter devoted to a tour of the user interface that will provide more details than we can cover here. Use the following URL to jump right to that: `http://download.oracle.com/docs/cd/E11882_01/owb.112/e10581/uitour.htm#BABFDIHH`

We'll briefly discuss the windows we can see in the image above as well as some of the additional available windows.

- **Navigator Windows**: We discussed the windows available for navigation in the last chapter, the Projects, Locations, and Global Explorer windows that show on the left in the above image. Each of these windows can be displayed or hidden as needed and if not visible, can be displayed by selecting **View** from the main menu and then choosing the window to display.

For any of these windows we'll discuss, if they are not currently visible, they can be displayed by selecting them from the **View** main menu so when we discuss any windows below that are not visible, that is how we can display them.

- **Canvas**: This is not really a separate window but is a feature of some editors such as the Mapping Editor, that provides an area in which the contents are displayed graphically. Each object is displayed in a box with the name of the object as the title of the box and attributes of the object listed inside the box. These boxes can be moved around and resized manually to suit our tastes. We'll see an example next when we look at an editor window.

- **Property Inspector:** This window is visible in the above image and is available for setting various properties of objects that have been selected in the Navigator windows or in the editors. It is context sensitive and will display or not display any properties depending on whether there are properties pertaining to the selected object.

- **Configuration:** The configuration window displays configuration information about a selected item. Display the Configuration window by right clicking an object in the **Project Navigator** and selecting **Configure...** from the pop-up menu. It is here that we can change the deployment option for the object to deploy OLAP metadata if we want a relational implementation to store the OLAP metadata. With the DATE_DIM dimension selected in the **Project Navigator**, right click on it and select **Configure** and in the Configuration window click the plus sign beside the **Identification** section to expand it. It contains a setting for the deployment option and we can see that it is set to deploy data objects only. For dimensions, the options are to deploy to catalog only (the OLAP catalog), deploy data objects only, or deploy all to do both. For cubes, there is an additional option to deploy aggregations.

- **Component Palette:** The Palette is primarily applicable to editing mappings and provides a list of the items that can be dragged and dropped to build a mapping. It contains each of the objects that can be used in the mapping. We can use this to create objects on our canvas in the editor by clicking and dragging to the canvas. This will create a new object where clicking and dragging from the **Projects Navigator** will place an already created object on the canvas. We'll discuss this more in detail when we start looking at mappings in the next chapter.

- **Bird's Eye View:** This window displays a miniature version of the entire canvas and allows us to scroll around the canvas without using the scroll bars. It is applicable only for editors that display a graphical canvas of objects. We can click and drag the blue-colored box around this window to view various portions of the main canvas, which will scroll as we move the blue box. We will find that in most editors, we will quickly outgrow the available space to display everything at once and will have to scroll around to see everything. This can come in very handy for rapidly scrolling the window.

- **Editor:** This is the actual editor window that contains details about the object we are currently editing. It is the center window in the above image. Various tabs will appear, which display information for us depending on the object being edited. The tabs from left to right are as follows when editing a dimension some of which we can see in the above image:

    ◦ **Name:** This tab displays the name of the dimension along with some other information specific to the dimension type we are looking at. In this case, it's a Time dimension created by the Time Dimension Wizard and so it displays the range of data in our Time dimension.

- ° **Storage**: Here we can see what storage option is set for our dimension object in the database, whether Relational or Multidimensional. If we wanted to switch between the two, this is where we could do it. For a relational implementation, we're able to specify a star or snowflake schema and whether we want to create **composite unique keys**. A composite key is one made up of more than one column to define uniqueness for a record. In most cases, it is a good idea to have this checked as it enforces uniqueness in the database for our dimension records. It will not make a difference in our particular case for the test data we'll be using. For a dimension, it will use the business identifiers we've specified as the key fields.

- ° **Attributes**: The attributes tab is where we can see the attributes that are designed for our dimension. It displays the attributes in a tabular form allowing us to view and/or edit them, including adding new attributes or deleting the existing ones. It is here that we can also change the description of our attributes if we wanted, or add descriptions the wizard did not add.

You may have noticed by now that the attributes in our Time dimension are not editable. They all appear as one solid background. We can scroll the window to display them and see what they are set to, but we can't change them. This is a feature of the Time dimension that was created by the wizard. It has created extra objects (as we saw earlier) to support the Time dimension, such as a mapping that could break if the wrong changes are made. So, it disallows changes. It is possible to modify the dimension behind the scenes to edit things, but that is a much more advanced topic. As mentioned earlier, we could have also defined our time dimension using the regular dimension wizard and these would all be editable, but we wouldn't have the mapping created automatically to populate it.

- ° **Levels**: This is where we view and/or edit the levels for our dimension. We are able to edit some of the information on this tab for the Time dimension created by the wizard, but not all. We can check and uncheck boxes to indicate which of the various level types we want to use and which attributes are applicable to which level, but that is it. We are not able to add or remove any levels or attributes. If we were to view one of the other dimensions we created, it would be fully editable. For those other dimensions we could also assign different names and descriptions to the attributes for each level.

- ° **Hierarchies**: This tab will let us specify hierarchy information for our dimension and will even let us create a new hierarchy. It's possible that we may have selected more levels on the previous page and now need to assign them to a hierarchy. There is also a **Create Map** button here that will automatically generate the mapping for us if we modify the hierarchies. This is one of the benefits of the Time dimension created by the wizard. Ordinary dimensions such as our Store and Product dimension will not have this **Create Map** button displayed on their **Hierarchies** tab.

- ° **SCD**: This tab is for specifying the Slowly Changing Dimension policy to use. The Time Dimension will not show this tab because its not applicable to that type of dimension since the contents are pre-loaded and won't change.

- ° **Orphan**: This tab will also not be available for the Time dimension but will be for the Product and Store dimensions. This is a new feature in the 11*g*R2 release of the Warehouse Builder that provides an automated way to manage what to do about dimensional records (dimensions and cubes) that can't be loaded because one or more records do not have a parent record. This is also known as **Early Arriving Facts** in industry and Orphan Management is OWB's answer to addressing this issue. Since we're working with a known set of canned test data, there aren't any orphans to worry about but for actual implementations this is a feature that can greatly improve productivity in loading data. For dimensions we have three main categories of Orphan Management to specify, for loading the dimension, removal of records from the dimension, and whether to deploy an error table for orphans.

There are three main options available for handling orphans:

- **No Maintenance**: This is the default setting and indicates that orphans will not be detected and nothing will be done about them.

- **Default Parent**: This setting indicates that a default parent record should be used if one is null or invalid and if a default parent doesn't exist, it will create one to use. There is a **Settings** button available to set the default level row to use.

- **Reject Orphan**: This will cause the orphan record to be rejected.

For more information, on the new Orphan Management policies available in the Warehouse Builder, see Chapter 3 in the *Warehouse Builder Data Modeling, ETL and Data Quality Guide* at the following URL: `http://download.oracle.com/docs/cd/E11882_01/owb.112/e10935/dim_objects.htm#BABEJGDC`

There is a blog entry in the Oracle Warehouse Builder Blog that talks specifically about Early Arriving Facts and Orphan Management which can be accessed for more details at the following URL:

`http://blogs.oracle.com/warehousebuilder/2010/06/owb_11gr2_-_early_arriving_facts.html`

- ○ **Physical Bindings**: This tab displays a canvas with the dimension represented graphically along with the underlying physical table showing how attributes of the dimension are mapped (or bound) to the table columns.

- **Data Viewer**: The Data Viewer is a more advanced feature that allows us to actually view the data in an object we are editing. This is only available for an object if it has been deployed to the database and has data loaded into it. It has a query capability to retrieve data and can specify a WHERE clause to get just the data we might need to see. For relational implementations, it will not display the data for a dimension or cube; but we can use it to view the data in the underlying table. It is accessible from the **View** menu by selecting the **Data...** menu entry when editing a data object.

- **Cube Editor:** If we edit the Sales Cube, the editor window has a slightly different set of tabs available to it which we'll cover briefly here:
  - ○ **Name**: It has a name tab like the dimensions to display its name.
  - ○ **Storage**: It has a storage tab as per dimensions. However, we see a different option here under the Relational (ROLAP) option where we can create **bitmap indexes**. An index is a database feature that allows faster access to data. It is somewhat analogous to the index of a book that allows us to get to a page in the book with the information we want much faster. A bitmap-type index refers to how it is stored in the database and is generally a better option to use for data warehouse implementations (so it is checked by default). There is also a composite unique key checkbox for cubes as there was for dimensions.

For a cube, checking this box will create a unique key out of the foreign keys for the dimensions referenced by the cube. We want to check this box to ensure we can't enter duplicate data into our cube, that is, more than one cube record with the same set of dimension attributes assigned.

- ° **Dimensions**: Instead of attributes, the cube has a tab for dimensions. The dimensions referenced by a cube are basically its attributes.

- ° **Measures:** The next tab is for the measures of the cube. It is for those values that we are storing in our cube as the facts that we wish to track.

- ° **Aggregations**: Instead of hierarchies, a cube has aggregations. There are various methods of aggregation that we can select, as seen in the drop-down box, the most common of which is sum, which is the default. This is where the default aggregation method referred to earlier can be changed. There will be no aggregations in a pure relational implementation, so we will leave this tab set to the defaults and not bother changing it.

- ° **Orphan**: This feature is available for cubes also and provides an automated way to manage what to do about cube records that can't be loaded because one or more dimension records cannot be found for it. There are two options to account for here, what to do if a dimension key is null and what to do if a dimension key is found to be invalid. In each case there are three options to choose from for how to handle the orphans:

    1. **No Maintenance**: This is the default setting and indicates that orphans will not be detected and nothing will be done about them.

    2. **Default Dimension Record**: This setting indicates that a default dimension record should be used if one is null or invalid and if a default dimension doesn't exist, it will create one to use. Default dimension records can be created from the **Orphan** tab of the dimension as discussed above.

    3. **Reject Orphan**: This will cause the orphan record to be rejected.

These are the main features of the Design Center interface and editors for dimensions and cubes. We can use it to view the objects the wizards have created for us, edit them, or create brand new objects from scratch. We can start with an empty canvas and drag new objects from the palette, or existing objects from the explorer, and then connect them. We will see other editors very similar to this from the next chapter when we start to look at ETL and mappings.

Summary

In this chapter, we dove right into creating our three dimensions and a cube using the Warehouse Builder Design Center. We used the wizards available to help us out, as well as investigated the flexibility to manually create, view, and edit objects using the data object editors for dimensions and cubes. In a relatively short amount of time, we were able to design a data warehouse structure that could be used as is, or expanded to support more detailed information.

Now that we have our sources defined and our targets designed, it's time to start thinking about loading that target. Next, we'll look at some **Extract, Transform, and Load (ETL)** basics to lay the groundwork for designing the ETL we'll use to actually load data into our data warehouse.

5
Extract, Transform, and Load Basics

We're moving along nicely into the process of designing and building a data warehouse. If you've been reading all the way through to here, you'll recall how we've introduced the Warehouse Builder software (how to install it along with the Oracle Database), looked at its architecture, and covered a short overview of the analysis and design phases for implementing a data warehouse project. We've defined our data sources and imported the metadata for them. We've designed our target structure into which we'll load the data. Congratulations for having read this far — don't give up now because we're not done yet. We still have to get data from our sources into our target. We will do that by:

- Designing *mappings* in OWB.
- Deploying the mappings to the database.
- Running the mappings.

This chapter will expose **ETL (Extract, Transform, and Load)** for the first time in this book. ETL is the first step in building the mappings from source to target. We have sources and targets defined and now we need to do the following:

- Work on *extracting* the data from our sources
- Perform any *transformations* on that data (to clean it up or modify it)
- *Load* it into our target data warehouse structure

We will accomplish this by designing mappings in OWB. **Mappings** are visual representations of the flow of data from source to target and the operations that need to be performed on the data. However, before we can do that, we need to be familiar with what OWB offers us so that we can make best use of it.

With this in mind, we'll spend this chapter looking at ETL in general and the Warehouse Builder features that support designing our ETL operations in particular. In the next chapter, we'll actually design our mappings in OWB.

ETL

The process of extracting, transforming, and loading data can appear rather complicated. We do have a special term to describe it, ETL, which contains the three steps mentioned. We're dealing with source data on different database systems from our target and a database from a vendor other than Oracle, Microsoft SQL Server in this case. Let's look from a high level at what is involved in getting that data from a source system to our target, and then take a look at whether to stage the data or not. We will then see how to automate that process in Warehouse Builder, which will relieve us of much of the work.

Manual ETL processes

First of all, we need to be able to get data out of that source system and move it over to the target system. We can't begin to do anything until that is accomplished, but what means can we use to do so? We know that the Oracle Database provides various methods to load data into it. There is an application that Oracle provides called **SQL*Loader**, which is a utility to load data from flat files. This could be one way to get data from our source system. Every database vendor provides some means of extracting data from their tables and saving it to flat files. We could copy the file over and then use the SQL*Loader utility to load the file. Reading the documentation that describes how to use that utility, we see that we have to define a control file to describe the loading process and definitions of the fields to be loaded. This seems like a lot of work, so let's see what other options we might have.

The Oracle Database allows us to create database links as we saw back in Chapter 2. When we define our sources, we can link them to other vendor's database systems via the heterogeneous services, which is exactly what we set up in Chapter 2. This looks like a better way to go. We could define a database link to point to our source database, and then we could directly copy the data into our database.

However, our target database structure doesn't look anything like the source database structure. The POS Transactional database is a relational database that is highly normalized, and our target consists of cubes and dimensions implemented relationally in the database. How are we going to get the data copied into that structure? Clearly, there will be some manipulation of the data to get it reformatted and restructured from source to target. We cannot just take all the rows from one table in the source structure and copy them into a table in the target structure for each source table. The data will have to be manipulated when it is copied. This means we need to develop code that can perform this rather complex task, depending on the manipulations that need to be done.

In a nutshell, this is the process of extract, transform, and load. We have to:

1. *Extract* the data from the source system by some method.
2. Load flat files using SQL*Loader or via a direct database link. Then we have to *transform* that data with SQL or PL/SQL code in the database to match and fit it into the target structure.
3. Finally, we have to *load* it into the target structure.

The good news here is that the Warehouse Builder provides us the means to design this process graphically, and then generate all the code we need automatically so that we don't have to build all that code manually.

Staging

We need to consider a practical aspect to this process that is related to ETL, as well as to the structure in our target database. This practical aspect is the question of whether to stage the source data in a temporary location before performing the transformations on it and loading it into the target structure. **Staging** is the process of copying the source data temporarily into a table(s) in our target database. Here we can perform any transformations that are required before loading the source data into the final target tables. The source data could actually be copied to a table in another database that we create just for this purpose, but it doesn't have to be. This process involves saving data to storage at any step along the way to the final target structure, and it can incorporate a number of intermediate staging steps. The source and target designations will be affected during the intermediate steps of staging. So we'll need to decide on a staging strategy, if any, before designing the ETL in OWB. Now, we'll look at the staging process before we actually design any ETL logic.

To stage or not to stage

There are a number of considerations we can take into account when deciding whether to use a staging area or not for our source data:

- The points to consider to keep the process flowing as fast as possible are:
    ◦ The amount of source data we will be dealing with
    ◦ The amount of manipulations of the source data that will be required
    ◦ If the source data is in another database other than an Oracle Database, the reliability of the connection to the database and the performance of the link while pulling data across

- If a failure occurs during an intermediate step of the ETL process, we will have to restart the process. If such a failure occurs, we will have to consider the severity of the impact, as in the following cases:
    ◦ Going back again to the source system to pull data if the first attempt failed.
    ◦ The source data is changing while we are trying to load it into the warehouse, meaning that whatever data we pull the second time might be different from what we started with (and which caused the failure). This condition will make it difficult to debug the error that caused this failure.

These points will determine whether it makes sense to create a staging area. Suppose that we have a large amount of data to load and many transformations to perform on that data while loading. This process will take a lot longer if we directly access the remote database to pull and transform data, particularly if that remote database is not an Oracle Database. We'll also be doing all of the manipulations and transformations in memory and if anything fails, we'll have to start all over again. Any access to a remote database like this is going to have an impact on the performance of the database. Having to do it again just compounds the potential impact.

For example, in one of my previous positions, I was responsible for the process of loading data into our customer's warehouse and each ETL run pulled approximately 150,000 records. After transforming, these turned into 1,350,000 records in the target warehouse. There were several transformations done on the data. When directly accessing the remote database, which is not an Oracle Database, the process literally took hours during its first run. This is not an acceptable situation by any means. Through making various changes to configurations, including first adding a step to stage the data in the Oracle Database, the process was streamlined to take a total of about 25 to 30 minutes. That is acceptable for a data load that at most happens two or three times a week.

The individual process to stage the data to a table in the Oracle database simply involves copying the data one-for-one over to the Oracle Database, and this runs in less than 30 seconds. This means the source database connection is only open for 30 seconds, whereas it had to constantly work for hours (previously) without a staging table. This is an example of how the source system is benefitted by using a staging table. An added benefit with the staging is that if the ETL process needs to be restarted, there is no need to go back to disturb the source system to retrieve the data.

Maybe there is only a small window of opportunity to grab the data at night when there is some downtime. Trying to perform all the transformations on the data at once while directly pulling it might cause the process to extend past the allowed time period. In this case, the above example of using a staging table in the Oracle Database will definitely be applicable. This will make the ETL process run very fast and the transformations can then be run on it without impacting the transactional system, or being impacted by it.

Configuration of a staging area

A staging area is clearly an advantage when designing our ETL. So we'll want to create one, but we will need to decide where we want to create it—in the database or outside the database. Outside the database, we would create a staging area in flat files on the file system that we could access to load data into the database. Back in Chapter 2, we discussed the pulling of data from flat files assuming that we weren't able to get access directly to the source database system and instead the DBA of ACME Toys and Gizmos company supplied us with a CSV file to import. For a staging area, we might want to consider storing the source data in a flat file ourselves, even if we have access to the source database. Our staging area in this case would be a folder on the file system and the data would be stored in a flat file.

When making a decision about whether to use a flat file, or create a table directly in the database, there are a number of particulars we'll want to take into account. As we are using OWB to design and implement our data warehouse, we've seen how it can directly support data stored in a flat file as a source (as if it was a table in the database) by using an external table. So this option of using OWB to directly support data stored in a flat file is open to us.

The external tables in the Oracle Database now render some of the reasons for keeping source staging data in tables in the database moot. We can treat a flat file as essentially another table in the database. This option is available to us in the Warehouse Builder for defining a flat file as a source, but not a target. So we must keep this in mind if we want to stage data at some other point during the process after the initial load of data. Earlier, we needed to have all our data in database tables if we were relying solely on SQL in the database. External tables allow us to access flat files using all the benefits of SQL for querying the data, so now that reason is not as big a factor as it once was.

If you would like to read more about staging areas and flat files versus database tables, you can refer to the book titled "*The Data Warehouse ETL Toolkit – Practical Techniques for Extracting, Cleaning, Conforming, and Delivering Data*", Ralph Kimball and Joe Caserta, Wiley Publishing, Inc. This book discusses a number of cases where it might be preferable to use flat files depending on the purpose at hand: things such as the storage and safekeeping of source data, sorting data, filtering it, or replacing text strings in data, and so on. Many of these purposes can be accomplished more efficiently outside the database with external tools and packages for manipulating text files. Unless you already have the packages or tools, it may make more sense to stick with database tables that can make full use of those features built into the database.

At the ACME Toys and Gizmos company, we are going to use a table in the database for the initial staging table. This way we can get some experience with how that would work in OWB using the Table Editor to create a table. One of our mapping tasks in the next chapter will be to create this table using OWB and use it as a part of our initial mapping from the source system. If needed, it is not difficult to switch to using a flat file later.

Mappings and operators in OWB

We are now going to look at the Warehouse Builder and its features for designing and building our ETL process. OWB handles this with what are called **mappings**. A mapping is composed of a series of **operators** that describe the sources, targets, and a series of operations that flow from source to target to load the data. It is all designed in a graphical manner using the **Mapping Editor**, which is available in the **Design Center**. Let's run the Design Center now and take a look at the Mapping Editor, its features, and some of the operators that are available to us. Launch the Design Center as we discussed in Chapter 2 in the *Overview of Warehouse Builder Design Center* section.

OWB Mappings

In the **Design Center | Project Navigator** window, expand the **ACME_DW_ PROJECT** project (if it is not already expanded) by clicking on the plus sign beside it. To access the **Mapping Editor**, we need a mapping to work on. So to begin with, we could create an empty mapping at this point.

There is no wizard for creating mappings as there is for importing source metadata, or creating dimensions and cubes. There are too many options to lay out the mapping for a wizard, so it's difficult to make any kind of intelligent guesses as to how to design. However, there are some cases where we get a mapping for "free" such as the **DATE_DIM_ MAP**, which was created for us automatically by the **Time Dimension** wizard — but that is the exception rather than the rule.

Mappings are created in the **Mappings** node. We can find it under the module we created to hold our data warehouse design under the **Databases | Oracle** node in our project. Expand that module, which we called **ACME_DWH**, and then expand the **Mappings** node underneath it. For reference, your **Project Navigator** should look like this now:

The **DATE_DIM_MAP** we see under Mappings is the mapping that was created for us automatically by the **Time Dimension** wizard. Instead of creating a new mapping, which will have nothing in it yet, let's open this mapping and take a look at it for our initial exploration of the features in OWB for designing mappings. Let's double-click on the **DATE_DIM_MAP** mapping. It will launch the **Mapping Editor** and load the **DATE_DIM_MAP** into it. We are not going to modify it, but we will use the displayed **Mapping Editor** window to familiarize ourselves with its features. This is a very similar concept to the data object editors we looked at in the last chapter but for mappings, not data objects. We're going to go into more detail in using the Mapping Editor simply because we need to use it to build our mappings; there is no wizard available to us. The **Mapping Editor** window looks like the following:

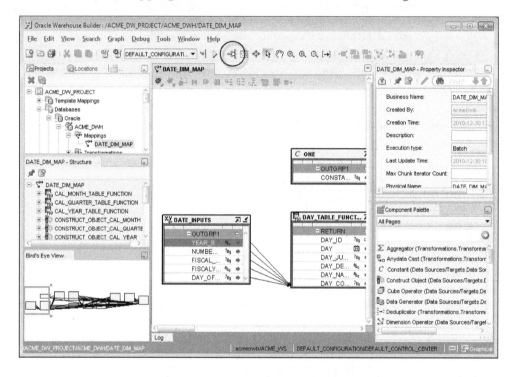

The **Mapping Editor** opens in the Design Center the same way as the **data object editors** we saw in the last chapter. The primary difference is the mapping editor is graphical where the data editors are primarily textual, with one tab, the Physical Bindings, displaying objects graphically. A few other additional windows are noticeable also, the **Component Palette**, the **Structure View**, and the **Bird's Eye View** windows.

The Component Palette should open automatically when a mapping is edited but the Bird's Eye and Structure views do not, but they are good to have open for quickly navigating around the canvas and viewing the objects in the mapping. Go ahead and open them from the **View** menu by selecting **Bird's Eye** and **Structure** if they are not already open. The window for the above image was re-sized to better fit here, but we're going to maximize the window while we work with it for ease of use as we can view more information on the screen. It is a good idea to make your screen resolution as high as possible so more screen real estate is available for displaying. Play around with the layout of the windows to come up with an orientation that works best for you. If the Structure and Birds Eye view are not being used, just close them to make more room. As you use the tool more you'll figure out what works best for you.

Your view might look different or be perhaps all jumbled from previous edits. It's very easy to move objects around on the canvas (that big window in the middle). We can go on clicking on the objects and dragging them into new locations to try to neaten it up but that's too much work. The **Mapping Editor**, as with all the graphical editors, provides a convenient Auto Layout option that will do all that for us. Click on the **Auto Layout** button in the toolbar to spread everything out. It is circled (at the top) for your reference in the previous image. The command is also available from the **Graph** menu entry under the Zoom and Layout sub-menu.

Let's briefly discuss some of the main features we can see in the **Mapping Editor** screen. The *Oracle Warehouse Builder Data Modeling, ETL and Data Quality Guide*, which is available at `http://download.oracle.com/docs/cd/E11882_01/owb.112/e10935/mappings.htm#BEIGDJAE`, covers each of these windows in greater detail in Chapter 5 on PL/SQL mappings along with other details about mappings. So we'll just touch upon them briefly, especially as we've seen some of them in the last chapter:

- **Mapping**

  The **Mapping** window is the main working area in the center of the above image where we will design the mapping. This window is also referred to as the **canvas**. This is the graphical display that will show the operators being used and the connections between the operators that indicate the data flow from source to target.

- **Structure View**

  We haven't seen this window yet. It provides a hierarchical view of the objects in the editor, including operators and attributes of those operators for a mapping. It will display the structure for a data object also if opened when editing a data object. This window is similar to the old **Explorer** window from the data and mapping editor windows in the previous release.

- **Property Inspector**

  The Property Inspector window displays the various properties that can be set for objects in our mapping. It is the same window we saw when looking at the data object editors in the last chapter. When an object is selected in the canvas, its properties will display in this window. We can resize any of these windows by holding the mouse pointer over the edge of a window until it turns into a double arrow, and then clicking and dragging to resize the window so we can see the contents better. To investigate the properties window a little closer, let's select the **DATE_INPUTS** operator. We can scroll the Structure View window until we see the operator and then click on it, or we can scroll the main canvas until we see it and then click on the top portion of the frame to select it. It is the first object on the left and defines inputs into **DATE_DIM_MAP**. It is visible in the previous image. After clicking on it, all the properties applicable to it will be displayed in the property inspector window. The only properties displaying for the **DATE_INPUTS** operator are the standard properties associated with any operator- name, description, and some creation and update information. Let's click on one of the attributes to see a better example of more specific attributes. Click on **YEAR_START_ DATE** within the **DATE_INPUTS** operator. It is the first attribute of the **DATE_INPUTS** operator and can be selected in the Structure View or on the canvas by clicking on it and is shown in the following image, which is a portion of the Design Center showing the Mapping Editor window and properties we're referring to. The windows have been resized to better display the information being referred to here:

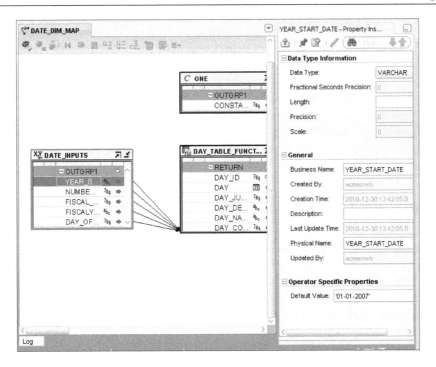

Now we can see some more interesting properties. **YEAR_START_DATE** is an attribute of the **DATE_INPUTS** object and defines the starting date to use for the data that will be loaded by this mapping. The properties that can be set or displayed for it include the characteristics about this attribute such as what kind of data type it is, its size, and its default value. Recalling our running of the **Time Dimension Wizard** in the last chapter, there was one option to specify the year range for the dimension and we chose **2007** as the start year and that is what formed the source for the default value we can see here. Do not change anything but just click on a few more objects or attributes to look around at the various properties.

- **Component Palette**

  The **Component Palette** contains each of the objects that can be used in our mapping. We can click on the object we want to place in the mapping and drag it onto the canvas. This list will be customized based on the category selection in the dropdown at the top of the window to view either all the components or subsets of the components by category/purpose.

- **Bird's Eye View**

  This window displays a miniature version of the entire canvas and allows us to scroll around the canvas without using the scroll bars. We can click and drag the blue-colored box around this window to view various portions of the main canvas. The main canvas will scroll as we move the blue box. Go ahead and give that a try. We will find that in most mappings, we'll quickly outgrow the available space to display everything at once and will have to scroll around to see everything. This can come in very handy for rapidly scrolling the window.

The canvas layout

Let's take a closer look at some of the general features of the operators we can see in our canvas, and then at some of the features specific to different operators. Operators on the canvas are represented by boxes with a title that indicates the name of the operator and an icon that indicates the type. In the canvas, we'll take a look at the operator that is on the far left of the canvas called **DATE_INPUTS**. This operator happens to be a **Mapping Input Parameter** operator.

It is shown in the following screenshot with the key features highlighted with callouts:

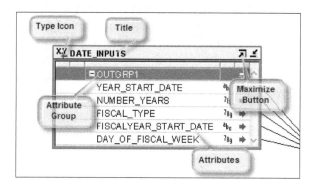

The box can be resized by clicking the left mouse button and holding it over an edge of the operator, and then dragging it to a new size. To show the entire contents at once, you can click on the maximize button to instantly expand the box, as shown in the above screenshot.

A handy feature available for viewing operators is to minimize them to better see the layout and mapping line connections. You can use the *Ctrl-A* key combination to select all operators on the canvas then select **Graph...Minimize** from the main menu to minimize them all and then **Graph...Zoom and Layout... Auto Layout** to automatically arrange them in a logical orientation.

We can see some lines of information listed inside the box, which are the attributes of this operator. There are two major types of attributes—an input group and an output group. In this case, we can see one group named **OUTGRP1** which tells us this operator has only an output group. This operator represents the input of information into the map at the beginning, so it is not meant to have any other operators mapped as input to it. Thus, it has no input attributes, but only output attributes.

Take a look at the operator on the right of the **DATE_INPUTS** operator called **DAY_TABLE_FUNCTION**. It has both input and output attributes as shown in the next screenshot, because this operator represents a PL/SQL function. A PL/SQL function takes the values supplied as input attributes in the Input group as parameters to the function and returns the value or values indicated in the Output group as a return value from the function.

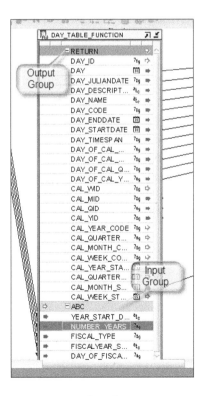

Renaming attribute group names

The names INGRP1 and OUTGRP1 are generic names that OWB uses as default names for input and output groups when there is only one of each. We can change those names if we want to and that is exactly what the Warehouse Builder has done with the DAY_TABLE_FUNCTION operator shown above. It has renamed the INGRP1 input group as ABC and OUTGRP1 output group as RETURN.

There are some operators that contain more than one input or output group. For instance, Joiner Operator is an operator to represent a join of two or more tables. This operator will have an input group defined for each table. In that case, each input group would have a different number incrementing from 1 (for example, INGRP2, INGRP3, and so on). It makes sense in this case to rename the input groups to match the tables being joined, but that is not a requirement.

An attribute group name is edited in the **Details** window for the group name. This window is accessible by right-clicking on the group name in the canvas and selecting **Open Details...** from the pop-up menu or by double clicking on the group name. It can also be edited by just clicking the group name and editing the name properties in the **Property Inspector** window. Using the Details window has the added benefit of displaying whether the group is an input group, an output group or both by including a column labeled **Direction** which we don't see in the **Property Inspector**. We'll be making use of that **Details** window in the next chapter when we actually start building a mapping.

We can also note with DAY_TABLE_FUNCTION that the number of attributes is greater than what's displayed in the operator window depending on how big we've made the window. We can scroll down through the list of attributes, or resize the operator in the canvas to see more of them.

That was a brief introduction to the user interface for the Mapping Editor and the operators as displayed in the canvas. The *Oracle Warehouse Builder Data Modeling, ETL and Data Quality Guide* includes additional details about the various windows and their purpose, as well as the toolbars and menus that are available. We will now look at the various operators that OWB provides us with in a little more detail.

OWB operators

We'll discuss here the various operators using the same category breakdown that the *Oracle Warehouse Builder Data Modeling, ETL, and Data Quality Guide* (http://download.oracle.com/docs/cd/E11882_01/owb.112/e10935/transformdata_intro.htm#i1127634) uses in its section on the types of operators in Chapter 4—**Source and Target Operators**, **Transformations (Data Flow Operators)**, and **Pre/Post Processing Operators**. All of the operators are available to us from the **Component Palette** window in the **Design Center** when editing a mapping, so we can refer to it as we discuss each operator. The Component Palette has a dropdown that contains the same categories of operators we mentioned above. There are a couple of other categories that are for more advanced topics than we'll cover here (Pluggable Mapping and Real-Time Data Warehousing). They are described in the above referenced documentation. The following screenshots display the complete list of operators in each of the three categories:

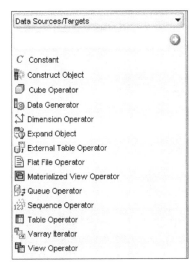

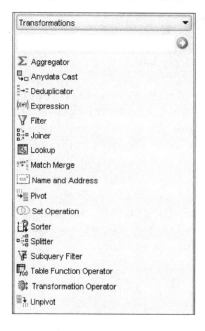

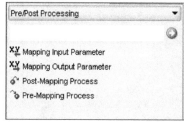

Earlier in the ETL section of this chapter, we discussed the various means at our disposal for performing ETL operations manually with applications such as SQL*Loader. We have also mentioned that OWB allows us to define the process graphically, and then generates the code for us as well. The bottom line is that OWB makes use of the existing facilities within the database and the utilities supplied with the database to accomplish the data load and transformations.

> The operators we use will determine the kind of code that gets generated by OWB. Keep this in mind as we study these operators because it will help us understand some of the explanations that are supplied for the operators in the documentation.

Most of the operators will result in a PL/SQL mapping. So the explanations are in terms of the SQL or PL/SQL code element that is created for an operator.

As we can see, we have quite an extensive list of operators available to us and we won't have room here to talk about all of them. We won't need them all, and that is usually the case when designing mappings in OWB. We will be focusing on the main ones that we will need for our application and discuss some of the more common ones along with the ones we can see in the DATE_DIM_MAP. The operators found in the DATE_DIM_MAP will be pointed out, so you can see an example by looking at that map. We'll talk about some of the operators in more detail as we actually begin to use them in the next chapter. As much as possible, we will try to discuss the operators from a functionality standpoint without getting too bogged down by the actual code that is generated.

For the adventurous out there, you can take a look at the code that the Warehouse Builder will create for the mapping in the database. But unless you are an SQL coding wizard, you will become quickly overwhelmed. There is OWB-generated code I've had to deal with in a previous position that contains SQL insert statements that are over 650-lines long for a single statement. This is definitely not for the faint-hearted. Have no fear, however; we don't have to dig into the code if we don't want to. This is the beauty of what a graphical interface does for us. For those who do love to delve into the code, there are ways to view it but that is definitely a more advanced topic.

Source and target operators

The Warehouse Builder provides operators that we will use to represent the sources of our data and the targets into which we will load data. We know we're going to be pulling data from non-Oracle database tables, and loading it into dimensions and cubes in our Oracle Database. We also saw in Chapter 2 how to import metadata from a flat file source. So there is another source type that we'll need to handle, a flat file. With that in mind, here are some of the operators we're going to potentially need:

- **Cube Operator**: An operator that represents a cube that we have previously defined. We defined our cube back in Chapter 4 and this operator will be used to represent that cube in our mapping. It encapsulates logic like surrogate key lookup and early arriving facts (orphan management).

- **Dimension Operator**: An operator that represents previously defined dimensions. As with our cube, our dimensions were defined in *Chapter 4* and this operator will be used in our mapping to represent them. We can see an example of **Dimension Operator** in DATE_DIM_MAP. This mapping is designed to load our DATE_DIM dimension, and so an operator of the same name was created in it at the end on the far right of the canvas. This operator includes logic for surrogate key generation also as well as support for slowly changing dimensions.

- **External Table Operator**: This operator represents external tables, which we have seen in Chapter 2. They can be used to access data stored in flat files as if they were tables. We will look at using an external table to access the flat file that we imported back in Chapter 2.

- **Table Operator**: This operator represents a table in the database. We will need to store data in tables in our Oracle Database at some point in the loading of data.

Those are the main operators we're going to need. There are a number of other operators that are defined for use as sources and targets in our mappings that can be very useful. The following are some of the more common operators:

- **Constant**: Represents a constant value that is needed. It can be used to load a default value for a field that doesn't have any input from another source, for instance. The DATE_DIM_MAP mapping contains a couple of constant values to represent hardcoded numbers. One is named ONE for the number 1, and one is named ZERO for a 0.

- **View Operator**: Represents a database view. Source data is frequently retrieved via a view in the source database that can pull data from multiple sources into a single, easily accessible view.

> In the latest release of OWB we can now have inline views using this View Operator which allow us to define SQL right in the mapping and not have a physical view in the database. We won't be covering that in this book but you can go to the OWB blog for more detailed information:
>
> http://blogs.oracle.com/warehousebuilder/2010/08/
> owb_11gr2_mappings_and_inline_sql.html

- **Sequence Operator**: Can be used to represent a database **sequence**, which is an automatic generator of sequential unique numbers and is most often used for populating a primary key field.

- **Construct Object**: This operator can be used to actually construct an Oracle object type in our mapping. There are examples of this in DATE_DIM_MAP, which builds the DATE_DIM dimension. An *object* in this context refers to a PL/SQL object. We can see three **Construct Object** operators in DATE_DIM_ MAP—for a calendar month (CONSTRUCT_OBJECT_CAL_MONTH), a calendar quarter (CONSTRUCT_OBJECT_CAL_QUARTER), and a calendar year object (CONSTRUCT_OBJECT_CAL_YEAR). If we click on the attribute in the **OUTGRP1** output group of one of those construct operators, we can see in the **Property Inspector** window that it is of type **SYS_REFCURSOR**. An example is shown in the next screenshot with the **CONSTRUCT_OBJECT_REFCURSOR_OUT** attribute selected in the **CONSTRUCT_OBJECT_CAL_MONTH** object:

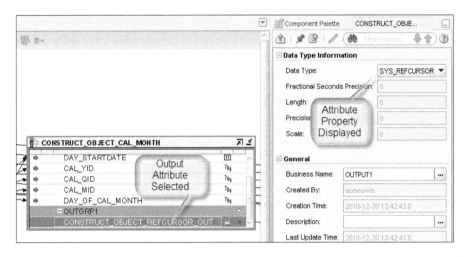

  A **SYS_REFCURSOR** is a PL/SQL type that represents a **cursor** in PL/SQL. A cursor is used to point to the row of the result of the query that is defined for that cursor. This is a rather advanced topic to be covered in this book, but is mentioned here as **DATE_DIM_MAP** contains some of this type.

These all represent sources and targets of data for our mappings. When we drag and drop one of these operators onto our canvas, it represents an actual database object. When created, every one of these will need to be bound to its underlying database object as we are using the relational storage option. For tables, attributes of the table operator will correspond to columns in the table, likewise for views and external tables. The same principle holds true for the cube and dimension operators. Attributes of the operator correspond to the attributes of the dimension or cube. If the dimension or cube is implemented relationally, they will correspond to the columns of the underlying table that is created.

A constant is implemented in the database as PL/SQL code using the PL/SQL syntax for representing a constant value. The value will be the value we would set on a constant's attribute. For sequences, constants are implemented as a database **sequence** object. The code is generated to invoke constants to retrieve the `currval` or `nextval` value from the underlying sequence as needed, depending on how we used it in our mapping. The `currval` variable will return the current value of the sequence, and the `nextval` variable will return the next value.

Transformations (data flow operators)

Sources and targets are good and we could end right there by connecting our sources directly to our targets. This would result in a complete mapping that would load our target from our source, but this would mean there needs to be a one-to-one correspondence between our source and target. If that were the case, why bother creating a data warehouse target in the first place if it's only going to look exactly like the source? Just query the source data.

The true power of a data warehouse lies in the restructuring of the source data into a format that greatly facilitates the querying of large amounts of data over different time periods. For this, we need to transform the source data into a new structure. That is the purpose of the **transformation** (or **data flow) operators**. They are dragged and dropped into our mapping between our sources and targets. Then they are connected to those sources and targets to indicate the flow of data and the transformations that will occur on that data as it is being pulled from the source and loaded into the target structure. Some of the common data flow operators we'll see are as follows:

- **Aggregator**: There are times when source data is at a finer level of detail than we need. So we need to sum the data up to a higher level, or apply some other aggregation type function such as an average function. This is the purpose of the **Aggregator** operator. This is implemented behind the scenes using an SQL `group by` clause with an aggregation SQL function applied to the amount(s) we want to aggregate.

- **Deduplicator**: Sometimes our data records will contain duplicate combinations that we want to weed out so we're loading only unique combinations of data. The **Deduplicator** operator will do this for us. It's implemented behind the scenes with the `distinct` SQL function, which returns combinations of data elements that are unique.

- **Expression**: This represents an SQL expression that can be applied to the output to produce the desired result. Any valid SQL code for an expression can be used, and we can reference input attributes to include them as well as functions.

It's possible to write expressions in an **Expression** operator for which separate operators are predefined such as functions. We will generally get better performance out of our mappings if we use the prebuilt operators whenever possible rather than implement code in expressions. So, if there is an operator available, we'll use it and use an expression only if we have to.

- **Filter:** This will limit the rows from an output set to criteria that we specify. It is generally implemented in a `where` clause in SQL to restrict the rows that are returned. We can connect a filter to a source object, specify the filter criteria, and get only those records that we want in the output.

- **Joiner:** This operator will implement an SQL `join` on two or more input sets of data. A `join` takes records from one source and combines them with the records from another source using some combination of values that are common between the two. We will specify these common records as an attribute of the `join`. This is a convenient way to combine data from multiple input sources into one.

- **Lookup:** A **Lookup** operator (previously known as a Key Lookup) looks up data in a table based on some input criteria (the key) to return some information required by our mapping. It is similar to a **Table Operator** that was discussed previously for sources and targets. However, a **Lookup** operator is geared toward returning a subset of rows from a table based on the key criteria we specify, rather than representing all the rows of a table, which the **Table Operator** does. It can look up data from a table, view, cube, or dimension.

The Lookup operator has been greatly enhanced in this new release of the Warehouse Builder. There is a blog posting that refers to the changes for additional reading at the following URL:

`http://blogs.oracle.com/warehousebuilder/2010/09/`
`owb_11gr2_lookup_operator.html`

- **Pivot**: This operator can be useful if we have source records that contain multiple columns of data that is spread across columns instead of rows. For instance, we might have source records of sales data for the year that contain a column for each month of the year. But we need to save that information by month, and not by year. The **Pivot** operator will create separate rows of output for each of those columns of input.

- **Set Operation:** This operator will allow us to perform an SQL set operation on our data such as a `union` (returning all rows from each of two sources, either ignoring the duplicates or including the duplicates) or `intersect` (which will return common rows from two sources).

- **Splitter**: This operator is the opposite of the **Joiner** operator. It will allow us to split an input stream of data rows into two separate targets based on the criteria we specify. It can be useful for shunting rows of data off to a side error table to flag them while copying the good rows into the main target.

- **Transformation Operator**: All these operators are transformation operators but there is one operator type specifically named "**Transformation**". This operator can be used to invoke a PL/SQL function or procedure with some of our source data as input to provide a transformation of data. For instance, the SQL `trim()` function can be represented by **Transformation Operator** to take a column value as input, and provide the value as output after having any whitespace trimmed from the value. This is just one example of a function that can be implemented with the **Transformation Operator**. There are numerous others available to us.

> A **Transformation Operator** is an example of an operator that could be implemented in an **Expression** operator by simply invoking the `trim()` SQL function directly on an input value. But as we can implement a `trim()` directly using its own operator, we should do so for efficiency and consistency.

- **Table Function Operator:** A **Table Function Operator** can be seen in the `DATE_DIM_MAP` map. There are three **Table Function** operators defined: `CAL_MONTH_TABLE_FUNCTION`, `CAL_QUARTER_TABLE_FUNCTION`, and `CAL_YEAR_TABLE_FUNCTION`. This kind of operator represents a **Table Function**, which is defined in PL/SQL and is a function that can be queried like a table to return rows of information. The **Table Function Operators** are more advanced than we will be covering in this book, but are mentioned here as `DATE_DIM_MAP` includes them.

These are just some of the operators available to us for performing transformations on our data as it flows from source to target. Others are described in the *Oracle Warehouse Builder Data Modeling, ETL, and Data Quality Guide* as mentioned previously (`http://download.oracle.com/docs/cd/E11882_01/owb.112/e10935/toc.htm`).

Other operators

There is a small group of operators that allow us to perform operations before the mapping process begins, or after the mapping process ends. These are the pre- and post-processing operators and mapping input and output operators. We can perform functions or procedures before or after a mapping runs, and can also accept input or provide output from a mapping process.

- **Mapping Input Parameter:** This operator allows us to pass a parameter(s) into a mapping process. It is very useful to make a mapping more generic by accepting a constant value as input that might change, rather than hardcoding it into the mapping. DATE_DIM_MAP uses a **Mapping Input Parameter** operator as its very first operator on the left, which we discussed earlier when talking about Mapping Properties.

- **Mapping Output Parameter**: As the name suggests, this is similar to the **Mapping Input Parameter** operator, but provides a value as output from our mapping.

- **Post-Mapping Process:** Allows us to invoke a function or procedure after the mapping completes its processing. There may be some cleanup we want to do automatically such as deleting all the records from a table we're done with—perhaps a staging table that was used during the mapping process.

- **Pre-Mapping Process**: It's not too hard to figure out what this operator does. It allows us to invoke a function or procedure before the mapping process begins. Maybe our mapping needs to do a key lookup of a data value that is going to be stored in every row of output. But we don't want to invoke a **Lookup** operator for every record of input. So we could use a **Pre-Mapping Process** operator instead to invoke the function once at the beginning, which will make the returned value available for every row that is processed without having to re-invoke the procedure.

That concludes our discussion of some of the main operators we're going to encounter. If you are looking at the *Oracle Warehouse Builder Data Modeling, ETL, and Data Quality Guide* section that discusses these categories of operators, you no doubt noticed the other two categories we mentioned previously. They are also visible in the **Component Palette** drop down. Pluggable Mappings (of which there are three operators) are a more advanced feature that allows us to create a grouping of operators that can function as a single operator and be reused in other mappings and Real-Time Data Warehousing mappings (of which there are only two operators) that are for creating real-time and batch mappings.

Summary

This chapter has given us an overview of the Extract, Transform, and Load (ETL) process as well as the Warehouse Builder's support for designing our ETL process. We discussed the process of mapping and a little of what that involves in OWB. We took a look at the OWB **Mapping Editor** in the **Design Center** to get a feel for the windows available to us, and also looked at a list of some of the operators OWB provides for us to use in our mappings.

We're laying the groundwork here for the real fun that comes in the next chapter where we get to put this knowledge to use in designing a mapping. In the next chapter, we will also get to use some of these operators.

6
ETL: Putting it Together

We had our first introduction to the process of ETL in the last chapter where we discussed what it is and saw the features the Warehouse Builder has for designing our ETL processes. We looked at the Mapping Editor, which is the main interface we'll use to build our ETL mappings. We also looked at the objects in OWB that we can use. However, we didn't get to do anything other than just look. We have all this new knowledge and are ready to use it. So let's work on designing a mapping, which will make use of some of the features we looked at in the last chapter.

We've looked in detail at the source structures in Chapter 2 and talked about staging data in Chapter 5. In the previous chapters, we've also talked about the concepts of extraction, transformation, and loading of data that will be required to get the source data from our source to our target structure. We will get to put all this together in this chapter as we begin to design and build our mappings. You may have already started thinking of some ideas to handle the mapping of information into our target, or some issues that we'll need to address. So without further ado, let's get started. We'll be covering the following main topics in this chapter:

- Designing a staging area
    - Designing staging area contents
    - Building a staging table with the Table Editor

- Reviewing the Mapping Editor
- Creating a mapping
    - Adding source table
    - Adding target table
    - Connecting source to target
    - Joiner operator attribute groups
    - Connecting operators to the Joiner
    - Defining operator properties for the Joiner
    - Adding an Aggregator operator

Designing our staging area

We are going to design and build our very first ETL mapping in OWB, but where do we get started? We know we have to pull data from the ACME_POS transactional database as we saw back in Chapter 2. The source data structure in that database is a normalized relational structure, and our target is a dimensional model of a cube and dimensions. This looks like quite a bit of transforming we'll need to do to get the data from our source into our target. We're going to break this down into much smaller chunks, so the process will be easier.

Instead of doing it all at once, we're going to bite off manageable chunks to work on a bit at a time. We will start with the initial extraction of data from the source database into our target database without having to worry about transforming it. Let's just get the complete set of data over to our target database, and then work on populating it into the final structure. This is the role a staging area plays in the process, and this is what we're going to focus on in this chapter to get our feet wet with designing ETL in OWB. We're going to stage the data initially on the target database server in one location, where it will be available for loading.

The first step is to design what our staging area is going to look like. The staging area is the interim location for the data between the source system and the target database structure. The staging area will hold the data extracted directly from the ACME_POS source database, which will determine how we structure our staging table. So let's begin designing it.

Designing the staging area contents

We designed our target structure in Chapter 3, so we know what data we need to load. We just need to design a staging area that will contain data. Let's summarize the data elements we're going to need to pull from our source database. We'll group them by the dimensional objects in our target that we designed in Chapter 4, and list the data elements we'll need for each. The dimensional objects in our target are as follows:

- Sales

  The data elements in the Sales dimensional object are:

  ○ Quantity

  ○ Sales amount

- Date

  The data element in the Date dimensional object is:

  ○ Date of sale

- Product

  The data elements in the Product dimensional object are:

    ° SKU

    ° Name

    ° List price

    ° Department

    ° Category

    ° Brand

- Store

  The data elements in the Store dimensional object are:

    ° Name

    ° Number

    ° Address1

    ° Address2

    ° City

    ° State

    ° Zip postal code

    ° Country

    ° Region

We know the data elements we're going to need. Now let's put together a structure in our database that we'll use to stage the data prior to actually loading it into the target. Staging areas can be in the same database as the target, or in a different database, depending on various factors such as size and space issues, and availability of databases. For our purposes, we'll create a staging area as a single table in our target database schema for simplicity and will use the Warehouse Builder's **Table Editor** to manually create the table.

> This is the same technique we used to create metadata for the source structures in the ACME_POS SQL Server database back in Chapter 2. We'll get to use it again as we build our staging table.

Building the staging area table with the Table Editor

To get started with building our staging area table, let's launch the OWB **Design Center** if it's not already running. Expand the ACME_DW_PROJECT node and let's take a look at where we're going to create this new table. We've stated previously that all the objects we design are created under modules in the Warehouse Builder so we need to pick a module to contain the new staging table. As we've decided to create it in the same database as our target structure, we already have a module created for this purpose. We created this module back in Chapter 3 when we created our target user, ACME_DWH, with a target module of the same name.

The steps to create the staging area table in our target database are:

1. Navigate to the **Databases | Oracle | ACME_DWH** module. We will create our staging table under the **Tables** node, so let's right-click on that node and select **New Table** from the pop-up menu. Notice that there is no wizard available here for creating a table and so we are using the **Table Editor** to do it.

2. Upon selecting **New Table**, we are presented with a popup asking us for the name of the new table and an optional description. Let's call it **POS_TRANS_STAGE** for Point-of-Sale transaction staging table. We'll just enter the name into the **Name** field, replacing the default **TABLE_1** that it suggested for us. We'll click the **OK** button and the **Table Editor** screen will appear in our **Design Center** looking similar to the following:

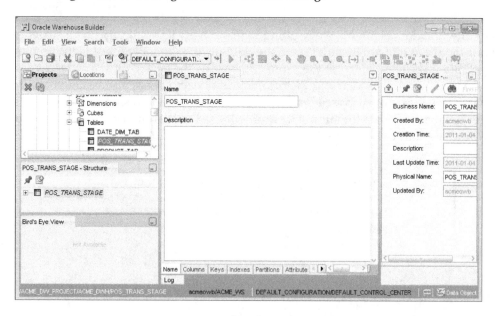

This will look different depending on what windows are open. For example, the Bird's Eye View is visible, since the Mapping Editor was the last editor we were using and the Design Center will load windows from the last time it ran. We can just close any windows we don't need and resize any that we do.

3. The first tab is the **Name** tab where it displays the name we just gave it in the opening popup.

4. Let's click on the **Columns** tab next and enter the information that describes the columns of our new table. Earlier in this chapter, we listed the key data elements that we will need for creating the columns. We didn't specify any properties of those data elements other than the name, so we'll need to figure that out.

One key point to keep in mind here is that we want to make sure the sizes and types of the fields will match the fields we want to pull the data from. If this is taken care of, we won't end up with any possible overflow errors generated by the database which could be caused by two character fields with different lengths for example.

Eventually, we know that we're going to have to use this new table that we're building as a source when we load our final target structure. This means we'll have to make sure our data sizes and types are compatible with our final structure also, and not just our sources. When we designed our target dimensions and cube, we made sure to specify correct sizes and types and so we shouldn't face any problem here. We can't change the source columns as they are fixed, which is another important consideration. The targets right now are only defined in metadata in the Warehouse Builder, so we can easily update them if needed.

 The Warehouse Builder will actually tell us if we have a problem with the data types and field lengths when we use this table in a mapping either as a source or target table. It knows the size and type of the fields in the sources and targets because we imported or created tables to represent the sources, and it does a comparison internally. It will tell us if we're trying to map something too big for a field, or to a field of an incompatible data type. We don't want to have to wait until then to specify the correct size and type, so we'll create them accordingly now.

The following will then be the column names, types, and sizes we'll use for our staging table based on what we found in the source tables in the POS transaction database:

```
SALE_QUANTITY NUMBER(0,0)
SALE_DOLLAR_AMOUNT NUMBER(10,2)
```

```
SALE_DATE DATE
PRODUCT_NAME VARCHAR2(50)
PRODUCT_SKU VARCHAR2(50)
PRODUCT_CATEGORY VARCHAR2(50)
PRODUCT_BRAND VARCHAR2(50)
PRODUCT_PRICE NUMBER(6,2)
PRODUCT_DEPARTMENT VARCHAR2(50)
STORE_NAME VARCHAR2(50)
STORE_NUMBER VARCHAR2(10)
STORE_ADDRESS1 VARCHAR2(60)
STORE_ADDRESS2 VARCHAR2(60)
STORE_CITY VARCHAR2(50)
STORE_STATE VARCHAR2(50)
STORE_ZIPPOSTALCODE VARCHAR2(50)
STORE_REGION VARCHAR2(50)
STORE_COUNTRY VARCHAR2(50)
```

There are a couple of things to note about these data elements. There are three groupings of data elements, which correspond to the three dimensional objects we created — our Sales cube and two dimensions, Product and Store.

We don't have to include the dimensional object names in the data element names, but it helps to organize the data elements for eventual load into the target objects. This way, we can readily see which elements go where when the time comes to map them into the target.

The second thing to note is that these data elements aren't all going to come from a single table in the source. For instance, the Store dimension has a STORE_REGION and STORE_COUNTRY column, but this information is found in the REGIONS table in the ACME_POS source database. This means we are going to have to join this table with the STORES table if we want to be able to extract these two columns.

We now have the information we need to populate the **Columns** tab in the **Data Object Editor** window for our staging table. We'll enter the above column names and types into the list of columns to complete the definition of our staging table.

Just as we saw back in Chapter 4 when entering column information for the product dimension, the Warehouse Builder attempts to make intelligent guesses of data types based on the name. That is actually controlled by a file containing regular expressions for various naming options and the data types, sizes and precisions to use. We can view that file to see what assumptions it is making and could even add our own entries or edit existing ones if we wanted. The file is in the `owb\bin\admin` folder under our Oracle home folder and is named `Oracle_ItemDefaults.properties`. Here is an example from the file for matching any column name that has the word NAME in it:

```
# Name Pattern
NameMatch = .*NAME.*
datatype = VARCHAR2
length = 30
```

When completed, our column list should look like the following screenshot:

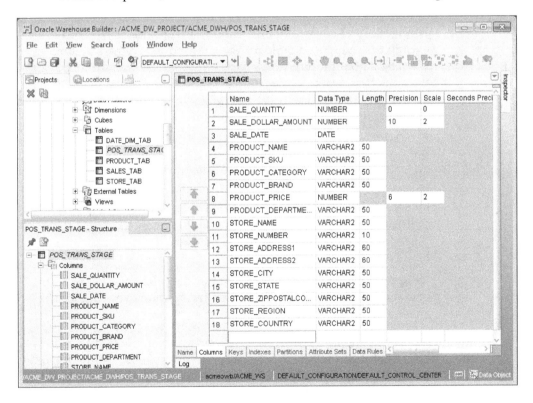

The **Property Inspector** has been minimized and the **Bird's Eye View** window closed to make more room for the main editor window in the above image. Feel free to position windows in any manner that is most useful to you.

6. We'll save our work using the *Ctrl+S* keys, or from the **File | Save All** main menu entry in the **Design Center** before continuing through the rest of the tabs. We didn't get to do this back in Chapter 2 when we first used the **Table Editor**.

The other tabs in **Table Editor** are:

- **Keys**

  The next tab after **Columns** is **Keys** where we can enter any one of the four different types of **constraints** on our new table. A constraint is a property that we set to tell the database to enforce some kind of rule on the table that limits (or constrains) the values that can be stored in it. There are four types of constraints:

  ○ **Check constraint**: A constraint on a particular column that indicates the acceptable values that can be stored in the column.

  ○ **Foreign key**: A constraint on a column that indicates a record must exist in the referenced table for the value stored in this column. We talked about foreign keys back in *Chapter 2* when we discussed the ACME_POS transactional source database. A foreign key is also considered a constraint because it limits the values that can be stored in the column that is designated as a foreign key column.

  ○ **Primary key**: A constraint that indicates the column(s) that make up the unique information that identifies one and only one record in the table. It is similar to a unique key constraint in which values must be unique. The primary key differs from the unique key as other tables' foreign key columns use the primary key value (or values) to reference this table. The value stored in the foreign key of a table is the value of the primary key of the referenced table for the record being referenced.

  ○ **Unique key**: A constraint that specifies the column(s) value combination(s) cannot be duplicated by any other row in the table.

  Now that we've discussed each of these constraints, we're not going to use any for our staging table. In general, we want maximum flexibility in storage of all types of data that we pull from the source system. Setting too many constraints on the staging table can prevent data from being stored in the table if data violates a particular constraint.

In this case, our staging table is a standalone table, so we don't have to worry about whether the data relates to any other tables via a foreign key. We want all the data available to our mapping, which will handle any transformations needed to make the data fit into the target system. So, no constraints are needed on this source staging table. In the next chapter, we'll have an opportunity to revisit this topic and create a primary key on a table.

- **Indexes**

    The next tab provided in the **Table Editor** is the **Indexes** tab. We were introduced to indexes at the end of Chapter 4 when we discussed the details displayed for a cube in the **Cube Editor** on the **Storage** tab. An index can greatly facilitate rapid access to a particular record. It is generally useful for permanent tables that will be repeatedly accessed in a random manner by certain known columns of data in the table. It is not desirable to go through the effort of creating an index on a staging table, which will only be accessed for a short amount of time during a data load. Also, it is not really useful to create an index on a staging table that will be accessed sequentially to pull all the data rows at one time. An index is best used in situations where data is pulled randomly from large tables, but doesn't provide any benefit in speed if you have to pull every record of the table.

Indexes are automatically created for us by the database in certain situations to support constraints. A primary key will have an index backing it up, consisting of the primary key column(s). A unique key is implemented with a unique index on the columns specified for the key. So if we were looking at creating indexes on a regular table, we would already have some if we'd specified these constraints. This is just something to keep in mind when deciding what to index in a table.

- **Partitions**

    So now that we have nixed the idea of creating indexes on our staging table, let's move on to the next tab in the **Table Editor** for our table, **Partitions**. **Partition** is an advanced topic that we won't be covering here but for any real-world data warehouse, we should definitely consider implementing partitions. A partition is a way of breaking down the data stored in a table into subsets that are stored separately. This can greatly speed up data access for retrieving random records, as the database will know the partition that contains the record being searched for based on the partitioning scheme used. It can directly home in on a particular partition to fetch the record by completely ignoring all the other partitions that it knows won't contain the record.

There are various methods the Oracle Database offers us for partitioning the data and they are covered in depth in the Oracle documentation. Oracle has published a document devoted just to **Very Large Databases (VLDB)** and partitioning, which can be found at `http://download.oracle.com/docs/cd/E11882_01/server.112/e16541/toc.htm`.

Not surprisingly, we're not going to partition our staging table for the same reasons we didn't index it. So let's move on with our discussion of the **Editor** tabs for a table.

- **Attribute Sets**

  The next tab is the **Attribute Sets** tab. An **Attribute Set** is a way to group attributes of an object in an order that we can specify when we create an attribute set. It is useful for grouping subsets of an object's attributes (or columns) for a later use. For instance, with data profiling (analyzing data quality for possible correction), we can specify attribute sets as candidate lists of attributes to use for profiling. This is a more advanced feature and as we won't need it for our implementation, we will not create any attribute sets.

- **Data Rules**

  The next tab is **Data Rules**. A **data rule** can be specified in the Warehouse Builder to enforce rules for data values or relationships between tables. It is used for ensuring that only high-quality data is loaded into the warehouse. There is a separate node — **Data Rules** — under our project in the **Design Center** that is strictly for specifying data rules. A data rule is created and stored under this node. This is a more advanced feature. We won't have time to cover it in this introductory book, so we will not have any data rules to specify here.

This completes our tour through the tabs in the **Table Editor** for our table. These are the tabs that will be available when creating, viewing, or editing any table object. At this point, we've gone through all the tabs and specified any characteristics or attributes of our table that we needed to specify. This table object is now ready to use for mapping. Our staging area is now complete so we can proceed to creating a mapping to load it. We can now close the **Table Editor** window before proceeding by selecting **File | Close** from the **Design Center** main menu or by clicking on the **X** in the window title tab.

Now that we have our staging table defined, we are now ready to actually begin designing our mapping. We'll cover creating a mapping, adding/editing operators, and connecting operators together, but first lets do a quick review of the Mapping Editor.

Review of the Mapping Editor

We were introduced to the **Mapping Editor** in the last chapter and discussed its features, so we'll just briefly review it here before using it to create a mapping. We will create mappings that are in the **Design Center** under an Oracle Database module. In our case, we have created an Oracle Database module called ACME_DWH for our target database. So this is where we will create our mappings. In **Design Center**, navigate to the **ACME_DW_PROJECT | Databases | Oracle | ACME_DWH | Mappings** node if it is not already showing. Right-click on it and select **New Mapping** from the resulting pop-up. We will be presented with a dialog box to specify a name and, optionally, a description of our mapping. We'll name this mapping **STAGE_MAP** to reflect what it is being used for, and click on the **OK** button.

This will open the **Mapping Editor** window for us to begin designing our mapping. An example of what we will see next is presented here:

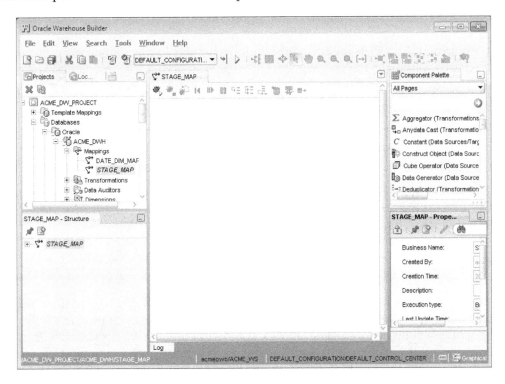

Unlike our first look at the **Mapping Editor** in the last chapter where we looked at the existing **DATE_DIM_MAP**, all new mappings start out with a blank slate upon which we can begin to design our mapping.

By way of comparison with the **data object editors**, the **Mapping Editor** has a blank area named **Mapping** which is the canvas. The **Table Editor** did not have a graphical canvas and the cube and dimension editors have a graphical depiction only on the Physical Bindings tab but were otherwise primarily text based. The mapping canvas performs the function of viewing and laying out objects. The other windows we can see above are the same ones we saw when using data object editors in the last chapter but now pertain to the Mapping Editor.

Although the data object editors are not graphical, there is a graphical way to view the objects provided by what is called the **Graphical Navigator** which can be opened from the **View** main menu. It provides a blank canvas onto which we can drag and drop any data object to get a graphical depiction of the object and any objects related to it. Dropping a cube for instance, will display the cube with any dimensions that it references. This is the functionality that was in the Data Object Editor in the previous release of the Warehouse Builder on the dimensional and relational tabs that used to be in the editor.

The **Mapping Editor** uses the **Structure** window similar to the **data object editors**. This window performs the same function for viewing operators/objects that we've already defined in our mapping. In the previous release this information was in the old Explorer window on the Selected Objects tab.

The **Properties Inspector** window is for viewing and/or editing properties of the selected element in the **Mapping** window. Right now we haven't yet defined anything in our mapping, so it's displaying our overall mapping properties.

The **Component Palette** displays all the operators that can be dragged and dropped onto the **Mapping** window to design our mapping. The objects in this case are specific to mappings, so we'll see all the operators that are available to us.

Creating a mapping

What we just saw was a brief review of the Mapping Editor. Now let's begin to use it to design our mapping of the staging table. In designing any mapping in OWB, there will be a source(s) that we pull from, a target(s) that we will load data into, and several operators in between depending on how much manipulation of data we need to do between source and target. The layout will begin with sources on the left and proceed to the final targets on the right of the canvas as we design it. Right now we know that we have to pull data from the ACME_POS transactional database in SQL Server as our source and load it into the POS_TRANS_STAGE table that we just defined as our target. So let's begin by including these objects into our mapping.

We need to look at the source data and determine what tables we will need to pull the data from so that we know which of the objects to include in our mapping. We first looked at the source data for the POS transactional database back in Chapter 2. So if you need to refresh your memory about what that looked like, now would be a good time to go back and review that quickly before moving on. In the next section, we'll start by adding a source table.

Adding source tables

We know that the first piece of information we need for loading into our staging table is the sales data—the quantity and dollar amount of each sale, and the date of the sale. Looking at our ACME_POS source database, we know that data is stored in the POS_Transactions table. Therefore, we'll start our mapping by including this table.

There are a couple of ways we can add a table to our mapping. One way is to use the **Projects Navigator** window and the other way is to use the **Palette** window. Which one we choose is really just a matter of preference.

We'll use the **Projects Navigator** window to find the table that we want to include in our mapping. To find an object in the **Projects Navigator**, we have to know what module it is located under.

Collections

Our project is not that big so it's easy to find objects but it's easy for projects to become very large. One feature we're not covering in this introductory book that can assist with that is Collections. That feature allows you to group objects from your project into arbitrary folders for ease in accessing them and for organizing them. For more information, consult the Oracle Warehouse Builder Concepts Guide, Chapter 3, at the following URL:

http://download.oracle.com/docs/cd/E11882_01/owb.112/e10581/uitour.htm#BABDCHCJ

In our case, we know the **POS_TRANSACTIONS** table is defined under the **ACME_POS** module. So let's navigate to the **Databases | Non-Oracle | ODBC | ACME_POS** node in the **Projects Navigator** tab to find the **POS_TRANSACTIONS** table entry.

We can also find things very quickly with the **Design Center** search function by clicking on the **Search** main menu entry and selecting **Find...** or by selecting *Ctrl-F* from the keyboard. Just enter the name of the object we're searching for and click the **Find** button and it will take us right to it. That's very helpful if we can't remember which module we created the object under.

Click and hold the left mouse button on **POS_TRANSACTIONS**, drag it over to the **Mapping** window, and release the left mouse button to drop the table into our mapping. Our **Mapping Editor** window should now look similar to the following:

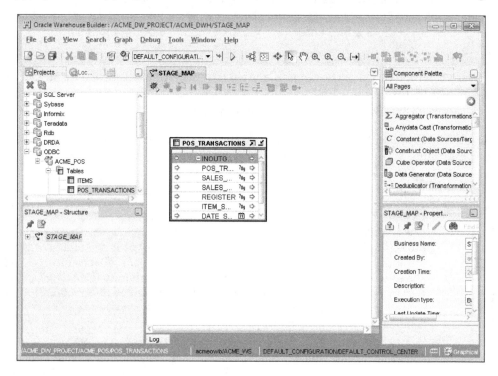

There are a couple of items to note about how the **Mapping Editor** window looks. The **Properties Inspector** window no longer shows the mapping information. It has changed to show the properties of the **POS_TRANSACTION** table as it is now highlighted in the **Mapping** canvas window.

If your **Properties** window does not show the **POS_TRANSACTIONS** properties, simply click on the **POS_TRANSACTIONS** operator in the **Mapping** window. Make sure you click on the title bar of the operator window because if you click inside the window, it will select one of the attributes or groups and display the properties for that instead of displaying the properties for the operator as a whole.

Another item to note is that now we have an object in our **Mapping** window instead of a blank canvas. These objects that make up a mapping are called **operators**. In this particular case, it is a Table operator that we have placed into the mapping to represent the POS_Transactions table.

Having just one operator in our mapping is not enough, so let's try including the remainder of the tables we'll need from our source database. We clearly need some product information to fill in. From our analysis in Chapter 2 of the ACME_POS source database structures, we know that product information comes from the Items table. We'll include that table in our mapping now, but instead of using the **Projects Navigator** window as we did for the **POS_TRANSACTIONS** table, let's see how the **Component Palette** window works for including objects into our mapping.

The operators in the **Component Palette** are sorted alphabetically, so we'll scroll the window until we see the **Table Operator**. Click and drag the **Table Operator** from the **Component Palette** window onto the **Mapping** window. As soon as we drag it onto the **Mapping** window, we are presented with a pop up like the following screenshot:

This pop up asks us which table we want to include as this table operator. We have a couple of options offered to us. We can create an unbound operator, which has no attributes; in other words, it is a blank table that we can define as we like, or we can specify an existing table from our project. An unbound operator is one which is not associated with (that is, bound to) an existing database object. The act of binding in OWB associates a generic operator with an actual defined object in the project. When we dragged our POS_TRANSACTIONS table from the Projects window, it did not ask us about this because we started with a specific named table. The operators in the **Component Palette** window are all generic and are not associated with any specific object of that type. With unbound operators, you can actually use the **Mapping Editor** to create a data object. We'll actually get to do this in the next chapter when we have to create a lookup table.

We're going to stick to the objects already defined for our operators. So we're going to select the **ITEMS** table under the **ACME_POS** entry in the list of table names that the pop-up window presents to us. We will click on the **OK** button to include the **ITEMS** table operator in our mapping. Notice how the **Add Table Operator** dialog box presents the information to us. It lists every possible table in our project and organizes them by module. ACME_DWH is our main data warehouse module that we created for our target in order to build our data warehouse. We can see the tables that were created for our cube and dimensions along with the staging table we created. ACME_WS_ORDERS is the web site order's database that we imported for source data from the web site, and ACME_POS is what we're working with right now to build a staging area.

Let's talk about organizing our tables in the **Mapping** window before we go any further. In general, it's always a good idea to place source operators on the left and the target operators on the right. So let's just make sure we keep the tables we're dropping into our **Mapping** window towards the left side of the window, one above the other. Click and hold on the header of the operator to drag it around.

We've seen how to include a table operator in our mapping using either of the two methods. Using either one now, we'll include the remainder of the source tables that we're going to need into our mapping—the REGISTERS, STORES, and REGIONS tables. It should be clear why we need the STORES and the REGIONS tables. These tables contain information about each store that we'll need, including the address, region, and country. But why do we need the REGISTERS table? We're not going store any information about the register used. From our analysis back in Chapter 2, we saw that the register information pointed to the store where the register was located in and the main POS_TRANSACTIONS table only had a foreign key column for the register—not the store or region. This information was kept in separate tables with a foreign key to the store, which is stored in the REGISTERS table. So, if we hope to be able to retrieve the store and region information out of the source database, we're going to need the REGISTERS table to get there.

Now go ahead and include those three tables into the mapping using either of the two methods we just discussed. When that is completed, make sure the tables are organized vertically on the left side of the mapping window in the following order: the ITEMS operator on top, then POS_TRANSACTIONS, then the REGISTERS operator next, then the STORES operator, and then the REGIONS operator at the bottom. We'll see soon why we are paying attention to the order in which we display the operators in the **Mapping** canvas.

You'll notice that while dragging objects around the **Mapping** window, it will grow in size automatically to hold the objects we are placing there. So we needn't be too concerned if our source tables are not all the way over to the left. When we place our target table, we'll put it to the right-hand side of the sources. Just make sure that the source tables are all together.

Your **Mapping Editor** window should now look similar to the following:

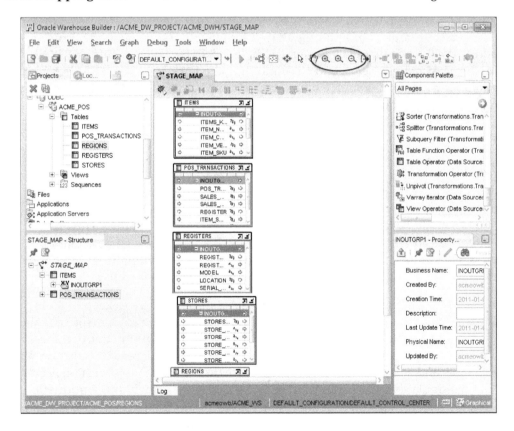

The five source tables may not all be visible at once as we saw in the previous screenshot. The **Mapping** view has been zoomed out, so mostly all are visible here. However, there is a trade-off in readability the more we zoom out. You can manipulate the zoom yourself to find a size that's comfortable for your viewing. The zoom buttons in the toolbar have been circled in the screenshot we just saw. Click on the magnifying glass with the plus sign to zoom in and the minus sign to zoom out. There are two magnifying glasses with a plus sign. The one on the left is an interactive zoom and the one on the right is the regular zoom in button.

Now that we have our source table all included and laid out in the **Mapping** window, we'll move on to discuss getting our target included in the mapping.

Adding a target table

Let's now turn our attention to the target for this particular mapping. As this is a staging-related mapping, we're going to be loading our staging table and so that will become our target. Let's find the **POS_TRANS_STAGE** table in the **Projects** window. We'll navigate to **Databases | Oracle | ACME_DWH | Tables | POS_TRANS_STAGE** in **Projects**, and click and drag the **POS_TRANS_STAGE** table to the righthand side of our source tables in the **Mapping** window. Let's leave some space between the source table and the target tables. We'll shortly see the reason behind this when we start connecting our source to the target.

Connecting source to target

The process of connecting the source to the target is the means of telling the Warehouse Builder which data fields from the source go in which data fields in the target. We might be tempted to just connect the data fields from the source tables directly to the corresponding fields in the target. For instance, we know that the ITEMS table has the ITEM_NAME field, which needs to be stored in the target in the PRODUCT_NAME column; so why can't we just connect the two directly?

The reason we can't connect the two directly is because we have to keep in mind what that means in terms of mapping. If we just connect a line from a source table attribute to a target table attribute, we're telling the Warehouse Builder that there is a one-to-one mapping from source to target. This means we can read a record from the source table and store the column values directly in the target table with no need of further manipulation. The problem in our case is that we're including information in our target table from multiple source tables, and the Warehouse Builder is not going to let us connect multiple source tables to a single target table directly as it won't know how to combine the data.

In addition to the joining of the tables, connecting directly from source to target would also imply that the data was at the granularity we need. We discussed granularity (or the level at which the data is stored) in Chapter 3 and decided that our warehouse would store the data by product, store, and date. However, looking at our source data, we can see that the data is actually stored by register. This is actually a lower level of detail than we need, so we'll need to sum up the data for each register in a store to get the total for the store.

This means we will have to provide some kind of intervening operators to get the data combined from the five source tables into the one target table, summed by product, store, and date. But what operators are we going to use? Remember our discussion in Chapter 5 that introduced us to the various operators available in the Warehouse Builder. We particularly mentioned in the *Transformations* section that directly connecting source to target would only work for a one-to-one mapping between a source table and a target table. Then went on to discuss some of the operators that can be used for data flows, and one of them was a **Joiner** operator. If you re-read the explanation, you'll see that a joiner is exactly what we need in this case because we have to take multiple source tables and combine (or join) them into one record in the target. We also discussed an **Aggregator** operator that can be used to aggregate data. In this case, we need to sum data at a higher level before storing it. So this should be exactly the operator we need for that purpose.

Now that we've settled on the two data flow operators we need, let's place them into our mapping between the sources and the target. Now you can see why we left some space between the sources and the target. Scroll down through the **Component Palette** window until the **Joiner** operator is visible, drag this operator into the **Mapping** window, and drop it between the sources and target.

Joiner operator attribute groups

We were introduced to the concept of attribute groups in the last chapter when we were looking at DATE_DIM_MAP in the **Mapping Editor**. It's time to talk about attribute groups again, because we can see that the **Joiner** operator has three groups defined, but the attributes in our table operators are all in one group. The groups in operators we saw are generally input groups, output groups, or both.

In our table operators we can see that there is only one group as we mentioned, called **INOUTGRP1**. The following screenshot is an example of that using the **POS_ TRANSACTIONS** table operator:

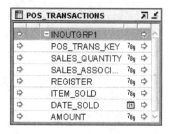

 There are actually two clues to identify the attributes that can be used for both input and output: one is the name of the group, which has both IN and OUT in it if the default names have not been changed, and the second is the little arrows that appear on each attribute line—one arrow on the left pointing in for input and one on the right pointing out for output.

If an attribute is in an input group, then we can connect an attribute from another operator on the left to let the data flow from that attribute to this one. These connections always enter an operator from the left. Now we can see why it's a good idea to put our sources on the left and targets on the right. This is the direction the data flows through the operators.

If the attribute can be used for output in either an output group or an in/out group, then it means the data from the attribute can be used as input into another operator. Output from an operator always flows out from the right side of the operator.

If we look at the **Joiner** operator we just dropped into our mapping, we can see that there are no attributes defined in any of the three groups. Before we add attributes, let's talk briefly about the groups in a **Joiner** operator. By default, the operator is created with two input groups and one output group. Each input group corresponds to a separate table or other data operator, and the output group represents the combined (joined) output from the input tables.

We have five source tables to join together, but this Joiner operator has only two input groups. Have no fear; a Joiner can have more than two input groups. We have to edit this Joiner to add three more input groups. To edit it, right-click on the header of the box and select **Open Details...** to open the **Joiner Editor** or just double click on the header . This dialog box will allow us to edit the number of groups as well as change the group names if we want something different from **INGRP1** and **INGRP2**.

The **Joiner Editor** can be used to edit not only the groups, but also the attributes that compose each group. So if we right-click inside the **Joiner** box on a group and select **Open Details...**, we will get the same dialog box with just the individual tab selected that corresponds to the group we clicked on.

With the **Joiner Editor** open, let's click on the **Groups** entry on the left. We'll add three new groups by typing their names in the empty box at the bottom of the Group column on the right. We could use INGRP3, INGRP4, and INGRP5 as the group names for our new groups but lets go ahead and use the actual table names. Enter registers then stores and then regions and hit the enter key after each. Notice how it automatically populated the group type as INPUT and doesn't allow us to change it. This means it knew we wanted input groups and not output groups. Did it read our minds? Well, not exactly. As it turns out, Joiners can have only one output group and no combined input/output groups. So the only kind of group left to add when we enter a group name is an input group.

While we're on the **Groups** tab, let's modify the names of our two default input groups to the other two table names. By just clicking on the name of the input group, we can type in a new name. So, let's rename each of those default input groups as follows:

- INGRP1 to ITEMS
- INGRP2 to POS_TRANSACTIONS

After entering three new names and renaming the two default names this is how it will look:

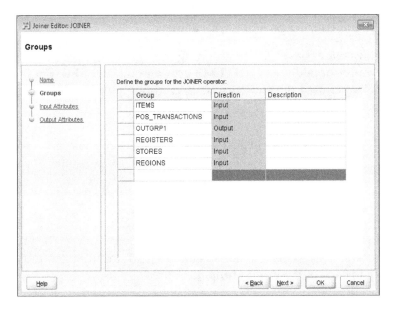

Now we'll click on the **OK** button to close out the **Joiner Editor** dialog box.

You may be wondering if there is a reason why we picked a particular sequence of input tables and paid attention to the order in which we displayed the table operators on the canvas. It's to match the sequence of tables that we set up in the **Mapping** window from top to bottom as displayed in the previous image. However, this is not a hard and fast requirement; they could be in any order. To ensure a good appearance, that is, keep lines from crisscrossing all over the mapping when we're done with it, it's a good idea to plan ahead and use the same order. We'll see this later.

Also, we don't have to worry about capitalization as the editor will automatically put everything we type into uppercase.

Connecting operators to the Joiner

Now that we have our Joiner groups defined, it's time to start making some connections between operators. The act of connecting operators is a matter of clicking and dragging a line from an output attribute of one operator to an input attribute of another operator, or from one output group in one operator to an input group in another operator. If we connect two attribute groups together, we're telling the **Mapping Editor** to go ahead and connect every attribute in the group. If we have several attributes, this is a convenient way to connect them. So, click and drag **INOUTGRP1** of the **ITEMS** table operator onto the **ITEMS** group of the **JOINER**. Immediately, it will add all the attributes from the **ITEMS** table to the **ITEMS** group in the **JOINER** and connect each one with a line.

Alternatively, we could have clicked and dragged a line from each attribute in the **ITEMS** table and dropped it on the **ITEMS** group in the **JOINER**. But it was quicker and more efficient to drag the entire group even though we won't be using every attribute.

Leaving attributes in the **JOINER** that we're not going to use will not affect the final result of our mapping. We're just going to drag the attributes we're going to need over to the target table in a moment. OWB will ignore the attributes we don't use when it builds its underlying code.

Notice that if we now scroll down our **JOINER** operator to where the **OUTGRP1** is visible, we can see that it automatically added attributes to the output group corresponding to each of the input group attributes.

To better view the attributes in the **JOINER** operator, we can make the box bigger by clicking and dragging the border of the box to a bigger size, either vertically or horizontally. Also, if we don't want to see all the attributes, we can click on the minus sign on a group to collapse it so that the attributes are not visible. Clicking on the plus sign then restores the attributes.

Now let's repeat the same procedure with the **POS_TRANSACTIONS**, **REGISTERS**, **STORES**, and **REGIONS** tables. That is, let's drag the **INOUTGRP1** group to the corresponding group in the **JOINER** for each table to connect them. Feel free to click on the minus sign on each group to collapse it to get a better view of the next group. If the ordering of the tables has been maintained between the **JOINER** groups and the table operators, and all the input groups of the **JOINER** have been collapsed (which is why the attributes are not visible), the mapping should look similar to the following screenshot:

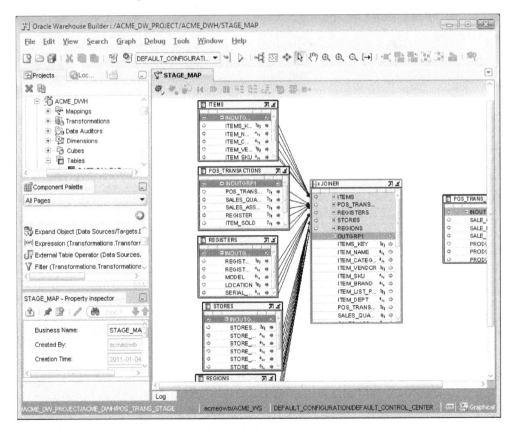

The **Component Palette** and **Property Inspector** windows have been moved over to the left side and the **Structure** window closed to make more room for the main canvas area of the Mapping Editor. Your overall window will probably look different but the important part is that your main canvas should look similar to how the objects are laid out above.

Defining operator properties for the JOINER

The next step in the process is to specify how we want the tables joined. We need to identify the attributes to use in the join condition. We will do that by modifying a property of the **JOINER**. This will be our first experience of working with the **Properties Inspector** window in the **Mapping Editor**. If the **JOINER** operator is not already selected, click once on the header of the box to select it and the **Properties** window will immediately change to display the properties of the selected object; in this case it's **JOINER**. We can see a property mentioned there, **Join Condition**. If it is not immediately visible, the properties can be scrolled down until it is.

If you click inside the **JOINER** operator on a group or attribute, the **Properties** window will display the properties for that group or attribute and not the **JOINER** operator as a whole. We want the **JOINER** properties, so make sure the **JOINER** itself is highlighted by clicking on the header of the **JOINER** window.

Click on the blank box to the right of the **Join Condition** label. The **Properties** window will now look like the following screenshot, which is ready for our input of the join condition:

Now we can type the join condition directly in the white box. This can get a bit tedious, especially as we'd need to know the correct syntax for specifying attributes. The Warehouse Builder refers to attributes by group as well as attribute name. So, to help us out with this, OWB provides the **Expression Builder**. This is a dialog box we can invoke to interactively build our Joiner condition.

We can invoke **Expression Builder** by clicking on the button with the three dots (**...**) to the right of the blank white box. It looks like the following screenshot before anything is filled in:

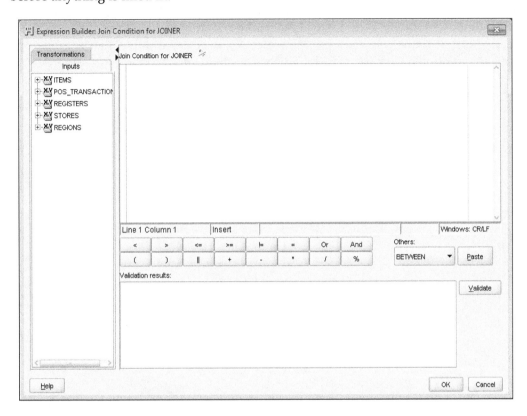

Notice on the left the list of input groups in the **JOINER**. From this list we're going to select the attributes we need and will include them in our expression in the correct format. We just need to make sure we specify the correct attributes and the correct join relation, which will be the equal to (=) symbol in our case.

We do need to know a little about SQL join syntax at this point. The **Expression Builder** provides us with the list of attributes and the relational operator buttons, which will insert the indicated relations. However, we need to insert them in the right order. Fortunately, the syntax is not very complicated. We just need to specify which column from one table equals which column from the table being joined to. Then include an equality for each table with each of the equalities separated by AND.

We've seen the ITEMS table from our analysis in *Chapter 2* of the source data structures in the ACME_POS database. So we know that the POS_TRANSACTIONS table contains a foreign key field pointing to the record in the ITEMS table for the particular item for that transaction. This gives us clues about which columns will be needed in the first join equality – the ITEM_SOLD attribute from POS_TRANSACTIONS and the ITEMS_KEY attribute from the ITEMS operator. So, we'll expand the **ITEMS** group on the left and double-click the **ITEMS_KEY** attribute to add it to the expression. As we want every record included where the **ITEM_SOLD** equals the **ITEMS_KEY**, we will include an equal sign next by clicking on the button with the = sign on it. We'll finish this first relation by expanding the **POS_TRANSACTIONS** group and double-clicking on the **ITEM_SOLD** attribute to include it. Our expression now looks like the following with the steps highlighted with callouts:

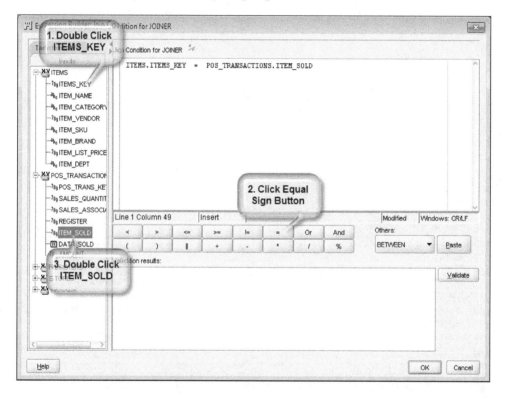

The attributes include the group name first. This is the syntax it uses to identify the specific attribute. It's common for the same attribute name to appear in more than one group, and this syntax will make it explicit which attribute is being referred to.

We're not done yet, because so far we've only accounted for two of the four tables in our join condition. We also need to include REGISTERS, STORES, and REGIONS tables. The REGISTER attribute of the POS_TRANSACTIONS group contains the foreign key to the REGISTERS_KEY attribute of the REGISTERS table, so let's add that one. But before we add it, we need an AND. So let's click on the **And** button (which is near the button labeled with an equal to sign) to enter it into our mapping, and then press the *Enter* key to advance to the next line. We move to a new line to prevent our expression from extending past the viewable window. The expression could extend past it and still work. But for ease of viewing, we'll enter it vertically instead of horizontally so that we don't have to scroll.

Now we'll enter the following:

- The **REGISTER** attribute by double-clicking on it in the **POS_TRANSACTIONS** group
- The equal to sign by clicking on the corresponding button
- The **REGISTERS_KEY** attribute by double-clicking on it under the **REGISTERS** group
- This expression is followed by another AND by clicking on the **And** button
- Press the *Enter* key

 The equal to sign and the And can be typed in manually if you prefer, rather than having to click on the buttons each time. Some people find that quicker to enter, and will just double-click the attributes needed and manually type the other operators that are needed.

Continue in the like manner with the LOCATION in the REGISTERS group equal to STORES_KEY in the STORES group, and REGION_LOCATED_IN in the STORES group equal to the REGIONS_KEY in the REGIONS group. Do not include **And** after this last part of the expression as it is the end. When completed, the expression should look like the one in the following screenshot:

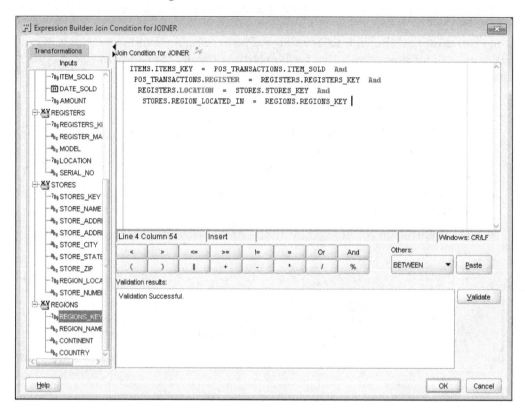

We can click on the **Validate** button now to make sure the expression we just entered is a valid expression, meaning that we used the correct SQL syntax. We should get the **Validation Successful** message.

Depending on what release number of the database you are running, you may get the following error message instead of the success message: **An error occured during expression validation. Bad expression return type**. This is a known bug, ID 7417869, which is reported to have occurred in Release 10.2.0.4 of the database and is fixed in 10.2.0.5. It also reports that the mapping will deploy and execute successfully even if this validation bug occurs. The bug report also says the error occurred in Release 11.1.0.7 of the database. However, it works in v11.2.0.1, which is the most recent publicly available version for download that we are using for this book. The screenshot we just saw was taken from 11.2.0.1 and we can see the **Validation Successful** message. So if you are using this version, you should not see the error.

Click on the **OK** button and we are done specifying the join condition for the **JOINER** operator. We can now see that it filled in the join condition text into the **Join Condition** entry in the **Properties** window. This completes the Joiner, but we still have to aggregate the data so that it's at the level we need for loading into the data warehouse. For aggregating data, we'll now include an **Aggregator** operator.

Adding an Aggregator operator

An Aggregator operator is used to apply an aggregate function to the data. Aggregation functions are documented in the *Oracle Database SQL Language Reference* at `http://download.oracle.com/docs/cd/E11882_01/server.112/ e17118/functions003.htm#i89203`. Chapter 5 of that online document has a section devoted to aggregate functions. In our case, we will need to add up the sales quantities and dollar amounts for every product, and the store and date combination to have data at the right level to load into the data warehouse. For this aggregation of data, we can use a `SUM()` function.

The **Aggregator** operator requires that we specify a few things for it to function correctly. As with any operator, there are attribute groups to set and an **Aggregator** operator has one input and one output group. For the input group, we will drag the output attributes of the Joiner operator. We have to specify a **group by clause** that the Aggregator operator is going to use to group the data, and it will create an output attribute for every attribute we use in the group by clause. We have to manually add output attributes for any of the values that are going to be summed up, and then specify the `SUM()` function to use for them.

We'll follow a similar process to add the Aggregator operator as we did for the Joiner; drag an **AGGREGATOR** operator onto the canvas to the right of the **JOINER** operator, connect output attributes from the **JOINER** operator to the input of the **AGGREGATOR** operator, define properties for the **AGGREGATOR** operator, and then connect the output of the **AGGREGATOR** operator to the **POS_TRANS_STAGE** table operator. Here we'll outline the steps to follow without going into as much detail as we did for the Joiner operator:

1. Drag an AGGREGATOR operator from the **Component Palette** window to the canvas and drop it to the right of the JOINER operator between that operator and the POS_TRANS_STAGE target operator. You may have to move the POS_TRANS_STAGE target operator further to the right to make enough room.

2. Connect the output attributes from the JOINER operator as input to the AGGREGATOR operator by dragging the OUTGRP1 output group and dropping it on the INGRP1 input group of the AGGREGATOR operator. This will map every output attribute at once, so we don't have to do each one individually.

> We have one issue we need to address with the input attributes for the Aggregator and that is related to the DATE_SOLD attribute from the Joiner operator. An attribute of the DATE type includes both date and time of day. We are going to sum up the data by date. But if we include the time of day, we'll get multiple dates occurring on the same day that are treated as distinct because the time is different. We want the sales for every product in a store for a single date to sum together regardless of the time of day the sale occurred. We need to strip out the time from the DATE_SOLD attribute, so we just have the date as input into the Aggregator operator. For that task, we need a Transformation Operator to apply the TRUNC() function to the value first. We'll discuss Transformation Operators in greater depth in the next chapter, but let's use one now to take care of the date.

3. We need to remove the line that got dragged to the input of the **Aggregator** operator for the DATE_SOLD attribute by clicking on the line and pressing the *Delete* key, or right-clicking and selecting **Delete** from the pop-up menu. Make sure the correct line is selected. Attribute groups can be expanded to spread the lines apart better so that it's easier to click.

4. Drag a **Transformation Operator** from the **Component Palette** window and drop it on the canvas between the **Joiner** operator and the **Aggregator** operator near the **DATE_SOLD** attribute. In the resulting pop up that appears, we'll scroll down the window until the Date() functions appear and then select the TRUNC() function. It will look like the following:

```
TRUNC(IN DATE, IN VARCHAR2) return DATE
```

Click on that line and then click on the **OK** button to select it. It will drop a **TRUNC** Transformation Operator on the canvas.

5. Connect the **DATE_SOLD** attribute in the **OUTGRP1** group of the **Joiner** to the **D** attribute of the **INGRP1** of the **TRUNC** transformation operator. Then connect the **VALUE** attribute of the **RETURN** output group of the **TRUNC** operator to the **DATE_SOLD** attribute of the **INGRP1** group of the **Aggregator** operator. We're not going to worry about mapping anything into the FMT input attribute. That is for the optional format parameter for the TRUNC() SQL function which if not provided defaults to truncate the date to the nearest day which is what we need. The above referenced *SQL Language Reference* explains all about that.

The canvas should now look similar to the following screenshot:

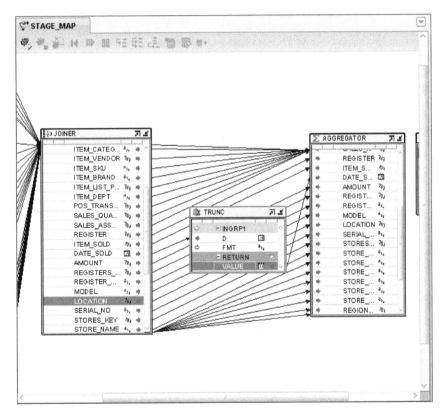

6. We have our input set for the Aggregator operator and now we need to address the output. Let's select the Aggregator operator by clicking on the title bar of the window where it says **AGGREGATOR**. The **Properties** window of the **Mapping Editor** will display the properties for the aggregator. If it doesn't, then make sure the title bar of the window was selected for the operator and not somewhere inside the operator.

7. The very first attribute listed is **Group By Clause**. We'll click on the ellipsis (...) on its right to open the **Expression Builder** for the **Group By Clause**. This is similar to how we launched it earlier to edit the join condition for the Joiner operator.

8. Enter the following attributes separated by commas by double-clicking each in the **INGRP1** entry in the left window:

   INGRP1.ITEM_NAME , INGRP1.ITEM_CATEGORY , INGRP1.ITEM_SKU , INGRP1.ITEM_BRAND , INGRP1.ITEM_LIST_PRICE , INGRP1.ITEM_DEPT , INGRP1.STORE_NAME , INGRP1.STORE_NUMBER , INGRP1.STORE_ADDRESS1 , INGRP1.STORE_ADDRESS2 , INGRP1.STORE_CITY , INGRP1.STORE_STATE , INGRP1.STORE_ZIP, INGRP1.REGION_NAME , INGRP1.COUNTRY , INGRP1.DATE_SOLD

   When completed, it should look similar to the following screenshot:

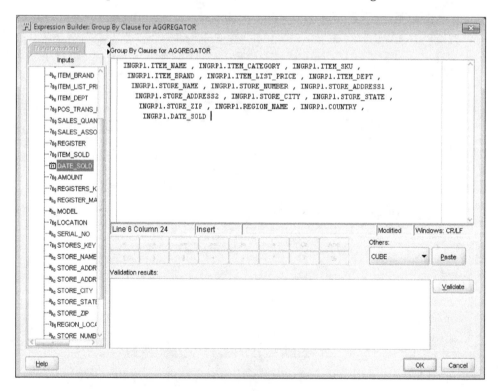

9. We'll click on the **OK** button to close the **Expression Builder** dialog box and looking at the **AGGREGATOR** now, we can see that it added an output attribute for each of these attributes in our group by clause. This list of attributes has every attribute needed for the **POS_TRANS_STAGE** operator except for the two number measures, SALE_QUANTITY and SALE_DOLLAR_ AMOUNT. So let's add them manually.

10. We'll right-click on the **OUTGRP1** attribute group of the **AGGREGATOR** operator and select **Open Details...** from the pop up. We used this editor earlier for the Joiner to edit the groups, and now we're going to use it for the Aggregator to edit the attributes in a group.

11. We'll click on the **Output Attributes** entry on the left, and then enter a new attribute in the blank line at the end called **SALES_QUANTITY** and leave the type **NUMERIC** with **0** for precision and scale. We'll enter **AMOUNT** next and make it type **NUMERIC** with precision **10** and scale **2**. Now we need to apply the **SUM()** function to these two new attributes. The Aggregator Editor has a column for the expression to be associated with each attribute and we can see that expressions have already been filled in for the other attributes we indicated as the "group by" attributes and now we need to provide the expressions to sum up the two new attributes we just entered. So we'll click on the expression for **SALES_QUANTITY** and then click on the ellipsis beside the **Expression** to launch the **Expression** editor for this attribute.

12. We'll immediately notice something different. The **Expression** editor for output attributes of an Aggregator is custom built to apply aggregation functions. We'll select **SUM** from the **Function** drop-down menu, **ALL** from the **ALL/DISTINCT** drop-down menu, and **SALES_QUANTITY** from the **Attribute** drop-down menu. We'll then click on the **Use Above Values** button and the expression will fill in showing the **SUM** function applied to the **SALES_QUANTITY** attribute. This is shown in the next screenshot of the **Expression** editor:

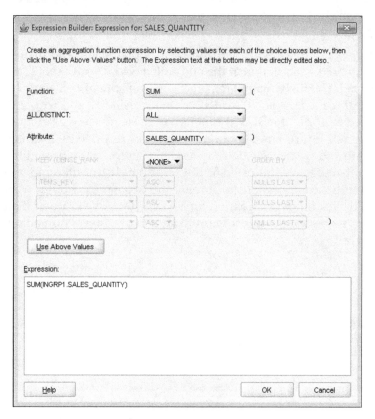

13. We'll click on the **OK** button to save the expression and close the dialog box. Then we'll do the same thing for the AMOUNT output attribute of the Aggregator, but will select **AMOUNT** for the **Attribute** drop-down menu. After making these changes, this is how the **Aggregator Editor** will look:

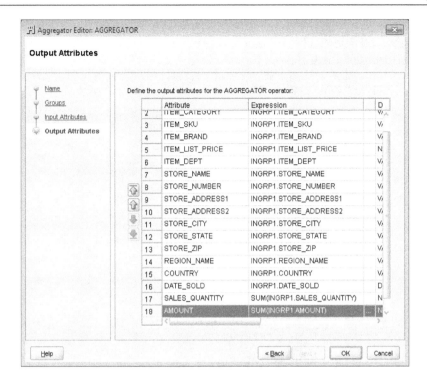

We'll click on the **OK** button to close the **AGGREGATOR Editor** dialog box.

We're almost done now. We've included the following:

- The source tables we need to pull the data from
- The target table we're going to store the data in
- A Joiner operator to join together the source tables
- An Aggregator to sum up the data

We have also connected the source tables as input to the Joiner operator and the Joiner as input to the Aggregator operator. The only thing left is to connect the output attributes of the Aggregator operator to the target input attributes. Before doing that, let's make the target table operator box big enough to display all its attributes at once without having to scroll. Just click and hold on the bottom edge of the **POS_TRANS_STAGE** window and drag the window down until all the attributes are visible. Do the same to the **Aggregator operator window**, but make sure only the output group is expanded. The input group should be collapsed because we're finished working with it for now.

Make the following attribute connections between the **Aggregator** and the **POS_TRANS_STAGE** table by clicking and dragging a line between attributes. We'll do individual attributes this time, not the whole group.

- SALES_QUANTITY to SALE_QUANTITY
- AMOUNT to SALE_DOLLAR_AMOUNT
- DATE_SOLD to SALE_DATE
- ITEM_NAME to PRODUCT_NAME
- ITEM_SKU to PRODUCT_SKU
- ITEM_CATEGORY to PRODUCT_CATEGORY
- ITEM_BRAND to PRODUCT_BRAND
- ITEM_LIST_PRICE to PRODUCT_PRICE
- ITEM_DEPT to PRODUCT_DEPARTMENT
- STORE_NAME to STORE_NAME
- STORE_NUMBER to STORE_NUMBER
- STORE_ADDRESS1 to STORE_ADDRESS1
- STORE_ADDRESS2 to STORE_ADDRESS2
- STORE_CITY to STORE_CITY
- STORE_STATE to STORE_STATE
- STORE_ZIP to STORE_ZIPPOSTALCODE
- REGION_NAME to STORE_REGION
- COUNTRY to STORE_COUNTRY

If we focus on just the **Aggregator** and the **POS_TRANS_STAGE** operators our mapping should now look like the following after making all those connections:

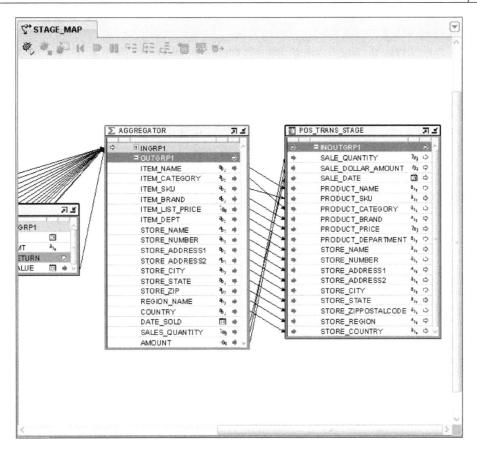

Notice that it's not always possible to avoid overlapping lines altogether, but we just want to avoid them as much as we can for readability. In this case, the overlapping lines are a result of different ordering of the attributes in the **AGGREGATOR** operator and the **POS_TRANS_STAGE** table. Changing this would involve recreating the table to reorder columns, and that is just not worth the effort. It will often be the case that sources and targets don't line up like that, but when we add intervening operators over which we have a more direct control, that is where we can focus our efforts on being neat and orderly. Also, your ordering of attributes in the **OUTGRP1** group of the **AGGREGATOR** operator may be different depending on the order in which you mapped the attributes from the Joiner. The order is not important as long as all the required attributes are present.

This completes the staging mapping. We've seen how to create a complete mapping in the Warehouse Builder. We'll make sure to save at this point so that we don't lose anything before we move on.

Summary

We saw how to create a mapping in the Warehouse Builder, including how to design a staging area table, build it with the **Table Editor**, design a mapping to populate it, and then create the mapping using source and target operators, and the intervening Joiner and Aggregator operators. We also got to use a Transformation Operator.

Now that we have completed our staging table mapping, we need to design mappings to get our dimensions and cube populated from the data in the staging table. We'll do that in the next chapter while taking a look at transformations, which are a key feature of the Warehouse Builder for loading and cleaning up data.

7
ETL: Transformations and Other Operators

Now we have completed our first mapping, but there is still more to do. The mapping we completed in the previous chapter was simple, as we just took data from our source database and loaded it into a staging table. We were not at all concerned about what format the data was in, and just wanted to get the data into our staging table in the target environment as quickly as possible. The only other operators we needed besides the source and target tables were a Joiner to pull together the source tables for storing in the staging table, an Aggregator to sum up the data, and a Transformation operator to truncate the date to remove the time portion. In the previous chapter, we made use of only a very small subset of the Warehouse Builder operators to load and transform data from source into target. We will continue building mappings in this chapter to make use of additional features.

We will be introduced to the concept of transformations and operators that are available in OWB, which can be used for transforming and manipulating data between source and target. We'll do this by building additional mappings for loading data into our STORE and PRODUCT dimensions, and loading of our SALES cube. Along the way, we'll get to build a quick mapping for creating and loading a table that will be used as a lookup table. As we build the mappings, we'll discuss in more detail some of the additional operators we'll need. Thus, we will begin to see the real power and flexibility the Warehouse Builder provides us for loading a data warehouse. When we complete the mappings in this chapter, we will have a complete collection of objects and mappings. We can deploy and run these to build and load our data warehouse.

The building of the mappings in this chapter will be very similar to those in the previous chapter, with the addition of a few more operators. The basic procedure is the same — start with adding a source and a target, and then include any operators in between needed for data flow and transformation. In the last chapter, we were introduced to a couple of data flow operators — the Joiner and the Aggregator. Let's start this chapter with the STORE dimension and we'll see some new operators that are involved in transformations. A complete list of the topics we'll cover this chapter is the following:

- STORE mapping
    - ° Adding source and target operators
    - ° Adding Transformation operators
    - ° Using a Lookup operator
        - ° Creating an external table
        - ° Creating and loading a lookup table
        - ° Retrieving the key to use for a Lookup operator
        - ° Adding a SUBSTR Transformation operator
        - ° Adding a Constant operator
        - ° Adding a TO_NUMBER transformation
        - ° Adding a Lookup operator
- PRODUCT mapping
- SALES cube mapping
    - ° Dimension attributes in the cube
    - ° Measures and other attributes in the cube
    - ° Mapping values to cube attributes
        - ° Mapping measures' values to the cube
        - ° Mapping PRODUCT and STORE dimension values to the cube
        - ° Mapping DATE_DIM values to the cube
        - ° Mapping an Expression operator
- Features and benefits of OWB

STORE mapping

Let's begin by creating a new mapping called STORE_MAP. We'll follow the procedure in the previous chapter to create a new mapping. In the **Design Center**, we will right-click on the **Mappings** node of the **ACME_DW_PROJECT | Databases | Oracle | ACME_DWH** database and select **New Mapping**. Enter **STORE_MAP** for the name of the mapping and we will be presented with a blank **Mapping Editor** window. In this window, we will begin designing our mapping to load data into the STORE dimension.

Adding source and target operators

In the last chapter, we loaded data into the POS_TRANS_STAGE staging table with the intent to use that data to load our dimensions and cube. We'll now use this POS_TRANS_STAGE table as our source table. Let's drag this table onto the mapping from the **Projects** window. Review the *Adding source tables* section of the previous chapter for a refresher if needed.

The target for this mapping is going to be the STORE dimension, so we'll drag this dimension from **Databases | Oracle | ACME_DWH | Dimensions** onto the mapping and drop it to the right of the POS_TRANS_STAGE table operator. Remember that we build our mappings from the left to the right, with source on the left and target on the right. We'll be sure to leave some space between the two because we'll be filling that in with some more operators as we proceed.

Now that we have our source and target included, let's take a moment to consider the data elements we're going to need for our target and where to get them from the source. Our target for this mapping, the STORE dimension, has the following attributes for the STORE level for which we'll need to have source data:

- NAME
- STORE_NUMBER
- ADDRESS1
- ADDRESS2
- CITY
- STATE
- ZIP_POSTALCODE
- COUNTY
- REGION_NAME

For the REGION level, we'll need data for the following attributes:

- NAME
- DESCRIPTION
- COUNTRY_NAME

For the COUNTRY level, we'll need data for the following attributes:

- NAME
- DESCRIPTION

The complete and fully expanded STORE dimension in our mapping appears like the following screenshot:

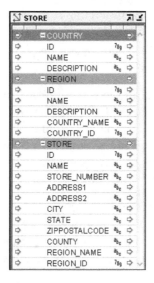

We might be tempted to include the ID fields in the above list of data elements for populating, but these are the attributes that will be filled in automatically by the Warehouse Builder. In fact, if we try to map a value to one of the IDs, the mapping editor will not let us. It will change the cursor into a "no entry" symbol, (a circle with a slash through it.) The Warehouse Builder fills them using the sequence that was automatically created for us when we built the dimension. This is one of the benefits of using the dimensional operators (cubes and dimensions). They handle the generation of the surrogate keys for a dimension and the lookup for a cube automatically for us. We don't have to be concerned with connecting any source data to the ID fields. We discussed the concept of using a sequence for the surrogate key back in *Chapter 4* when we designed our dimensions.

Now that we know what we need to populate in our STORE dimension, let's turn our attention over to the POS_TRANS_STAGE dimension for the candidate data elements that we can use. In this table, we see the following data elements for populating data in our STORE dimension:

- STORE_NAME
- STORE_NUMBER
- STORE_ADDRESS1
- STORE_ADDRESS2
- STORE_CITY
- STORE_STATE
- STORE_ZIPPOSTALCODE
- STORE_REGION
- STORE_COUNTRY

It is easy to see which of these attributes will be used to map data to attributes in the STORE level of the STORE dimension. They will map into the corresponding attributes in the dimension in the **STORE** group. We'll need to connect the following attributes together:

- STORE_NAME to NAME
- STORE_NUMBER to STORE_NUMBER
- STORE_ADDRESS1 to ADDRESS1
- STORE_ADDRESS2 to ADDRESS2
- STORE_CITY to CITY
- STORE_STATE to STATE
- STORE_ZIPPOSTALCODE to ZIP_POSTALCODE
- STORE_REGION to REGION_NAME

There is another attribute in our STORE dimension that we haven't accounted for yet—the COUNTY attribute. We don't have an input attribute to provide direct information about it. It is a special case that we will handle after we take care of these more straightforward attributes and will involve the lookup table that we discussed earlier in the introduction of this chapter.

We're not going to directly connect the attributes mentioned in the list by just dragging a line between each of them. There are some issues with the source data that we are going to have to account for in our mapping. Connecting the attributes directly like that would mean the data would be loaded into the dimension as is, but we have investigated the source data and discovered that much of the source data contains trailing blanks due to the way the transactional system stores it. Some of the fields should be made all uppercase for consistency.

Given this additional information, we'll summarize the issues with each of the fields that need to be corrected before loading into the target and then we'll see how to implement the necessary transformations in the mapping to correct them:

- `STORE_NAME`, `STORE_NUMBER`: We need to trim spaces and change these attributes to uppercase to facilitate queries as they are part of the business identifier

- `STORE_ADDRESS1`, `ADDRESS2`, `CITY`, `STATE`, and `ZIP_POSTALCODE`: We need to trim spaces and change the `STATE` attribute to uppercase

- `STORE_REGION`: We need to trim spaces and change this attribute to uppercase

All of these needs can be satisfied and we can have the desired effect by applying pre-existing SQL functions to the data via Transformation Operators.

Adding Transformation Operators

The Transformation Operator is a generic operator that is used to represent several built-in or custom-built functions or procedures for operating on data in order to make some kind of change or transformation to it. Let's take a look at the available list of transformations. In the **Design Center**, we can look at a list of available transformations either custom or pre-built in the database in the **Globals Navigator** panel under **Public Transformations**. There are several categories of transformations available to us as shown in the following screenshot:

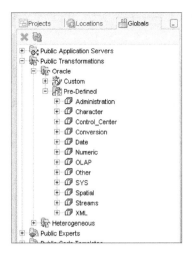

We are primarily interested in the **Character** category because that is where we'll find functions that operate on character strings, and that can convert them to uppercase and remove whitespace. We can expand any of these lists to take a look at the names of the various transformations names available. We can also go to the online help for explanations of all the functions in the **Warehouse Builder Transformations Reference** heading under the **Data Modeling, Data Quality and Performing ETL** section of the online help table of contents. You can access this by selecting **Help | Table of Contents** from the main menu of the Design Center, or by pressing the *F1* key. The particular transformation names we need under the character heading are the `upper()` function to convert to uppercase and the `trim()` function to remove whitespace.

We can now move back to the Mapping Editor where we're creating our `STORE_MAP` mapping and begin to add the transformations, and through them connect source to target. The first data element we'll map is the store name, so let's drag a Transformation operator onto the mapping and drop it between the `POS_TRANS_STAGE` table and the `STORE` dimension. We can find the **Transformation Operator** in the **Component Palette** window as shown in the following screenshot:

After dropping the **Transformation Operator** on the mapping, it will pop up a dialog box where we select the transformation we want to use. We have two options in this dialog box—create an unbound operator (basically, one that is not tied to an existing repository object) or select from an existing object. We'll select an existing one because we know that the function that will suit our purpose already exists. We'll scroll the window down until we see the **TRIM()** function as shown in the following screenshot:

Searching for a function

If we want to find the function quickly, rather than manually scrolling the window down, there's a not-so-obvious feature of this dialog box called the search capability. If we start typing the name of the function we want, it will automatically scroll down the list with each letter typed, until it settles on the one we want. For example, type a *T* and it highlights the line for the **TRANSLATE** function. Type an *R* next and it jumps to the TRUNC() function. But type an *I* next and it jumps right to the **TRIM** function we need. This option is much better to quickly find what we're looking for than manually scrolling the window. This option is a great help as it's so easy to scroll right by what we're looking for without realizing it.

If you click anywhere on the window before typing, the search string will start the search at that point.

We'll now click on the **TRIM** function in the window and then on the **OK** button. This will display a **TRIM** Transformation operator window on our mapping. It is like any other operator in that it has attributes, which are in groups depending on whether they are input, output, or both. In this case, a **TRIM** operator has one input attribute and one output attribute. The input attribute is the string we want to trim the whitespace from and the output attribute represents the result of applying the **TRIM** operator to the input string. It looks like the following screenshot:

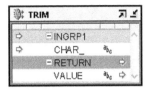

 With all of these Transformation operators that we can select from, the attribute names will appear similar to the above character attributes named CHAR_, a return value named VALUE. We can change these if we want, but this will become tedious when large numbers of Transformation Operators are required. Leaving the Transformation operator's attributes as they are will not affect the operation of the mapping.

We can now connect our STORE_NAME attribute in the POS_TRANS_STAGE mapping table operator to this new **TRIM** operator. We'll drag a line from STORE_NAME to **CHAR_** in the **TRIM** operator. This succeeds in mapping the input for our new **TRIM** Transformation operator, but now we need to map the output somewhere. We could just drag a line from the **VALUE** output attribute over to the **STORE** dimension. But we've said before that we need to apply an **UPPER** transformation on this value as well as a trim, so the value that ultimately gets loaded into our dimension will be in all uppercase letters.

 Upper and lowercase issues

When working between an MS SQL Server Database and an Oracle Database, we will frequently find that the case of the strings we're working with becomes an issue. The Oracle Database is very case sensitive. If we store a string in the database as 'Some String', then searching for 'some string' will not get a match. It will match in SQL Server, even though the case is different. This is why it is a good idea to store key fields that uniquely identify a record in the database in all uppercase. By doing so, we won't encounter a possible situation where two records get loaded into our data warehouse that differ by only the case of the key identifier, or we don't get a match at all because of a different case.

Now we need an **UPPER** transformation added for our `STORE_NAME`, so let's drag another Transformation operator onto the mapping and drop it to the right of the **TRIM** operator. It is perfectly acceptable and very common, in fact, to have to map the output from one Transformation operator into the input of another Transformation operator. We will select the **UPPER()** function this time from the resulting pop-up window. It is close to the **TRIM** function in the dialog box as shown in the following screenshot:

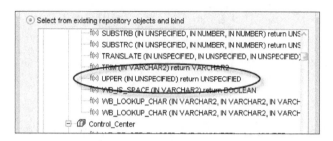

The **UPPER()** function is similar to the **TRIM()** function in the number of arguments it takes and the value it returns—which is one in both the cases. It is different in that the **UPPER()** function does not specify the type of the arguments as the **TRIM()** function does. We can see from the previous screenshot that the type is listed as **UNSPECIFIED**. We know these are character functions because that is where we found them in the list. As a **TRIM** function removes characters (blank characters) from a string, this string must be a `varchar2` string and not a string of a `char` type. A `varchar2` string is a variable length string up to the maximum length it was defined with; so if you remove some characters from it, it just shrinks in size. However a `char` string is a string with a fixed length.

The database will fill up a char string with blanks up to the maximum size of the string if you store a string that is smaller than the defined size of the `char` string. A **TRIM()** will have no effect on this kind of field. An **UPPER()** function, on the other hand, will work on a string of any type. The *Oracle Database SQL Language Reference* manual (which can be found at `http://download.oracle.com/docs/cd/E11882_01/server.112/e17118/functions.htm#i1482196`) indicates that the parameter can be any of the following: `CHAR`, `VARCHAR2`, `NCHAR`, `NVARCHAR2`, `CLOB`, or `NCLOB`. When we look up the **TRIM()** function, we see that it can only be a **VARCHAR2** for input.

Thus, the **UPPER** transformation is not able to know beforehand the exact type of the input and output parameters. It will know about that only when we drag an actual value to it. There is also a difference in how the operator looks on the mapping just after being dropped. We can see in the following screenshot that unlike other operators in our mapping, the attribute type indicators in this operator (that appear to the right of the attributes) show as blank boxes:

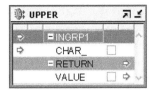

These blank boxes will fill in automatically at some point after an attribute gets mapped to it, so let's continue. We will need the output of the **TRIM** operator to be the input of this one, so we'll drag a line from VALUE in the **TRIM** operator to CHAR_ in the **UPPER** operator. The type indicator in the window on the mapping will eventually update automatically to reflect the type that was connected to it, which is VARCHAR2 in this case.

We can now connect to the STORE dimension as we don't have any more transformations that we need to do to the STORE_NAME, but we need to decide where in the STORE dimension to connect. This is where it could be easy to make the wrong connection because looking at the **STORE** dimension we see that it has three **NAME** attributes, all of which can be used as input, as circled in the following screenshot:

Here the key in deciding which attribute to use is to recall our discussion of the design of our dimension back in Chapter 4. There we talked about the levels and hierarchy that can exist in a dimension, and how certain attributes can be designated as **dimension attributes**, which can be found at every level of the dimension. In this case, the **NAME** attribute is just such an attribute. The hierarchy in this case is COUNTRY, REGION, STORE; and each level of the hierarchy has a NAME associated with it. This is the name of the store, so let's make sure to drag the line to the **NAME** attribute in the **STORE** group of the **STORE** dimension operator, which is the bottommost operator in the above screenshot.

At this point, our mapping should look roughly similar to the following. The placement of the operators on the mapping will vary, but it should generally be similar to the **POS_TRANS_STAGE** mapping table on the left as input, the **TRIM** and **UPPER** operators in the middle connecting the **STORE_NAME** attribute from input to the **NAME** attribute of the **STORE** group in the **STORE** dimension as output:

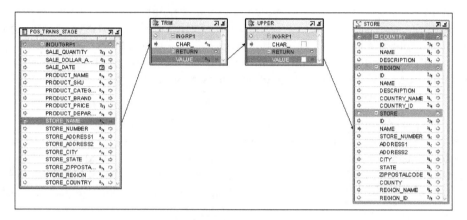

To keep our mapping from becoming too cluttered, collapse the transformation windows into their icon view after making all the connections through them. The icons take up much less space on the mapping and can always be opened again by double-clicking on them if needed in the future. We can click on the down arrow in the upper-right corner of the window to collapse them into the icon view.

Another option to un-clutter the mapping would be to use a single expression operator to implement the functions for each attribute. We mentioned back in Chapter 5 how we could implement a prebuilt operator in an expression operator just by creating an expression that used the function. An expression operator can actually include more than one expression so we could do one for each attribute that needed transforming. We'll take a quick look at that option in a moment when we complete this mapping.

Next, we'll take care of the STORE_NUMBER as it is the second part of the business identifier for the store. The name and number of the store are what uniquely identify a single store in the ACME Toys and Gizmos company, and are handled similarly in our mapping. The same two transformations are needed for the STORE_NUMBER field as for STORE_NAME from the POS_TRANS_STAGE input table, but we can't reuse the existing two transformations we just dropped onto our mapping. We will need to drag two more transformations to our mapping, making one a **TRIM** and another an **UPPER** just as we did for the STORE_NAME. We'll connect them in a manner similar to how we connected the previous two transformations. We'll start with the POS_TRANS_STAGE mapping table operator. We will connect the STORE_NUMBER attribute to the input of the **TRIM**, the output of the **TRIM** to the input of the new **UPPER** we just dropped onto the mapping, and the output of the **UPPER** to the STORE_NUMBER attribute of the STORE dimension. There is only one STORE_NUMBER attribute in the dimension, unlike the name, because the STORE_NUMBER is not defined as a dimension attribute; it exists only at the STORE level as a level attribute.

At this point we have our STORE_NAME and STORE_NUMBER attributes connected to the dimension, and we'll continue with the two address fields, the city, the state, and the zip/postal code field. We determined that these fields will need to have spaces trimmed, but we do not want to make them uppercase except for the state field. They are not a part of the unique business identifier for an individual store and, apart from the state field, can be any combination of characters and/or numbers, which make them less likely to be queried for. The state field contains states in the US, which are commonly expressed as two uppercase characters, and so we'll apply the **UPPER** transformation to it.

We will need six more Transformation operators dropped into our mapping, with five being for **TRIM** operators for each of those five fields and one for an UPPER() function to use for the state field. The following attributes of the POS_TRANS_STAGE mapping table operator will provide the input for the five **TRIM** operators:

- STORE_ADDRESS1
- STORE_ADDRESS2
- STORE_CITY
- STORE_STATE
- STORE_ZIPPOSTALCODE

The output of the **TRIM** operators for all but the STORE_STATE attribute will be connected directly to **STORE** level attributes of the **STORE** dimension as follows:

- ADDRESS1
- ADDRESS2
- CITY
- ZIP_POSTALCODE

The **TRIM** output for the STORE_STATE attribute will be connected to the **UPPER** Transformation operator, and the output from the **UPPER** operator will be connected to the **STATE** attribute in the **STORE** dimension.

After making all these connections, our mapping should now look similar to the following with all the Transformation operators collapsed into their icon views:

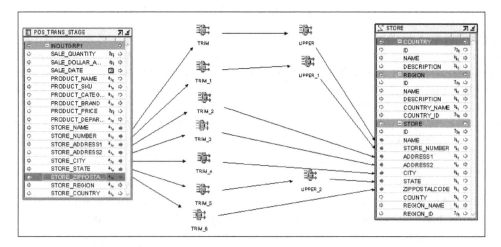

We're not done with this mapping yet as we still have to map the STORE_REGION attribute to the **STORE** level, and map both the **REGION** and **COUNTRY** levels. Before continuing, let's save our work so far with the **Mapping | Save All** menu entry on the **Design Center**. We can also use the *Ctrl+S* key combination.

Information about both the region and country comes from two attributes in our source staging table, the STORE_REGION and STORE_COUNTRY attributes. These are character fields for the name of the region and country the store is located in. When we designed our STORE dimension in Chapter 4, a NAME and DESCRIPTION field were created for us by default. We decided to leave it that way as that is a common design technique for dimensions and avoids the error we mentioned back then about not having any updatable fields. As we don't have separate name and description fields to draw from at this point, we'll just fill the same information into both fields in the STORE dimension.

The NAME field is identified as the business identifier, so we'll put the value we store there into uppercase and leave the description in whatever case the source was in.

Let's start with the region attribute. We can see in our STORE dimension that there is a REGION_NAME attribute in the **STORE** group (level). This attribute indicates in which region on the **REGION** level this store is located. Looking at the **REGION** level we can see that there is a **COUNTRY_NAME** located there, which indicates the country from the **COUNTRY** level where the region is located. In terms of our mapping, this determines where we map the STORE_REGION and STORE_COUNTRY attributes to.

The first mapping change we'll do for the region is to finish up the **STORE** level attributes by mapping the STORE_REGION from the stage table to the REGION_NAME attribute in the STORE dimension, **STORE** level. We indicated earlier that names should be capitalized and spaces trimmed, so we'll drag two more Transformation Operators into our mapping—TRIM and UPPER—and map the STORE_REGION to the **TRIM**, the **TRIM** to the **UPPER**, and the **UPPER** to the REGION_NAME field.

This completes the **STORE** level except for the COUNTY attribute, and we still have this attribute plus the **REGION** and **COUNTRY** levels to complete. At this point, we've become more proficient in doing our mapping and including transformations. So we'll just continue to the **REGION** level and add the following connections and transformations without having to walk through each one in detail. Be sure to read the tip below before completing these:

- STORE_REGION to NAME in the **REGION** level using **TRIM** and **UPPER** transformations
- STORE_REGION to DESCRIPTION in the **REGION** level using a **TRIM** transformation
- STORE_COUNTRY to COUNTRY_NAME in the **REGION** level using **TRIM** and **UPPER** transformations
- STORE_COUNTRY to NAME in the **COUNTRY** level using **TRIM** and **UPPER** transformations
- STORE_COUNTRY to DESCRIPTION in the **COUNTRY** level using a **TRIM** transformation

But we'll want to implement the following tip to make our mapping easier and less cluttered.

We have had a couple of instances earlier where the same input attribute needs to be mapped to more than one target attribute. We learned previously that we couldn't reuse a Transformation operator on two different input attributes. However, we can reuse a Transformation Operator if the output goes to two different attributes. Multiple connections can be created from an output attribute in an operator, but only one input connection is allowed.

For example, we can use just one **TRIM** operator on the REGION_NAME and have its output go to an **UPPER** operator and also directly to the DESCRIPTION attribute in the **REGION** group of the **STORE** dimension. The output of the **UPPER** operator can then be connected to both the REGION_NAME of the **STORE** level and the NAME attribute of the **REGION** level. The same technique can be applied to the mappings for the COUNTRY_NAME.

The bottom line is to reuse the **TRIM** and **UPPER** operators just added for the NAME in the **REGION** level, and add one **TRIM** and one **UPPER** operator for the COUNTRY_NAME.

After adding the two additional transformations and making the connections already mentioned, our mapping should now look similar to the following screenshot:

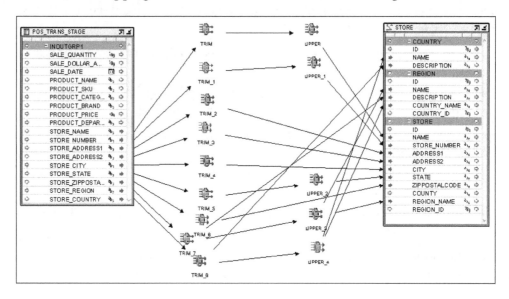

Our **STORE** dimension is now mapped for every attribute except for the COUNTY attribute. We've saved this one for last because it is the most complex of our attributes to map for this dimension. The reason is that we don't have an exact match with an attribute from our input staging table to use. Let's save our work at this point and then investigate further how we need to map this attribute.

Using a Lookup operator

Lookup operators, as the name implies, are used for looking up information from other sources based on some key attribute(s) in a mapping. This is exactly what we will need to do to get the information for the **COUNTY** attribute of our **STORE** dimension. However, only tables, views, dimensions, and cubes can be used as the source for this operator. This means we need a table that can be used to look up the required county information. Back in Chapter 2, we imported the source metadata for a flat file called `counties.csv`, creating a file in our `ACME_FILES` module in Design Center for this file that contains the names of counties. It looks like we ought to be able to use the information in that file to build a lookup table, so that's exactly what we're going to do right now. We will use a simple Warehouse Builder mapping to do it in a couple of easy steps. First, we will need to create an external table to represent the `counties.csv` file. We could use the `counties.csv` file directly, but as we discussed back in Chapter 2 that would require using the SQL*Loader utility, which would not be consistent with the PL/SQL access that can be used for all the other sources. So we will create an external table using the simple steps outlined in the next section, and then follow that by using that external table as the source in a new mapping to load a lookup table.

Creating an external table

In Chapter 2, we imported metadata from the `counties.csv` file which was created in a module separate from our main database module because a file is not a part of the database. However, external tables are created in the database as they are accessed just like regular database tables. However, unlike a regular table whose data is stored in the database, an external table's data is stored in a flat file that is external to the database.

External tables are created under the **Oracle | ACME_DWH | External Tables** node in the **Design Center**, so we'll right-click on it and select **New External Table** from the pop-up menu. This will launch the **External Table** wizard, which will guide us through the process. It is a three-step process that involves providing a name to use for the external table, specifying the file to use, and specifying the default location. The steps are as follows:

1. By clicking on **Next** on the **Welcome** screen, we come to the screen labeled **Step 1**. We'll name this external table **COUNTIES** and click on **Next** to continue to the screen labeled **Step 2**.

2. In this step we'll select the file that contains the metadata for the external table. It will display the name of any files that have been defined in our **Files** module. We can see our **COUNTIES_CSV** file listed, so we'll select that and click on **Next** to continue.

3. This brings us to the screen labeled **Step 3** where we will select the default location to use for this table. The drop-down menu on this screen will display the file locations that have been defined in the Design Center. We will select the **ACME_FILES_LOCATION** entry, which is for the files that exist for this project. Clicking on **Next** will bring us to the **Summary** screen where we can verify the information we just specified. It should look similar to the following screenshot:

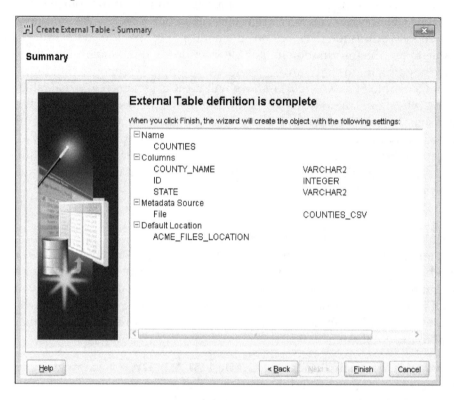

If we see anything we'd like to change, we can click on the **Back** button to move back through the screens to make any changes and click on **Next** until we get back here.

4. When we click on the **Finish** button, it will create a new entry called **COUNTIES** under the **External Tables** node in our project in the Design Center.

The wizard has created an external table with the column attributes that were listed in the **Summary** screen. These attributes correspond to the fields that are stored in the counties.csv flat file. We can query this table just as we query a table in the database.

Creating and loading a lookup table

Now that we have our source table defined for our new lookup table, let's create a new mapping called COUNTIES_LOOKUP_MAP using the same method we've used previously. The steps to create a lookup table are:

1. Right-click on the **Mappings** node, select **New Mapping**, enter **COUNTIES_ LOOKUP_MAP** in the name field, and click on the **OK** button.

2. In the **Mapping Editor** that pops up, let's drag an **External Table Operator** from the **Component Palette** window onto the mapping.

3. On the **Add External Table Operator** pop-up window that appears, our **COUNTIES** external table is visible. We will select that and click on the **OK** button to continue. This will drop an External Table Operator on our mapping that is bound to our **COUNTIES** external table.

4. We need to get that data loaded into a regular table in the database, so next we'll drag a **Table Operator** onto the mapping.

As this table doesn't yet exist, there are a few different ways we can go about creating it to hold our county information. We could create the table in the Design Center in the **Tables** node under our database module, and then drag that table into our mapping. Alternatively, we could create the table in the database and then import the metadata for that table as we imported source metadata back in Chapter 2, or we can take the path we're taking now to make full use of the Warehouse Builder's automation and flexibility and create the table as we need it.

5. In the resulting **Add Table Operator** pop up that appears, we specify what table we want to add. We've seen this add operator dialog box before, but we've always been choosing an existing object to add. This time we're going to check the first option to **Create unbound operator with no attributes** and we'll give it the name **COUNTIES_LOOKUP** by typing that name into the box. This is shown in the following screenshot:

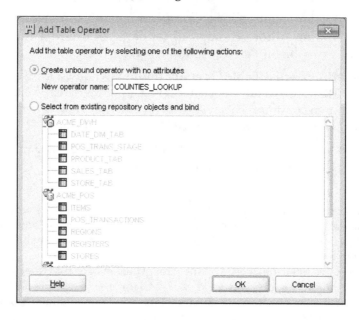

6. We'll click on **OK** and it will drop a Table Operator onto our mapping with no attributes defined in it.

We need to define the attributes and we know we need the data loaded from the external table, so let's use these attributes in our example. We might think we have to enter each of these attributes individually into the Table Operator and then drag a line from the corresponding attribute in the external table over to the new table. But the Warehouse Builder makes this very easy; with one drag we can map an attribute group instead of individual attributes.

Let's drag a line from the output group (OUTGRP1) of our COUNTIES external table over to the input/output group (INOUTGRP1) of our new COUNTIES_LOOKUP table. With that one action, the new table operator immediately goes from being empty to having three attributes defined in it. These attributes have names that are the same as the external table attribute names and have the same data types which have been copied over for us also. Connecting lines are drawn for all three attributes to map them from the external table. This is very neat, and it just saved us a bunch of time.

This mapping is done. However, there is one more step we need to take to actually create the lookup table definition. Remember we created our table operator as an unbound operator, which means it's not associated with any database object. If we look in the **ACME_DWH | Tables** node, there is no table named COUNTIES_LOOKUP. The steps to create a new table object and to bind this operator to it are as follows:

1. When we right-click on the unbounded operator, the pop-up menu has a menu selection called **Create and Bind...**. With this option we will create a new table object in the OWB **Tables** node and bind this operator to it.

    Let's select that menu entry from the pop-up menu and it will present us with the following dialog box:

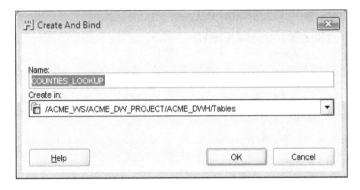

2. The name is the same as what we gave to the operator. We could name the underlying bound table something different, but it's best to leave it with the same name for clarity.

3. The **Create in:** text field is to specify the module in which to create the new table under our project in the **Design Center**. It has defaulted to the **Tables** node under the current ACME_DWH module, and that is exactly where we want it. The drop-down option provides a listing of every **Tables** node in all the modules that are currently defined in our current project if we want to create it in one of those other modules.

4. When we click on the **OK** button on this dialog box, a table is created in the **Tables** node and is bound to the operator.

To verify that, we can navigate to the **ACME_DWH | Tables** node under our database module and there is the new **COUNTIES_LOOKUP** table now. This completes the mapping and table creation. Our new table is now ready to include in a mapping as a Lookup operator.

To ensure that we don't end up with duplicate records in our new lookup table, we can take an extra step to define a primary key on this table.

When we use the option to create a table in this manner, it creates a basic, no-frills table with no constraints defined on it. To add a primary key, we'll perform the following steps:

1. In the **Design Center**, open the **COUNTIES_LOOKUP** table in the **Table Editor** by double-clicking on it under the **Tables** node.

2. Click on the **Keys** tab.

3. Click on the **Add Constraint** button.

4. Type **PK_COUNTIES_LOOKUP** (or any other naming convention we might choose) in the **Name** column.

5. In the **Type** column, click on the drop-down menu and select **Primary Key**.

6. Click on the **Local Columns** column, and then click on the **Add Local Column** button.

7. Click on the drop-down menu that appears and select the **ID** column.

8. Close the **Table Editor** window.

The new table and mapping is now complete. It is very basic, but gives us an idea of the power of the Warehouse Builder to make our data warehouse design job easier. The mapping just handles inserts into the lookup table from the external table. We could add more bells and whistles to our lookup to handle updates or changes to the existing rows, but that is for more advanced topics.

We'll save our work up to this point with the *Ctrl+S* key combination, and then move on to make use of this new lookup table to retrieve the county information.

Retrieving the key to use for a Lookup operator

We now have a table definition created and a mapping completed that can load the table to use to look up the county name. But we need a key that will uniquely identify a record in the table and with which we can look up a county. The key has to be a data element that is unique in the file, and it would be the ID column we defined as the primary key for the table. It is a number that does not repeat itself for any of the rows in the file; so given a particular value of that number, we can find the county and the state that the county is in.

We recall from our analysis and importing of source metadata back in *Chapter 2* that the STORE_NUMBER data element contained in the STORES source table has a code that indicates the county the store is located in for stores in the USA. This is actually a fixed known format, and the positions three through six of the number are actually the code for the location of the store in the county. This number is actually the ID number found in the counties.csv flat file, and which is the ID in the lookup table. So, we now have a key value that we can use to look up the county. However, there are still some more issues we have to work out before we can use it.

The county ID is only a portion of the entire STORE_NUMBER field, so we can't just use the STORE_NUMBER from input as the direct key to a Lookup operator. We will have to extract the ID number out of it and then convert it to a number before we can use it to look up the county. This implies that some more transformations will be needed, so let's work on getting that county ID extracted from the STORE_NUMBER field.

Adding a SUBSTR Transformation operator

The Transformation operators available to us in OWB include a SUBSTR (or substring) transformation that will do exactly what we need to extract the county ID value out of the STORE_NUMBER field. The SUBSTR transformation takes three parameters—the string we want to extract the substring from, a number indicating the start position of the substring within the string, and a number indicating the length of the substring to extract.

So, let's drag a Transformation operator onto the STORE_MAP mapping between the POS_TRANS_STAGE table and the STORE dimension below all the other Transformation operators. On the resulting **Add Transformation Operator** pop-up window, select the **SUBSTR()** transformation and it will place the following operator into our mapping:

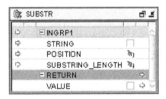

For the **SUBSTR** operator, we need to make sure we select the correct version as there are five different variants of SUBSTR we could choose from. They are SUBSTR, SUBSTR2, SUBSTR4, SUBSTRB, and SUBSTRC. The main SUBSTR version is the one we want because it works on regular character strings. The others only vary in the type of input character string they operate on. A more in-depth description of the SUBSTR() function and its variants is in *the Oracle Database SQL Language Reference Manual*, which is available online at the **Oracle Database Documentation** website (http://www.oracle.com/technology/documentation/database.html).

When first dropped on the mapping, this operator may not look exactly like the above screenshot in which the operator is fully expanded. To see the whole operator contents at once, we can click and drag an edge to manually make the window bigger or click on the symbol in the upper-right corner with the arrow pointing upwards as indicated in the following screenshot, which shows the operator before being expanded fully:

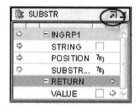

We didn't have this issue with any of the Transformation operators we included earlier, but it's helpful here for being able to see the entire contents of the operator.

All windows on the mapping, and not just the Transformation operators, have this feature for expanding the window size. We'll find that the table, dimension, and cube operators need to be expanded frequently to see the entire contents, and this is a quick way to do it. If we wanted to maximize or minimize all the operators at once, we could use the Ctrl-A key combination and then select **View...Maximize** or **View...Minimize** from the main menu.

Let's continue mapping attributes to the **SUBSTR** operator. The **STRING** attribute is easy, which will be the STORE_NUMBER from the POS_TRANS_STAGE table. So let's drag a line from STORE_NUMBER down to **STRING**. The position and length are not so obvious. We don't have any values in the source table to use for those two so we need to create something to use.

The second and the third parameters—the position and length—these need to be constant integer values that we supply. By looking at the list of operators available to us in the **Component Palette** window, we see that there is a **CONSTANT** operator as shown in the following image. We can use this operator by dragging it from the **Palette** window in the **Design Center**:

Adding a Constant operator

We'll click and drag a **Constant** operator onto the mapping to the left of the **SUBSTR** Transformation operator. We can see that it has an output group called **OUTGRP1** by default. We'll right-click on it and select **Open Details...** from the pop-up menu. This opens an editor on the **CONSTANT** operator, which should look like the following screenshot:

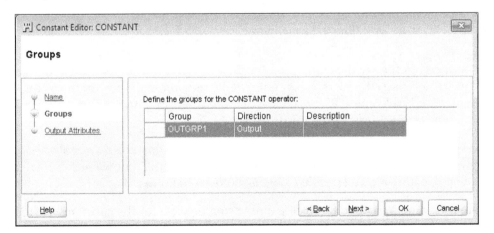

The sub-window that is highlighted when the dialog box opens depends on what was right-clicked. As we can see, this editor has windows for editing the **Name** of the operator, the **Groups**, and the **Output Attributes** of the output group. The **Constant** operator only allows output, so there is no input group defined or allowed. If it was an operator that allowed input, such as a function or procedure that took parameters (for example, the **SUBSTR** operator), there would be an additional tab for **Input Attributes** also.

Clicking on the **Output Attributes** entry on the left we see that there are no attributes currently existing for this operator. This is where we will add our constants that we need for the **SUBSTR** operator. We can actually enter more than one constant in the same operator (which is a good thing to do if we are using those constants together anyway), which we are doing in this case. We could just as easily drag another **Constant** operator onto the mapping for the other constant we need; it's really just a matter of preference. Functionally, the result will be the same when OWB deploys and executes the mapping.

To add an attribute, we just type the names in the name column. This will create an output attribute in the group with that name and data type that we can then edit to suit our purposes. We'll name this first constant attribute to reflect the destination for this value, that is the position attribute of the **SUBSTR** operator, so we'll name it **POSITION** also. Click on the first empty space under the name column and we can then type in what we want it to be. We'll name it **position**.

> We don't have to worry about capitalization as the Warehouse Builder will automatically convert everything to uppercase anyway. We'll see this when we click elsewhere on the dialog box and the focus moves out of that field, or if we close the dialog box and then look at the name in the operator on the mapping.

Next we need to specify the expression for this constant. The expression in this case since we're defining constants, is just going to be the number we want to use for the constant value. We'll enter a **3** since we know the position of the county value in the store number string starts at the third position.

Next, we need to make sure the data type is correct. The position value to which we're going to map this constant in the **SUBSTR** operator is defined as a **NUMBER** with no precision or scale specified (that is, both set to zero).

We are not going to bother specifying a precision or scale for the constants we're creating because we don't need the extra data integrity checks in the database and the **SUBSTR** position attribute is defined that way. We'll leave the precision and scale set to zeros, which is the default.

We need another constant value defined to indicate the length of the substring, so let's add another attribute on the **Output Attributes** window of the **CONSTANT Editor** dialog box. We'll name this attribute **LENGTH** to reflect its purpose and enter the name in the next available blank name field. We'll enter a value of 4 for the expression and leave the data type set to **NUMERIC**, and the default precision and scale set to zero as we did for the POSITION attribute. We'll click on the **OK** button on the dialog box to close it.

The next step is to connect our constants to the corresponding attributes of our **SUBSTR** operator. We'll drag a line from **POSITION** in the **CONSTANT** operator to the **POSITION** attribute of the **SUBSTR** operator, and from the **LENGTH** attribute to the **SUBSTRING_LENGTH** attribute.

Adding a TO_NUMBER transformation

The **SUBSTR** value is ready and we can use it to look up the county ID, but there's one more transformation we need to apply before we can use it to look up the county name. First, it needs to be converted into a number to match the data type of the ID field in the COUNTIES_LOOKUP table. To do this, we will use the **TO_NUMBER()** function. So let's drag a **Transformation Operator** onto our mapping to the right of the **SUBSTR** operator and select **TO_NUMBER** from the resulting pop up.

This operator needs three parameters, only one of which is absolutely necessary — the expression we wish to convert to a number. The other two parameters are optional and include a format string that we can use if we have a particular format of number we want (such as a decimal point in a certain place) and a parameter that allows us to set a certain national language format to default to if it's different from the language set in the database. We'll just map the input expression because our number is a straight integer format number. So let's drag a line from the **VALUE** attribute of **SUBSTR** to the **EXPR** input attribute of the **TO_NUMBER** operator.

We are now ready to look up the number to find the county name. The final step we need to perform now is to actually add the Lookup operator that we'll use to do that, so let's continue with that task.

Adding a Lookup operator

After that little side trip to quickly create our lookup table and add a **SUBSTR** operator with a **TO_NUMBER** transformation to convert the result to a number, we can now add a **Lookup** operator to our mapping for looking up the county name. Let's drag a **Lookup** operator onto the mapping and drop it to the right of the **TO_ NUMBER** operator. We can find the **Lookup** operator in the **Palette** window just as we did for the other operators we've added. After we drop it in the mapping, the **Add Lookup** popup appears similar to the one that appeared when we dragged a table operator and dropped it on the mapping. We get to select an unbound operator or select an existing object to bind to this operator. Since we've created our table to use for the lookup we'll use the option for binding to an existing repository object and select the **COUNTIES_LOOKUP** table as shown next:

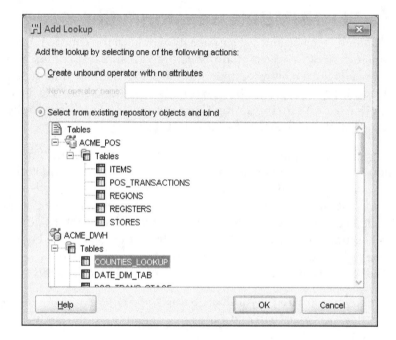

After clicking the OK button the Lookup Wizard will be launched.

1. After the welcome screen, the first step asks us for a name for this Lookup. Since we just chose the COUNTIES_LOOKUP table to bind to, it shows that name here. We could change it if we wanted but it's a good idea to leave it the same as the bound table. We'll click on the **Next** button to proceed to the screen labeled **Step 2**.

2. This screen is for defining input and output groups for the Lookup operator. There is one input and one output group by default, and here we have an opportunity to rename the groups if we desire or add new groups. Lookups can take input from more than one source and lookup data from more than one table. We'll leave just the two default groups and leave them with their default names `INGRP1` and `OUTGRP1`, and click on **Next** to continue.

3. This is where we can specify the lookup table to use for each output group. Since we only have one output group and already chose a table in the opening popup, it will be preselected for us. We can just click **Next** to continue.

4. In this step we will specify the input attribute(s) we want to use. We have just one value we need to use, the county identification number that was stored in the store_number field so we'll define one input attribute called **COUNTY_ID** and make it a type **NUMERIC** with no precision or scale. This will be the output of the **TO_NUMBER** operator that we've already mapped. We'll click **Next** to continue.

5. This step is where we specify the output attributes for our lookup. We can see that it has already filled in output attributes for us based on the columns of the **COUNTIES_LOOKUP** table that we specified as the lookup table. We will use these without modification and click **Next** to continue to the next step.

6. This step is where we will specify the lookup conditions. Since we could have specified more than one input and output group, we have to specify which input group to use with which output group. It defaults to our two default groups so we don't have to do anything with the dropdowns. We do however need to configure the lookup table column to use and the input attribute to match against it. There are two options for doing that, **Simple Editing** or **Freestyle Editing** which can be chosen using the appropriate radio buttons. We'll leave it set to the default of Simple Editing which provides drop down menus to select from below.

7. We'll click in the first row under **Lookup Table Column**. In the resulting drop-down menu that appears (which may take a moment or two to appear, so we'll be patient), we'll select the primary key we defined on the **COUNTIES_LOOKUP** table. We could also have selected an individual column if we did not have a primary key on the table.

8. Having selected the primary key, we now have to specify an input attribute. We'll click in that box and see that it has added a row beneath with the **COUNTY_ID**. It might not be readily apparent so just click row two under the **Input Attribute** column and we'll see it as the column to use for the Lookup Table Key.

It may seem redundant to make this selection here, but there could be more than one input attribute used in a lookup. Therefore, we have to go through this step to indicate which input attribute matches with which lookup table key. In this case, we happen to have only a single attribute to use for the lookup.

Now our dialog box should look similar to the following:

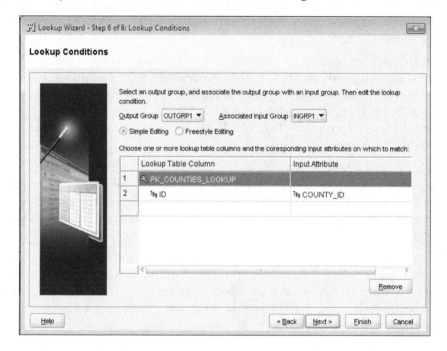

1. Now we're going to specify what to do if multiple rows are returned by our lookup. Since we're looking up a single value using the primary key of the lookup table there will only be one row returned but it's possible to specify general lookup conditions using other than the primary key which will cause more than one row to return. We have several options for how to handle this situation. We'll choose the option that makes the mapping error out if multiple rows are returned since we do not want that situation to occur. Step 7 should look like the following for us:

The other options we could specify are to return all the rows or to select a single row from the multiple that are returned. If we select single row, then we have a number of additional options we can specify to tell it what row to return. The following illustrates the options we can specify for the row position drop down if we've chosen single row:

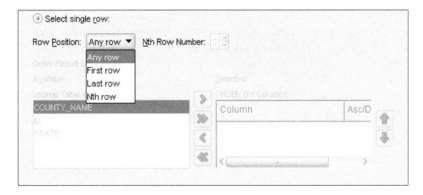

The options are to pick any row meaning the system will just return a row that is not guaranteed to be any particular row. If something more specific is desired, **first, last,** or **Nth** rows can be specified and the other criteria that is grayed out above will be selectable to specify the conditions to use for determining which is the first, last, or Nth row. We don't have to worry about any of that for our implementation so we'll just click **Next** to continue. It would not have mattered if we left **Single Row** selected with **Any row** as the option either because it would have had no effect due to only returning one row anyway.

2. We will click on the **Next** button to proceed to the final step where we will specify what to return if no record is found in the lookup table. Here we are only concerned with the **COUNTY_NAME** column as that is the value we need to map to the **SALES** cube. We'll specify a default value of **UNKNOWN** rather than just leave it **NULL**. So we'll click on **NULL** that currently appears as the default for the **COUNTY_NAME** value and type in **'UNKNOWN'** in the box.

 We have to make sure we include the single quotes around this string because it is a character string and the Oracle Database requires single quotes around character literals.

It also has an editor available to give us more power over the expression we might want to use to determine the value. Select the ellipsis beside the column value to invoke the editor. But in our case, we only want a single string to be used, so we can just type it in.

3. We will click on the **Next** button to proceed to the **Summary** screen. It should look similar to the following screenshot:

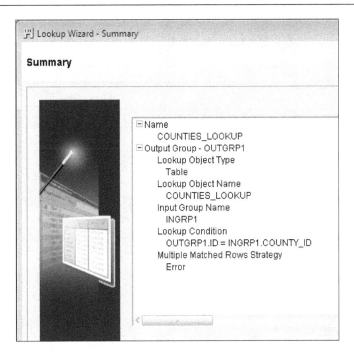

4. We will click on the **Finish** button and the wizard ends and drops a Lookup operator on our mapping. We now need to draw a connection line from the output attribute of the **TO_NUMBER** operator to the **COUNTY_ID** input attribute of the lookup operator we just created.

5. Finally we'll connect the **COUNTY_NAME** field from this Lookup operator to the **COUNTY** attribute in the **STORE** level of the **STORE** dimension and we are done with this mapping.

Now we have a completed mapping that will populate our **STORE** dimension. Our final mapping should look similar to the following screenshot:

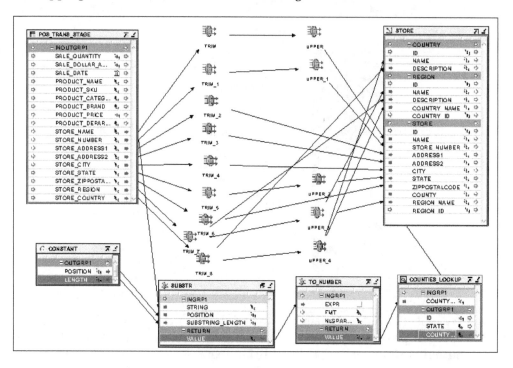

Of course, there are an almost infinite number of ways we could have organized our mapping. The mapping we just saw was somewhat compressed to better fit the available size for the image, so we won't focus on making the mapping look exactly like that. The important thing is that all the connections are made as they are shown in the mapping and not where each individual operator appears on the mapping.

Another option to clear up clutter would be to use an Expression operator. We referred to that option back in chapter 5 when we first discussed that operator and how it can be used to implement the same functions the stand-alone function Transformation operators implement. We'll take a look at an **Expression** operator soon when we do the cube mapping.

Having completed our STORE mapping, we'll save our work with the *Ctrl+S* key combination. Now we need to move on to address the mapping for our PRODUCT dimension.

PRODUCT mapping

The mapping for the **PRODUCT** dimension will be similar to the **STORE** mapping, so we won't cover it in as much detail here. We'll open the Design Center if it's not already open and create a new mapping just as we did for the STORE mapping earlier and the STAGE_MAP mapping from the last chapter. We'll name this mapping PRODUCT_MAP.

The source for the data will again be our staging table, POS_TRANS_STAGE, just as it was for the STORE mapping. Only the target will change as we're loading the PRODUCT dimension this time. We'll drag the **POS_TRANS_STAGE** table from the **Projects** window and drop it on the left of the mapping, and drag the **PRODUCT** dimension from **ACME_DWH | Dimensions** and drop it to the right of the mapping. Not surprisingly, the data elements we'll now need from the staging table are the attributes that begin with PRODUCT. We created our PRODUCT dimension with four levels—DEPARTMENT, CATEGORY, BRAND, and ITEM—which we will need to populate. Let's start with the **ITEM** level and jump right to listing the attributes from the source to the target along with the issues we'll have to address with the data elements for this level:

- PRODUCT_NAME to NAME (in the ITEM level)—needs trimmed spaces and conversion to uppercase

- PRODUCT_NAME to DESCRIPTION (in the ITEM level)—needs trimmed spaces

> We don't have a separate description field to map from the source. So for now we'll just map the name to it, but without converting to uppercase as we did for the STORE mapping. We'll do that for each of the other levels where description also appears.

- PRODUCT_SKU to SKU—needs trimmed spaces and conversion to uppercase

- PRODUCT_PRICE to LIST_PRICE—no transformation needed

- PRODUCT_BRAND to BRAND_NAME—needs trimmed spaces and conversion to uppercase

We'll add the needed transformations to accomplish the changes as indicated in the list we just saw, and then move on to the BRAND level. For the BRAND level, we need to map the NAME, DESCRIPTION, and CATEGORY_NAME as follows:

- PRODUCT_BRAND to NAME (in the BRAND level)—needs trimmed spaces and conversion to uppercase

- PRODUCT_BRAND to DESCRIPTION (in the BRAND level) — needs trimmed spaces
- PRODUCT_CATEGORY to CATEGORY_NAME — needs trimmed spaces and conversion to uppercase

When we have added these transformations and made these connections to the BRAND level, we'll move on to the CATEGORY level. It will be mapped in a similar manner to BRAND, but using the PRODUCT_CATEGORY attribute as input:

- PRODUCT_CATEGORY to NAME (in the CATEGORY level) — needs trimmed spaces and conversion to uppercase
- PRODUCT_CATEGORY to DESCRIPTION (in the CATEGORY group) — needs trimmed spaces
- PRODUCT_DEPARTMENT to DEPARTMENT_NAME — needs trimmed spaces and conversion to uppercase

Finally, we'll map the DEPARTMENT level, which has just two attributes we need to be concerned about — the NAME and the DESCRIPTION:

- PRODUCT_DEPARTMENT to NAME (in the DEPARTMENT level) — needs trimmed spaces and conversion to uppercase
- PRODUCT_DEPARTMENT to DESCRIPTION (in the DEPARTMENT level) — needs trimmed spaces

When we have completed these additional connections and transformations, we will have completed the mapping for the PRODUCT dimension. It should look similar to the following screenshot, which shows all the transformations and connections in place that were described earlier:

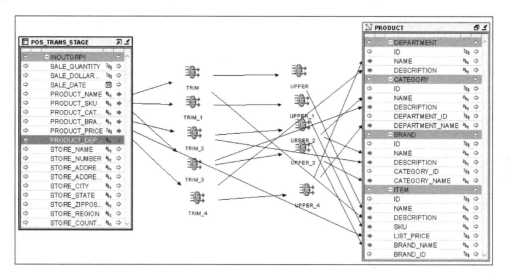

We have conserved on the usage of Transformation operators by making multiple connections from some of them as we did for the STORE_MAP previously. For instance, the topmost **TRIM** has a connection to the **UPPER** transformation to convert its output to uppercase before connecting to the **NAME** attribute of the **ITEM** group. But it also connects directly to the **DESCRIPTION** attribute of the **ITEM** group. It was not necessary to have the description in all uppercase, so the output of the **TRIM** was used. We could have just as easily dragged another **TRIM** as well as another line from the **PRODUCT_NAME** in **POS_TRANS_STAGE** to the mapping, but we would have ended up with more clutter than necessary. The functioning of the mapping would have been the same in either case.

We have completed the mapping for our PRODUCT dimension, and that completes all the mappings for our dimensions we will need to do. There is a third dimension we'll be using, the DATE_DIM mapping, but that mapping was created automatically for us. Let's save our work with the *Ctrl+S* key combination, or with **File | Save All** from the **Design Center** main menu. Moving on, we'll now create a mapping to populate our cube and that will be all the mappings we'll need for our data warehouse.

SALES cube mapping

Turning our attention to the cube, we have one more mapping to create. It will be created in the same way as we created the previous maps, but let's call this one SALES_MAP. In this mapping, we will need to draw data from the POS_TRANS_STAGE table as input as we did for the other two dimension maps, and we will have the SALES cube as the output target to load our data. Let's drag each of these onto our mapping using **Table Operator** for the POS_TRANS_STAGE table and **Cube Operator** for the SALES cube.

The POS_TRANS_STAGE table is very familiar to us as we have used it for the two dimensions, but the SALES cube is new. It looks slightly different than the dimensions we worked with earlier in this chapter, so let's take a moment to go over it in a little more detail. When dropped onto our mapping and expanded completely, it should look similar to the following:

The top group with visible attributes is the main group for the cube and contains the data elements to which we'll need to map. The other groups represent the dimensions that are linked to our cube. We mapped data to these dimensions (except for the DATE_DIM dimension) earlier. So there is no need to map any data to these groups in the cube now and, indeed, it doesn't even provide a way to do that here. The data we map for the dimensions will be to attributes in the main cube group, which will indicate to the cube which record is applicable from each of the dimensions.

Dimension attributes in the cube

Each dimension is represented in the cube attributes by a surrogate identifier, which is the primary key for the dimension, and the business identifier(s) defined for the dimension. This is where we will see the real usefulness of the business identifiers that we specified when we designed our dimensions in Chapter 4. They identify the dimension record for this cube record and the surrogate identifier will be used as the foreign key to actually link to the appropriate dimension record in the database. Let's take a look at these attributes for the dimensions.

For the PRODUCT dimension, we have seen three attributes earlier that are product related — PRODUCT_NAME, PRODUCT_SKU, and PRODUCT. If we were to open our PRODUCT dimension in the Table Editor to view its attributes, we wouldn't see any attributes with exactly these names. The Warehouse Builder has provided us with attributes that represent the corresponding attributes from the dimension, but with a slightly different naming scheme. The PRODUCT_NAME and PRODUCT_SKU attributes correspond to the NAME and SKU attributes from the dimension that are the business identifiers we defined. The PRODUCT attribute corresponds to the ID attribute that was created automatically for us as the surrogate identifier for the dimension. It prefixes the name of the dimension onto the name of the attribute for the business identifiers and uses the name of the dimension as the surrogate identifier. The same name can be used for attributes in more than one dimension included in a cube so it does this renaming scheme to make the names unique and to tell which dimension they correspond to.

> Another reason dimension attributes are renamed in the cube is that the underlying implementation for the cube in the database uses relational tables when ROLAP is selected for the storage option, and the database will not allow the same name to be used for more than one column in a table.
>
> **Renaming dimension attributes**
>
> The names for dimension attributes in cubes that OWB comes up with can be changed if we desire. We would just have to click on the name in the cube operator in the mapping and view the Property Inspector window. We could type in a new name for the Business name and/or the Physical name. Of course, we would have to make sure we didn't choose something already taken. But if we do, the Warehouse builder will definitely let us know immediately by popping up an error dialog box, and will change the name right back to what it was and give us another chance.

For the STORE dimension, we identified NAME and STORE_NUMBER as the business identifiers. Looking at the list of attributes for the STORE dimension that OWB created for us, we see STORE_NAME and STORE_STORE_NUMBER. Remember about the prefixing of the dimension name. In most cases that will work out OK, but in some cases where we might have included the dimension name as a part of our attribute name in the dimension (as we did for the STORE_NUMBER), we will end up with the dimension name repeated twice. It doesn't hurt anything to leave it as is; but if we want to change it, we can simply use our tip above about editing the name. Let's go ahead and make that change, changing both the Business Identifier (what the attribute is known by in the design) and the Physical Identifier (what the attribute will be known by physically in the database when deployed). So now we have STORE_NUMBER instead of STORE_STORE_NUMBER. We also have a third attribute, which we recall is for the surrogate identifier. It is named for the dimension, which is STORE in this case.

Another clue that can help us figure out what attribute is what is to look at the type that was defined for the attribute. The type icons just to the right of the name in the Cube Operator show us that the STORE and PRODUCT attributes are numeric. From our dimension design we know that the ID surrogate identifier was also defined as numeric.

The third dimension we have defined for our cube is the DATE_DIM dimension. In this chapter, we have been focusing mainly on the PRODUCT and STORE dimensions because we had to define them ourselves, but we still have to work with the DATE_DIM dimension because it's also a part of the cube. We can see only one attribute defined for it, a date field. There is no surrogate identifier created for a Time Dimension so the only attribute for the DATE_DIM dimension will be the business identifier, DATE_DIM_DAY_START_DATE. We discussed this lack of a surrogate identifier back when we were looking at the date dimension back in Chapter 4.

Let's verify the business identifier for the DATE_DIM dimension by opening it in the data object editor for a dimension. To open it in the editor, navigate in the Design Center to **ACME_DWH | Dimensions | DATE_DIM** and double-click to open it. Looking at the **Attributes** tab, we see that there is a business identifier called **DAY_START_DATE** as shown in the following screenshot:

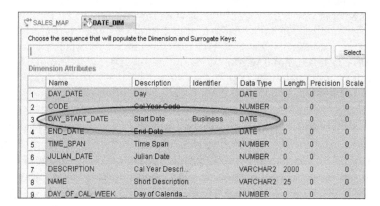

Scrolling that window down a little further would reveal actually three other business identifiers that can be used also, one each for the calendar month start date, the calendar quarter start date, and the calendar year start date. The day start date is the one it uses to link to the cube because when we defined the cube, the DAY level was the level specified for referencing the DATE_DIM dimension. If we had specified the **CALENDAR_MONTH, CALENDAR_QUARTER** or **CALENDAR_YEAR** levels to map to the cube, it would have used the business identifier from one of those levels.

Measures and other attributes in the cube

Two of the remaining attributes we can see in the SALES cube are the measures we defined for our cube—the quantity of the items sold and the dollar amount of the sale. We specified these names explicitly in the **Cube Wizard** when we defined our cube in *Chapter 4*, so they appear here as we named them.

We can see one final attribute that we haven't accounted for yet, and that is called ACTIVE_DATE. It's created automatically for us and is designed to support Type 2 **Slowly Changing Dimensions (SCD)**. It is used as the time to determine the active record in a Type 2 SCD. This is a more advanced topic and there is a more thorough explanation of this field in the *Oracle Warehouse Builder Users Guide*. However, you'll have to look back to the documentation for the 11.1 version of OWB since the 11.2 version appears to have a documentation bug, in that it has left out the explanation of this field. The 11.1 users guide is at the following URL: http://download. oracle.com/docs/cd/B28359_01/owb.111/b31278/toc.htm. If you would like more information about this field, read Chapter 17 in that guide on Source and Target operators where the Cube operator is discussed. For our purposes, we don't need to do anything with it as we have no Type 2 SCDs. If we don't map anything to this field, the Warehouse Builder will simply populate it using the SYSDATE Oracle function, which sets it to the current system date/time.

Mapping values to cube attributes

Now that we've taken a look at the attributes in our cube, we need to turn our attention to getting values mapped to them. We'll begin by mapping values for the measures because they are the simplest, and then proceed to map values for the two dimensions we created mappings for earlier, the PRODUCT and STORE, then we'll do the DATE_DIM dimension last.

Mapping measures' values to a cube

The measures that get mapped to a cube are most often numbers, so we don't have to be concerned with the TRIM and UPPER operators for them. Sometimes we may need to do calculations on values from input before storing them in output, but in our case now we just want to map the values from the input as they are. The SALE_QUANTITY from our POS_TRANS_STAGE table is going to provide the value for the QUANTITY in the SALES cube, and the SALE_DOLLAR_AMOUNT is going to supply the value for the SALES_AMOUNT attribute.

We'll drag a line directly from SALE_QUANTITY to QUANTITY, and another line directly from SALE_DOLLAR_AMOUNT to SALES_AMOUNT. This completes the measures. We saw earlier that the ACTIVE_DATE attribute didn't need anything mapped to it, so we'll move right to the dimensions.

Mapping PRODUCT and STORE dimension values to the cube

When mapping values for a dimension in a cube, we only need to concern ourselves with mapping the business identifiers. The Warehouse Builder will take care of the lookup to determine the identifier to fill in for the key value (surrogate identifier), so we don't have to worry about it. We get this for free by using OWB's Cube and Dimension operators where we'd have to do a manual lookup if we were to use regular Table operators.

So for the PRODUCT dimension-related attribute values, we have the PRODUCT_NAME and PRODUCT_SKU to which we need to map values to. We can leave the PRODUCT attribute alone as it will be populated automatically behind the scenes based on a lookup using the values we provide for name and SKU.

> The PRODUCT_NAME and PRODUCT_SKU attributes were chosen as business identifiers because they uniquely identify a single product. No two products in the ACME Toys and Gizmos company inventory are assigned the same name and SKU. This is why they can be used here to look up the dimension record key for us.

Looking back at our source table now, which is the POS_TRANS_STAGE mapping table, we need to find the name and SKU attributes to map to the corresponding attributes in the cube.

> Here it's very important to make sure whether there were any transformations applied to the values when mapping them to the dimension in the dimension mapping. If there were transformations, the same transformations need to be applied here to ensure a match will be made.
>
> If we had a name in mixed case and stored it in the dimension using the UPPER transformation, but used the value without applying the UPPER to it for a lookup, we would not get a match.

Earlier in this chapter where we mapped these fields in the dimension mappings, we decided we would apply a TRIM and UPPER to them before storing. So this is what we'll need here also. Our Mapping Editor must be already open from when we dragged in the source and target operators. So let's now drag a Transformation Operator to our mapping and make it a **TRIM**, and drag a second Transformation Operator to our mapping and make it an **UPPER**. We'll connect the **PRODUCT_ NAME** from our source to the input of the **TRIM**, the output of the **TRIM** to the input of the **UPPER**, and the output of the **UPPER** to the **PRODUCT_NAME** attribute in the cube. The PRODUCT_SKU attribute needs to be mapped in the same way to the PRODUCT_SKU attribute of the SALES cube.

We'll do the same steps for the STORE_NUMBER and STORE_NAME fields from input to the same named attributes in the cube. This will take care of these two dimensions. The PRODUCT and STORE attributes in the cube will be automatically populated with the key value for the corresponding dimension record. Finally, we'll look at the DATE_DIM dimension values for mapping.

Mapping DATE_DIM values to the cube

We saw earlier that the DATE_DIM_DAY_START_DATE was the business identifier value for the DATE_DIM dimension, so we need to map a value to it. Looking at our POS_TRANS_STAGE mapping table for input, the only date-related value we have is the SALE_DATE field so that is what we will use to map to the DATE_DIM_DAY_START_ DATE field. Since this is a date field, trims and upper functions have no effect on it so we could just drag it directly to the cube and be done; however there would be a slight problem. An Oracle DATE value has both a time of day and a date value associated with it and if the time values don't exactly match between two DATE values, there will not be a match even if the date value matches.

 To read more about the Oracle DATE data type, consult the *Oracle SQL Language Reference* at the following URL:
http://download.oracle.com/docs/cd/E11882_01/
server.112/e17118/sql_elements001.htm#sthref154

As it is clear that we will not be able to connect the SALE_DATE directly to the cube, we must do something to it first to fix that time issue but how will we know what time is being used so we can make sure they match? The answer lies in the fact that we can actually remove the time value from a DATE using the trunc() function (for truncating a number or date). That function when applied to a DATE value doesn't physically remove the time portion from the value but just sets it to a default of 00:00. That is how the dates are all stored in the **DATE_DIM** dimension. The simple solution then is to just apply the trunc() function to the **SALE_DATE** value before mapping it to the cube.

The `trunc()` function is a function just like `trim()` or `upper()` so we could use the Transformation operator and specify `trunc()` as the function but we're going to do it a little differently this time to gain some exposure to another commonly used Transformation operator we haven't used yet and that is the **Expression operator**. We discussed expressions back in Chapter 5 when being introduced to the main operators that are available. We said then that these functions like `trunc()` could be done in expressions and that is what we're going to do now.

Mapping an Expression operator

Let's now turn our attention back to the Mapping Editor and map the SALE_DATE to the cube using this expression. To include an expression in our mapping, the Mapping Editor provides an **Expression** operator in the **Palette** window as shown in the following screenshot:

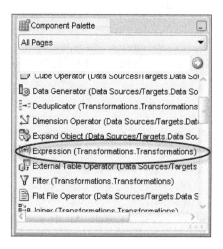

The steps to perform for the required expression are:

1. Drag the **Expression** operator onto our mapping, and drop it between our source and target operators. Initially, it doesn't display any defined attributes, but it does have two groups defined — an input group, INGRP1 — and an output group, OUTGRP1. Expression operators are for defining any type of valid Oracle PL/SQL expression and, therefore, provide us tremendous flexibility in defining our own transformations, which we will do now.

2. Let's drag the **SALE_DATE** from the **POS_TRANS_STAGE** mapping table to the **INGRP1** of the **EXPRESSION** operator we just dropped into our mapping. This will now make the SALE_DATE available to us to use in the expression.

3. First, we need to create an output attribute that will hold the results of our expression. It will be used to map to the cube. Right-click on **OUTGRP2** and select **Open Details...** from the pop-up menu or double click on it.

4. This will display an **Editor** window for the expression, so we'll click on the **Output Attributes** entry on the left because we need to add an attribute as output. It is initially blank as no attributes are defined, so we will enter an attribute name into the first row under the **Attribute** column. Let's call it **DAY_DATE** to reflect what it is for.

5. We haven't entered an expression yet to tell it what we actually want this operator to do. We'll click in the box under the **Expression** column and it changes to allow us to enter text into that block. We could just enter it directly. For simple expressions this works well, but for most expressions we'll want to make use of the powerful **Expression Builder** tool that the Warehouse Builder provides to construct expressions. We can launch the **Expression Builder** by clicking on the button with three dots to the right of the **Expression** input field that appeared when we clicked on it. The **Expression Builder** dialog box appears and we can create our expression. We've seen this before in the previous chapter when we were specifying the join condition to use for the Joiner operator in our STAGE_MAP. It is basically the same dialog box, as join conditions are also simply expressions. We'll type the following into the expression window labeled **Expression for DAY_ DATE** to begin our expression:

   TRUNC(

6. The next item to enter is the name of the input to use and for that we want to specify the SALE_DATE input attribute. This is the real benefit of using the Expression Builder. We can now just double-click on the **SALE_DATE** attribute under the **INGRP1** heading in the left pane to enter it into our expression at the point where the cursor is currently located, which should be right after the last open parenthesis we entered. We don't have to worry about using the correct syntax to specify it, as it gets entered for us.

 We can notice a feature of the Expression Builder that when the cursor is just to the right of that last parenthesis, it turns red. This is the bracket matching feature of the Expression Builder. It helps us make sure we have corresponding closing parentheses for any open parentheses. When it finds a matching closing parenthesis, it will highlight them both in yellow.

7. We'll now finish entering our expression by typing in the following text which is just a closing parenthesis to close out the expression. Alternatively, we could just click the right bracket button in the list of buttons to enter it.

8. We'll click on the **Validate** button to make sure our expression is correctly entered and our **Expression Builder** window will now look like the following screenshot:

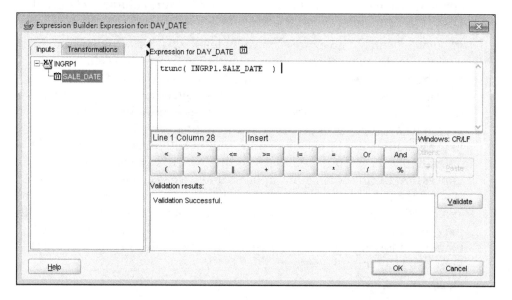

9. We'll click on the **OK** button to close the **Expression Builder** and the expression editor now shows an expression filled in for the **DAY_DATE** attribute.

10. We'll click the **OK** button to close the **Expression Editor** and our **Expression operator** will now be complete.

11. The final step is to connect our expression with the cube by dragging a line from the **DAY_DATE** output attribute of the expression to the **DATE_DIM_DAY_START_DATE** attribute.

With that we have completed mapping all the attributes that are needed for our cube. Our mapping should now look similar to the following with all our transformation operators collapsed into their icon view and the **EXPRESSION** operator left open:

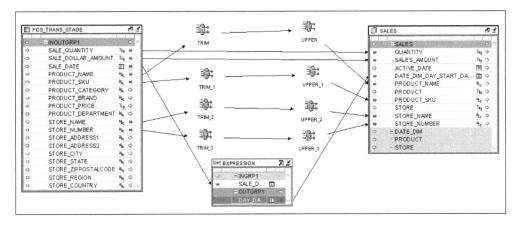

Now that we have used an **Expression** operator let's discuss briefly the use of it to replace individual Transformation operators like **TRIM** and **UPPER**. We mentioned that in Chapter 5 when first discussing **Expression** operators and then briefly alluded to it earlier in this chapter for helping de-clutter our mapping. We only created one input and one output attribute in the above expression operator but it can hold as many attributes as we need. We could create one input and output attribute for every source attribute that we needed to apply a trim and/or upper function to and then define the expression to use as the TRIM() and/or UPPER() SQL function. The procedure would be similar to what we walked through above but just repeat steps 2 through 9 for each source attribute we need to apply the trim and upper functions to. The expression we'd enter in the Expression Builder would be similar to the following using an attribute in the STORE mapping as an example:

```
trim(upper( INGRP1.STORE_NAME )
```

It would look like the following if just using the TRIM() function:

```
trim( INGRP1.STORE_ADDRESS1 )
```

Our dimension mappings were completed earlier in the chapter, so we now have all the mappings completed that we'll need to populate our data warehouse. This means we are now ready to deploy them to the database and try them out. This will be the main topic of the next chapter. Let's make sure we save our work before continuing.

Features and benefits of OWB

Before we move on to the next chapter, let's take a moment to recapitulate some of the features that the Oracle Warehouse Builder provides to us to make our job easier. This is why we made the choices we did for our design and implementation. By providing us with the option to implement our cubes and dimensions either relationally with ROLAP or fully multi-dimensionally with MOLAP, OWB allows us to design one way in OWB and implement either way in the database with a simple change of a storage option.

- By providing us the **ROLAP option**, the Oracle Warehouse Builder opens to us the design features of cubes and dimensions even though we'll be implementing them relationally with tables in our database. Choosing that option rather than just implementing tables directly saves us from having to worry about dimension keys, sequences to populate them, and providing lookups of dimension record keys to fill in for our cube. When loading a dimension, all we have to do is map data to it and it handles constructing the levels and assigning keys automatically. When mapping to the cube, all we have to do is specify business identifier attributes in our dimensions and map values to them in the cube. The rest is all handled for us.

  The underlying tables and sequences are all built automatically for us, so we need not be concerned with building any tables or sequences.

- The **Expression Builder** provides us a powerful tool to use for interactively building expressions.

- Support for **Slowly Changing Dimensions and Orphan Management** (late arriving facts) is built in with the Enterprise ETL option. Although we didn't make use of that feature in this introductory book, the support is there if we need it and have paid for it when we build more advanced data warehouses and want to implement SCDs.

These are just some of the benefits the Warehouse Builder provides to us and were the basis for many of our decisions throughout the book regarding how we chose to implement our data warehouse using OWB.

Summary

Now we are real close to actually having a data warehouse built in our database. We've completed all the mappings that we will need for the Warehouse Builder to create the code that will run to actually pull data from our source system, load our staging table, and then load our target data warehouse structure from our staging table.

We've seen how to use Transformation operators to apply functions to our data to change it before loading. We've also seen the Expression operator for entering custom expressions. We've taken a look at how to connect them together with source and target operators to complete a mapping and successfully validate them.

Now we're ready to deploy these mappings to the database and execute them to actually load our data, which we will do in the next chapter.

8
Validating, Generating, Deploying, and Executing Objects

We have reached the last step in the process of building our data warehouse. We've done a large amount of work so far, which includes designing target schemas, creating objects in the Warehouse Builder, and creating mappings to load data into our target. However, we have yet to actually create a single real database object. What we have is the complete design stored in the Warehouse Builder. Let's think of ourselves as architects of new houses; only instead of designing a house, we're designing a data warehouse. Before any house can be physically built, someone has to design it and create a model of the house that the builders will then use for construction. That's what we've been doing up until this point, that is, creating the model of our data warehouse.

Now we are at the point where the model is complete and we're ready to actually build the data warehouse in an actual database, and load data into it. So, we get to be the builders also and not just the architects and that is what this chapter is all about. The process of building the data warehouse from our model in the Warehouse Builder involves the following four steps:

- **Validating**: Checking objects and mappings for errors
- **Generating**: Creating the code that will be executed to create the objects and run the mappings
- **Deploying**: Creating the physical objects in the database from the logical objects we designed in the Warehouse Builder
- **Executing**: Executing the logic that is found in the deployed mappings for mappings and transformations

The first three steps—validating, generating, and deploying—generally go together as all objects and mappings are deployed. A deployment will automatically do a validation and generation first before deploying. The fourth step—execution—is an independent process that is performed on those objects that contain ETL logic and mappings after they've been deployed. It doesn't happen for everything that we design in the Design Center. The Design Center has menu entries that will allow us to validate, generate, and deploy objects, but not execute them. We will be introduced to a new interface called the **Control Center Manager**, which is the tool for controlling the deployment of objects and execution of mappings.

 Throughout the remaining chapter, the word "objects" will generally be used to refer to any type of object or mapping that can be built in the Warehouse Builder.

We will discuss each of the four processes separately in more detail in this chapter although we'll frequently find ourselves doing just deployments and executions, as the deployment process includes a validation and generation. We need to understand each of these processes, so let's get started by talking more about the validation of objects and mappings. The specific main topics we'll cover are listed next:

- Validating
  - Validating in the design center
  - Using the toolbar icon in the Mapping Editor

- Generating
  - Generating in the Design Center
  - Generating using the icon from the mapping editor
  - Default operating mode of the mapping
  - Selecting the generation style

- Deploying
  - The Control Center Service
  - Deploying in the Design Center and Data Object Editor
  - The Control Center Manager
    - The Control Center Manager window overview
      - The Object Details window
      - The Control Center Jobs window
      - Deploying in the Control Center Manager

- Deploying and executing remaining objects
  - ○ Deployment order
  - ○ Execution order

Validating

Error checking is what validation is for. The process of validation is all about making sure the objects and mappings we've defined in the Warehouse Builder have no obvious errors in design.

Let's discuss how we go about performing a validation on an object we've created in the Warehouse Builder. There are a number of places we can perform a validation. One of them is the main Design Center.

Validating in the Design Center

There is a context menu associated with everything we create. You can access it on any object in the Design Center by right-clicking on the object of your choice. Let's take a look at this by launching our Design Center, connecting as our **ACMEOWB** user, and then expanding our ACME_DW_PROJECT. Let's find our staging table, POS_TRANS_STAGE, and use it to illustrate the validation of an object from the Design Center. As we can recall, this table is under the ACME_DWH module in the **Oracle** node and right-clicking on it will present us with the following pop-up menu:

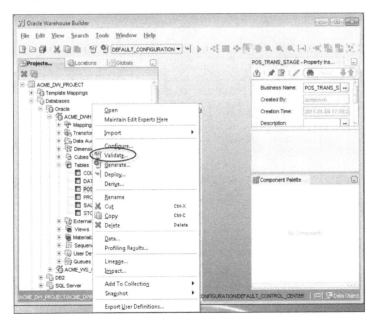

The **Validate...** entry has been highlighted. If we click on it, it will perform the validation of the metadata entered for the object and will present us with the results in the **Log** window on the **Results** tab. It will look similar to the following:

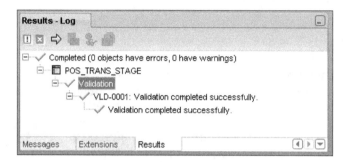

This window is resizable and the entries have all been expanded so that we can focus on the important parts. If the Log window is not visible, it can be displayed from the **View** main menu entry by selecting **Log** or by using the *Ctrl-Shift-L* key combination. Our POS_TRANS_STAGE table has validated successfully. But if we had any warnings or errors, they would appear in this window.

One more option for invoking the validation command on an object is to click the validate icon in the toolbar when the object is selected or opened for editing. The icon is highlighted in the following image for reference:

The validation will result in one of the following three possibilities:

- The validation completes successfully with no warnings and/or errors as this one did

- The validation completes successfully, but with some non-fatal warnings

- The validation fails due to one or more errors having been found

The icons on the toolbar in the upper left of the results window have options for viewing all objects, just warnings, or just errors. The yellow exclamation point is selected to view warnings and the red x is selected to view errors. They are both selected by default which means it will display all objects that have been validated, whether or not there were warnings or errors. We have the option to validate more than one object at a time by holding down the *Ctrl* key and clicking on several objects in the Design Center, and then with the *Ctrl* key still held down, right-clicking on one of them and then selecting **Validate**. All the selected objects will be validated and the results for all of them will appear in the **Results** tab of the Log window. If we select **Warnings (yellow exclamation point)**, only the objects that have warnings will be displayed, and if we select **Errors (red X)**, only the objects with errors will be displayed.

If we have warnings or errors that we need to fix, we can double-click on the object name in the **Results** tab of the **Log** window to launch the appropriate editor on the object – the data object editor or the Mapping Editor. With one of these editors, we can make any modifications and revalidate the object.

We can close the **Log** window now before moving on to discuss validating from the editors or we can minimize it. To close it we can click on **X** in the window header, or use the *Shift+ESC* key combination. To minimize it, just click the minimize button in the upper right corner of the window. The Log window will reappear automatically the next time we perform a task like validation that requires it to display a message to us. At any time we can also open it from the **View** menu as we've mentioned before.

We mentioned the icon on the main **Design Center** toolbar that can be clicked on to validate a data object or mapping if one is selected in the project navigator. For a data object that icon will behave just as if we'd selected Validate from the pop-up menu whether the item is open in an editor or not. However, if we're editing a mapping and have it open in an editor window when we press the icon, the validation will display its results differently.

Validating using the toolbar icon in the Mapping Editor

Let's double-click on the STORE_MAP mapping name in the Design Center to launch the Mapping Editor so that we can discuss validation in the editor. We can press the validate icon on the **Main** toolbar, which is circled in the above image of the toolbar icons.

When we validate a mapping using that icon while the object is open in the editor, we do not get the **Results** tab in the Log window as we did when validating from the Design Center without the object open in an editor. Here we get another window created, the **Generation Results** window, which appears in the **Log** window. The window that is produced will look similar to the following:

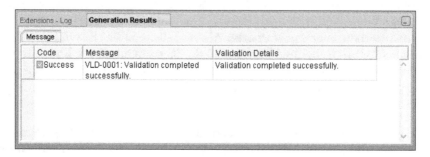

In many cases, the error message will be long and the window will display the message truncated in the window. We can double-click on the message and it makes the box containing the message expand until the entire message is visible.

A curious thing we'll find about validating is that the log window may appear and then disappear when it's all done. That's a feature of the new interface. It just means the log window has been minimized and it will display it temporarily to alert us that a message was logged. We can hover the mouse pointer over the minimized **Log** window and it will appear again. We can make it stay visible by clicking the **Restore** button on the left side of the window.

Another curious thing is the title says **Generation** instead of **Validation** in the results window. It's where both the validation and generation results will appear. As we'll soon see when we discuss the process of generation, it is closely tied to validation. Indeed, when we generate an object one of the steps it performs is validating the object. The Generation Results window is fulfilling two purposes here, displaying the validation results and displaying the results of the generation when that option is selected.

That is validation of mappings. We can go through our remaining objects and mappings now and validate them. The order we validate objects in is not critical. Unless we've made a typographical error, missed a selection we should have made, missed a column we should have added, or something like that, all the objects and mappings should validate successfully or have warnings that can be safely ignored.

This process of validation only checks the logical design within the metadata in the Warehouse Builder. It can't check for any errors that might occur when the object is deployed and/or executed in the database. We haven't got to that point yet. We don't want to get the attitude that our objects and mappings are perfect just because they have passed validation. This is only the first step.

The validations can even be misleading between objects. The STORE dimension would validate successfully if we removed the DESCRIPTION attribute that we talked about in Chapter 4. However, the STORE_MAP that used the dimension would give the error we talked about without the DESCRIPTION there to map to. So, validation is just one step along the way to getting a working data warehouse, but doesn't guarantee that there won't be further errors at a later point in the process.

When we are satisfied that everything is ready, we can move on to the generation step.

A final tip about the **Log** window — As each object is validated, it will add a new **Results** tab to the log window. Just close them by clicking the X on the tab if they start getting too cluttered, especially if they are all success messages.

Generating

This step can happen in conjunction with the validation step as we've discussed previously, but the Warehouse Builder does provide a separate menu entry to select for generating. We will discuss it here to see what it's all about. Let's talk about generation; and no, we're not talking about baby boomers, Gen X-ers, Gen Y-ers, Millenials, or whatever they come up with for future generations. Here we're talking about the other meaning of the word, which is the act or process of generating. Dictionary.com says to generate means *to bring into existence; cause to be; produce*. With the generation step in the Warehouse Builder, we are going to bring into existence the code that we need to use to build and load our data warehouse. The objects — dimensions, cube, tables, and so on — will have **SQL Data Definition Language** (or **DDL**) statements produced, which when executed will build the objects in the database. The mappings will have the PL/SQL code produced that when its run, will load the objects. The Warehouse Builder can also create configuration files for the SQL*Loader utility to load data or ABAP scripts, which are for interfacing to a SAP system. We're not going to make use of the SQL*Loader utility and we're not going to interface with a SAP system, so we won't need those options. We are going to use DDL and PL/SQL code for our project.

Generating in the Design Center

When we generate an object or mapping in the Design Center using the popup menu on the object name in the **Projects Navigator**, we'll get the same **Results** tab appearing in the **Log** window as we got when we validated, but in this case we'll have some extra information displayed. Let's go to the Design Center now and generate the code for the POS_TRANS_STAGE table. We'll right-click on it and select **Generate...** from the pop-up menu. Just as for validation above, we can also click on the table name and click the generate icon in the main toolbar. It is just to the right of the validate icon that we discussed above. It will present us with the following **Results** tab, which looks very similar to the one we got when we validated it:

There is the list of the objects that we've generated; in this case only one appears. Notice that the validation messages appear here when doing a generation. The messages that would appear when doing a generation are really validation messages from the validation that is automatically done whenever we choose to generate.

When we expand all the entries in the main **Results** tab as in the above image we can see something extra this time that we didn't see when we just validated. There is an extra entry called **Scripts** that was not there before. This is where we can view the script that was generated, and which will create this object for us in the database. For a database object, a DDL script is generated for us. We see that it has generated a DDL script called POS_TRANS_STAGE.ddl as shown above.

Let's click on the script name and then click the **View Script** button, the circled one on the left in the above image, or right click the name and select **Go to Source** from the pop-up menu or just double click on it to view the script. The circled icon on the right will allow us to save the script to a file if desired. We'll be presented with an editor window displaying the code as shown next after clicking the **View Script** button:

We can see that it has generated an SQL CREATE TABLE statement for us. It contains the name of our POS_TRANS_STAGE table along with column names and types as they are defined in the Warehouse Builder. Since this is an editor window, certain tasks are available to us:

- Saving this code to a file (select **File…Save as File** from the main menu)
- Copying portions of the code and pasting them into another window using the **Edit** main menu
- Searching through the code for text strings using the **Search** main menu

However, we can see if we try to make changes to anything in the window that the script is displayed in a read-only mode. In other words, we are not allowed to make any changes to it. It is code that is automatically generated by the Warehouse Builder, so there is no way for us to edit it directly.

To deploy our objects and mappings to create and populate our data warehouse, we really need not be concerned with what the code looks like. This is because the Warehouse Builder takes care of generating it all for us. However, we're checking this out for the first time to get an appreciation of what it is doing for us behind the scenes. The data object code is not complicated in this case, but let's take a look at the code for the mapping to populate this data object. We can close out the code editor window for the POS_TRANS_STAGE table.

We'll right-click on the STAGE_MAP mapping in the Design Center and select **Generate** from the pop-up menu or we can click the generate icon in the main toolbar. There may be something different that is noticeable on the **Scripts** entry in the **Results** tab of the log window, depending on whether we've generated and actually deployed this mapping before:

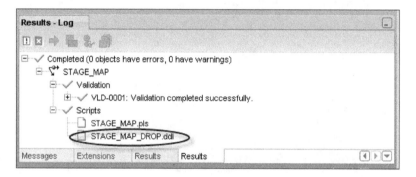

There may be an extra script that gets generated for us here to do a drop of the object first. If we've deployed the mapping previously and have now made some edits to it to regenerate and redeploy, it defaults to a replace option for the deploy action and creates the script to drop the mapping along with any temporary tables that got generated to support the execution of the mapping.

Whether we've deployed the mapping or not, we still get the code generated that will create the mapping code for us in the database. This is the STAGE_MAP.pls package that appears in the window. We'll discuss the deployment actions a little later in the chapter. If we view this code, we'll see that it is more complicated than the DDL script that was generated for our previous table. Let's double click on the STAGE_MAP.pls line to view the code. The same editor window is used to view this mapping code as we saw before when we viewed the DDL script for the table. However, the code is quite different as it is PL/SQL code as shown in the following image:

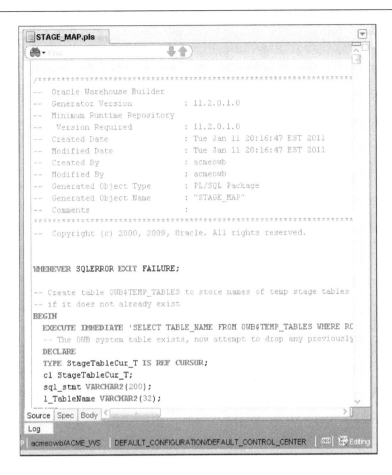

For a mapping, the code that is generated is a PL/SQL Package. A package is a code construct that contains variables and procedures to perform some work in the database. It is a way to group variables and procedures together that all contribute to the performance of a particular task. In this case, the task is the loading of the POS_ TRANS_STAGE table. All the code necessary to accomplish that task is contained in this package's script. We have the same features available to us for copying, searching, and saving as a file and the script is also read-only, as it was for the table object we displayed previously. Unlike the DDL script we viewed for a table object previously, this one has three tabs available to us labeled **Source**, **Spec,** and **Body** which are visible at the bottom of the code viewing window. This is PL/SQL package code and a package is composed of a specification portion (the description of what is in the package) and the body of the package (the actual code that does the work). With these tabs we are able to jump right to the specification portion or right to the body portion or just view the entire package source script as a whole.

If we scroll this window all the way to the bottom, we see that the Warehouse Builder has generated about 4,500 lines of code.

 Line numbers can be displayed in the editor window by right clicking the mouse along the left hand edge of the window between the thin vertical line and the edge of the window and selecting **Toggle Line Numbers**.

This is much more than it generated for the table object previously, and makes us real glad we didn't have to write all that code ourselves.

This completes our look at the process we would follow to generate our objects and mappings from the Design Center without having the objects open in an editor window. If we were to encounter any errors that needed to be fixed, we could jump to the appropriate editor by double-clicking on the object or mapping name in the **Results** tab of the **Log** window.

As with validation, there is an icon available on the main Design Center toolbar that will invoke the generation process on objects and mappings. As long as the object is not being edited it will behave just as if the validate or generate menu selection had been made from the popup menu; however, if we're editing a mapping at the time we click the generate icon, it will behave differently from the pop-up menu. So let's take a look at that now after closing out the script window and the **Results** log window.

Generating using the icon from the mapping editor

When we generate a data object using the toolbar icon, it will display the results in the **Generation Results** window within the log window just as it did for the validation. The same **Generation Results** window in which the validation results appeared will be used for the actual generation results.

Let's open the Mapping Editor on the STAGE_MAP mapping now. From the Design Center, we can just double-click on the STAGE_MAP mapping to launch the Mapping Editor and load the STAGE_MAP mapping. The process for generating the mapping using the icon in the toolbar is the same as for validation, but we just select the **Generate** icon instead of Validate from the **main toolbar** as shown next:

Looking at the **Generation Results** window now, we can see that we have additional information displayed. Instead of the validation messages appearing in the window, we now see the script that was generated. We also have a couple of extra drop-down menus, which we didn't have when we were just validating. An example of what we'll see is shown next:

We have two tabs available in the window, a **Script** tab that displays the script and a **Message** tab that displays the validation messages. 1Looking at the Script tab we can see that it is just a view only window. There is no saving of the code or searching through the code like we could do when viewing the generated code in a full viewer window. The reason can be found in this comment we see in the script window as a note:

```
/****************************************************************
****************
-- Note: This generated code is for demonstration purposes only and
may
--        not be deployable.
****************************************************************
****************/
```

The code generated for a mapping is far more complex than the DDL code generated for data objects as we saw when we looked at it from the Design Center. One of the main reasons the code for mappings is so complex is because we have five options to choose from for the **default operating mode** of the mapping when we execute it, and it has to be able to support all five. There are three operating modes the mapping can run in, and two that indicate failover options for switching between them. One of the drop-down menus at the top of the **Script** tab window is labeled **Operating mode**, and allows us to view the code for each of the operating modes separately.

For this reason, some different functionality is available to us in the **Script** tab and it displays code that is not quite the complete script we saw in the Design Center code view window. If we scroll down the **Script** tab, we'll see that it is not displaying as many lines as were displayed when viewing the code in the code view window. That is what the note we mentioned previously is referring to. Viewing the script from the Design Center in a code view window shows us the complete script, which includes support for the code of all operating modes. As we mentioned before, if we want to see that, we can click on the script name in the **Results** tab and then click the **View Script** icon in the **Results** toolbar, or right click and select **Go to Source** from the popup menu.

Default operating mode of the mapping

The Warehouse Builder provides three possible modes that the mapping code can run in when executing in the database. In addition, it also provides two options for failover execution should one mode have errors. These modes are based on the performance we expect from the mapping, the amount of auditing data we require, and how we designed the mapping. The *Warehouse Builder Data Modeling, ETL and Data Quality Guide* has a much more detailed discussion of this topic in Chapter 10 — Understanding Performance and Advanced ETL Concepts. (http://download.oracle.com/docs/cd/E11882_01/owb.112/e10935/etl_performance.htm#BBAHFHBC) For more advanced mappings, we'll definitely want to be familiar with concepts from that chapter. But for our purpose here, we'll only cover a very high-level view with just enough information to explain the different options we have in the Script tab of the **Generation Results** window for viewing the code.

The three modes are as follows:

- Set-based
- Row-based
- Row-based (target only)

In set-based mode, the Warehouse Builder will generate a single SQL statement that performs all the operations of our mapping in one statement. It processes the data as a single set of data. This is good for performance, but the drawback is that runtime auditing information is limited. If any errors are generated, it is not able to tell us which row generated the error. We can view the code that is set-based by selecting **SET_BASED** in the **Script** tab from the **Operating Mode** drop-down menu.

In row-based mode, the Warehouse Builder generates code to process the data row by row. It uses a combination of SQL Cursors and PL/SQL code. It does not provide as big a performance benefit as the set-based mode, but we gain much greater auditing capability of the execution results. There are also additional parameters that can be set to improve the performance of this mode, which are documented in the User's Guide and online help if we choose to use this mode. We can select **ROW_BASED** from the drop-down menu to view the row-based code.

The final of the three options is row-based (target only) mode. This option creates a SQL select cursor and tries to include as many operations as it can into that cursor to process the source data and operations on it as a set, but then writes the rows to the target one row at a time. This will limit the auditing available for input and operations, but provides greater auditing of the output to the target. We can select **ROW_BASED_TARGET_ONLY** from the drop-down menu to view the code for the option.

The following two additional options for operating modes are available, which are based on the previous three:

- Set-based fail over to row-based
- Set-based fail over to row-based (target only)

These options are used to run the mapping in set-based mode, but if an error occurs, try the mapping in row-based mode—either regular or target only. We can view the code for either of these options by selecting **SET_BASED_FAIL_OVER_TO_ROW_BASED** or **SET_BASED_FAIL_OVER_TO_ROW_BASED_TARGET_ONLY** from the drop-down menu.

Changing that drop-down menu does not change the actual mode that will be used to run the mapping. For that we have to view the configuration options for the mapping from the Design Center. The options are available via right-clicking a mapping in the **Projects Navigator** and selecting **Configure....** This will display the following window where we can see that the default operating mode set for our mapping is **Set based fail over to row based**. To see that, click the plus sign beside the **Runtime parameters** entry. This is the default that is set for all mappings, as shown next:

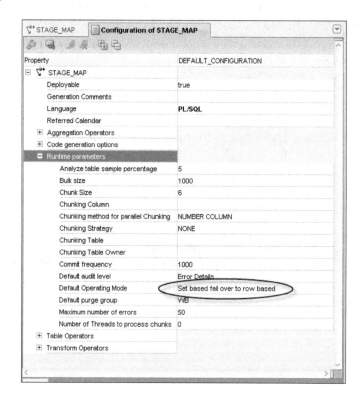

We will not have to modify any of these options for our mappings and so will not spend any more time with this window. More information about these options can be found in the Warehouse Builder Data Modeling, ETL, and Data Quality Guide in Chapter 10. We'll move on to discuss the other drop-down menu that appears in the **Script** tab of the **Mapping Editor Generation Results** window, the **Generation style** drop-down menu.

Selecting the generation style

The generation style has two options we can choose from, **Full** or **Intermediate**. The Full option will display the code for all operators in the complete mapping for the operating mode selected. The Intermediate option allows us to investigate code for subsets of the full mapping option. It displays code at the attribute group level of an individual operator. If no attribute group is selected when we select the intermediate option in the drop-down menu, we'll immediately get a message in the **Script** tab saying the following:

```
Please select an attribute group.
```

When we click on an attribute group in any operator on the mapping, the Script window immediately displays the code for setting the values of that attribute group. The following is an example of what we would see by clicking on the **INOUTGRP1** group of the **REGIONS** table operator:

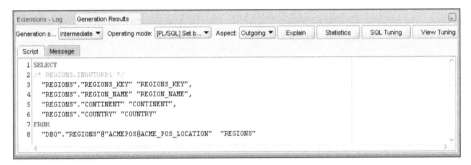

It is a standard SQL SELECT statement that has the four attributes of the REGIONS table selected. The FROM clause indicates that the source of the data for these attributes is the REGIONS table in the ACME_POS database at our location defined as ACME_POS_LOCATION. In Chapter 2, we discussed the non-Oracle Database module we created for the ACME POS transactional database. We called it ACME_POS with a location defined as ACME_POS_LOCATION. The Warehouse Builder implements this location as a database link in the Oracle Database and calls it ACMEPOS@ACME_POS_LOCATION. The ACMEPOS text string is from the service name we used to refer to the location and ACME_POS_LOCATION is the name we gave to the location. To reference a table in that database, the table name is prefixed to the database link name, which is separated by another @ symbol. To further specify the exact table, the schema name is prefixed to the table name separated by a period. Looking back at Chapter 2 where we defined the ACME_POS_LOCATION, we specified DBO as the schema name in the **Edit non-Oracle Location** dialog box along with ACMEPOS as the service name and ACME_POS_LOCATION as the location name. This is where all that information used in the previous script came from.

When we selected the **Intermediate generation** style, the drop-down menu and buttons on the right hand side of the window became active. We have a number of options for further investigation of the code that is generated, but these are beyond the scope of what we'll be covering in this book. One final point we'll make about these options is in reference to the drop-down menu labeled **Aspect**. When an attribute group is selected, it may be used as input, output, or both. This drop-down menu lets us see the code that is defined for either one of these options for an attribute group that has more than one of these options. If we select **Incoming**, we get to see what code selects the values that are used as input for the group. If we select **Outgoing**, we get to see the code that will select the values for output. There is another option that can appear in the menu, and that is **Loading**. If we click on the INOUTGRP1 attribute group of the POS_TRANS_STAGE mapping table operator, we'll have that option in addition to **Incoming** and **Outgoing**. This is the final target operator in the mapping, and so must actually load data into the target table. The loading aspect will show us the SQL INSERT statement that loads the data into the target table.

This concludes our discussion about generating code for mappings and objects. So let's close the Mapping Editor and proceed to the next step, which is to deploy our objects and mappings to the database.

Deploying

The process of deploying is where database objects are actually created and PL/SQL code is actually loaded and compiled in the target database. Up until this point, no objects exist in our target schema, ACME_DWH, in our Oracle database. Everything we've talked about so far about importing metadata for tables, defining objects, mappings, and so on has referred totally to the Warehouse Builder repository, where it keeps a record of everything we've defined so far in metadata. Not a single actual database object has been created yet. Everything we've done until now has been done entirely in the OWB Design Center client. But to perform the process of deployment, now we're going to have to communicate to the target database. For that we need to be introduced to the **Control Center Service**, which must be running for the deployments to function.

The Control Center Service

If we briefly look all the way back at Chapter 1, we talked about the architecture of the Warehouse Builder and looked at a diagram that laid out the main components of the Warehouse Builder software and where they were located—either on the client or on the server. The Control Center Service is a process that runs on the server and provides the interface to our target database for controlling the deployment process. It is also possible to run the Control Center Service on another remote computer to implement a remote runtime. If it's running in this configuration, it doesn't start automatically by default. So we would need to manually start it. It is available from the Windows **Start** menu as shown next:

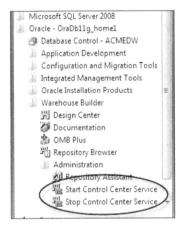

We will not need to run it because we're running locally on the same machine as the database is running, and will be interfacing with the Control Center Service that is running locally in the database. If we were to implement a remote runtime and had to run this **Start Control Center Service** menu entry, it would start up a command window with the window title Start Control Center Service and would pop-up a dialog box asking us for connection information for the OWBSYS schema in our database. We would enter the password, host name, and service name for connecting to that schema.

The local Control Center Manager on the database server is controlled using scripts, which are run in the database while connected as the OWBSYS user. The scripts are located in the ORACLE_HOME\owb\rtp\sql\ folder. They can be run using the SQL*Plus command-line utility for executing SQL commands and scripts. Open a command-prompt window and enter the following command to run it and connect to the OWBSYS schema:

```
sqlplus OWBSYS
```

Enter the password for OWBSYS when prompted, and then enter the following command at the SQL*Plus command prompt to display the status of the service:

`@ORACLE_HOME\owb\rtp\sql\show_service.sql`

Substitute your actual ORACLE_HOME location in the previous command.

A few of the other scripts available in the previous folder are as follows:

- `start_service.sql`: Starts the Control Center Service
- `stop_service.sql`: Stops the Control Center Service
- `service_doctor.sql`: Analyzes the state of the service and reports the status

The Control Center Service normally starts when the database starts up. So if we are running the database server locally, we don't need to bother with running any of the scripts. However, it is good to be informed should there be any problem in the future involving connections to the service. Let's give the Control Center Service some work to do now by doing an actual deployment from the Design Center.

Deploying in the Design Center and Data Object Editor

As with validation and generation, we can deploy objects and mappings from the Design Center. Let's deploy our POS_TRANS_STAGE table from the Design Center. We'll right-click on it and select **Deploy** from the pop-up menu. If the Control Center Service is not running for some reason, we'll be presented with an error dialog box as shown next:

If we get this pop-up window when we click on the **OK** button, we'll get another pop-up window prompting for connection information for the Control Center Service where we can provide connection information. That dialog box looks like the following:

The only items we can modify here are the **User Name** and **Password** to use. These items default to the repository workspace owner that we've been using all along to connect in the Design Center, and we should not change them. Mostly, this dialog box appears because the Control Center Service is not running, and not because of incorrect connection information. Let's take a quick look at where that connection information is specified. We'll press the **Cancel** button in the dialog box to close it if it appears.

The Control Center Service connection information is set in the **Design Center**, which is in the **Locations Navigator** window under the **Control Centers** entry. If we expand it, we can see that a default Control Center Service was created for us called DEFAULT_CONTROL_CENTER. We did not have to create it separately. If we double-click on this, we get a dialog box that shows the connection information. However, we're not able to edit anything in it. When this entry was created it was specified, and it can't be changed. Therefore, it is unlikely that incorrect connection information caused the Control Center Service error dialog box to appear. We could have more than one control center defined. But the default will work fine for us, so we will not modify it.

If our Control Center Service is running, which will usually be the case, we won't get the previous dialog boxes. However, we may get a dialog box telling us that our location is not registered.

The act of registering a location is to associate all the previous information with a location defined in the Warehouse Builder so that the Control Center Service knows how to find the location. The connection details in the dialog box are what it uses to connect to the location. Simply provide the password for the target schema and ensure that the rest of the information is correct, and then click on **OK**. The location will be registered and the object will deploy. We can register and un-register locations at any time by using the Control Center Manager. We'll be looking at the Control Center Manager very soon.

So, we have deployed our POS_TRANS_STAGE table in the Design Center. Assuming the Control Center Service is running and we don't get any of the previous dialog boxes, we will actually not get any dialog box when we deploy an object, unless we have set a certain option to tell the Warehouse Builder to display a dialog box upon completion of the deployment. If this option is not set (which is the default), it will not tell us whether the deployment succeeded or failed. If we want to see a completion message, we have to set this option in the preferences for the Design Center and tell it to show this message to us when the deployment is completed. We can set this option under the Tools menu entry by selecting the **Preferences...** menu entry. The resulting dialog box will look similar to the following, which has been scrolled down so that the needed entry is visible and the column has been expanded so that the whole description is visible. We need to check the box beside the option for displaying the completion status as follows:

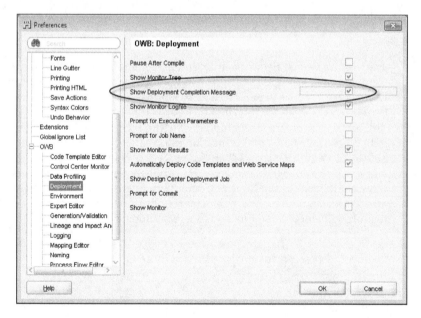

It will show us the completion message after this option has been checked, which will look similar to the following:

This shows us that the deployment processed successfully with no errors or warnings. But what if the count of errors or warnings was not zero? There would be nothing but a count that would display with this dialog box, so we need a feature to see what these warnings and error messages are. If we look at the Log window, we'll see that it has created a tab with some results of our deployment. The tab name will be named for the object we're deploying and it will look very similar to the results we viewed previously for validating and generating but with the addition of a new entry for deployment results. It will look similar to the following:

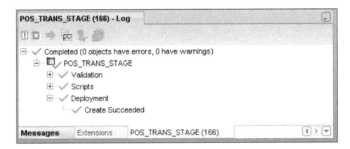

The number you will see beside the object name in your log window will most likely be different since that's a randomly assigned ID number the warehouse builder gives to deployment jobs. We'll see that in a moment. There must be some way to give us more control over the deployment process as the Design Center only shows us design information and these messages. This feature of the Warehouse Builder is the **Control Center Manager**.

The Control Center Manager

The Control Center Manager is the interface the Warehouse Builder provides for interacting with the target schema. This is where the deployment of objects and subsequent execution of generated code takes place. The Design Center is for manipulating metadata only on the repository. Deployment and execution take place in the target schema through the Control Center Service. The Control Center Manager is our interface into the process where we can deploy objects and mappings, check on the status of previous deployments, and execute the generated code in the target schema.

We launch the Control Center Manager from the **Tools** menu of the **Design Center** main menu. We click on the very first menu entry, which says **Control Center Manager**. This will open up a new window to run the Control Center Manager, which will look similar to the following:

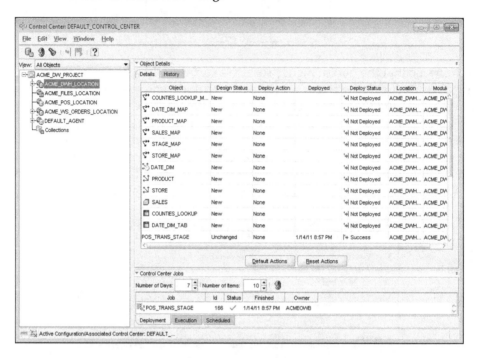

The Control Center Manager window overview

The Control Center Manager interface is organized in a similar manner to the Design Center with multiple windows appearing in the main window. But only two windows are available: the **Object Details** window and the **Control Center Jobs** window. The subwindow on the left that displays the tree hierarchy for our project and the locations defined within it is a permanent part of the interface, and so it does not have a separate window title like the other two.

Beginning with the left subwindow, we see our project name displayed there with a list of the locations that have been defined within our project. The primary location of concern for deployment and execution will be ACME_DWH_LOCATION. This is the location we have defined for our target database and selected as default.

This is where we can control the registering and un-registering of a location. If we right-click on a location, we see a **Register...** menu entry. When it is selected, it pops up the same dialog box as we have seen previously. If the location has not been previously registered it's connection details will all be editable. But if the location was previously registered successfully, only the password can be set. The **Unregister...** menu entry will remove the connection details for the location.

All the objects defined for this location can be found by clicking on the plus sign to the left of the location name to expand the tree, and then clicking on the plus sign next to the **ACME_DWH** module to display for us a hierarchy of the object types that can be deployed. An example is shown next:

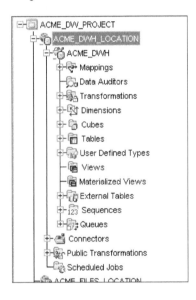

Clicking on the plus sign beside any of the subcategories, such as **Mappings** or **Tables**, will show us the list of the objects of that type defined within our project. If we click on an entry in the hierarchy, the Object Details window will update to display the associated objects. In the previous image of the entire **Control Center Manager** window, we can see that the **Object Details** window contains the entire set of objects defined in our project for the main location because that is what is selected in the tree view on the left. Now as we click on the subcategories, the Object Details window updates to display just the objects within that subcategory. If we further expand the tree view on the left to view the objects in a subcategory, we can click on an individual item and the Object Details window will display the details for just that item.

If this looks familiar, it is because the module view for the ACME_DWH module in the tree is very similar to the view we get in the Design Center when viewing that module. All the objects represented here can be deployed and correspond exactly to the same item in the Design Center.

The Object Details window

Let's click on the ACME_DWH_LOCATION again in the left window and look at the complete list of objects for our project. The statuses will vary depending on whether we've done any deployments or not, when we did them, and whether there are any warnings or failures due to errors that occurred. If you're following along exactly with the book, the only deployment we've done so far is the POS_TRANS_STAGE table and the previous image of the complete Control Center manager interface shows it as the only one that has been deployed successfully. The remainder all have a deploy status of **Not Deployed**.

The columns displayed in the Object Details window are as follows:

- **Object**: The name of the object
- **Design Status**: The status of the design of the object in relation to whether it has been deployed yet or not
  - **New**: The object has been created in the Design Center, but has not been deployed yet
  - **Unchanged**: The Object has been created in the Design Center and deployed previously, and has not been changed since its last deployment
  - **Changed**: The Object has been created and deployed, and has subsequently undergone changes in the Design Center since its last deployment
- **Deploy Action**: What action will be taken upon the next deployment of this object in the Control Center Manager
  - **Create**: Create the object; if an object with the same name already exists, this can generate an error upon deployment
  - **Upgrade**: Upgrade the object in place, preserving data (only on objects able to be upgraded)
  - **Drop**: Delete the object
  - **Replace**: Delete and recreate the object; this option does not preserve data

- **Deployed**: Date and time of the last deployment
- **Deploy Status**: Results of the last deployment
    - **Not Deployed**: The object has not been deployed yet
    - **Success**: The last deployment was successful, without any errors or warnings
    - **Warning**: The last deployment had warnings
    - **Failed**: The last deployment failed due to errors
- **Location**: The location defined for the object, which is where it will be deployed
- **Module**: The module where the object is defined

    Some of the previous columns will allow us to perform an action associated with the column by double-clicking or single-clicking in the column. The following is a list of the columns that have actions available, and how to access them:

- **Object**: Double-click on the object name to launch the appropriate editor on the object.
- **Deploy Action**: Click on the deploy action to change the deploy action for the next deployment of the object via a drop-down menu. The list of available actions that can be taken will be displayed. Not all the previously listed actions are available for every object. For instance, upgrade is not available for some objects and will not be an option for a mapping. The deploy action is what determines the scripts that get generated for an object. The **Create** option will generate only a script to create the object. The **Replace** option, in addition to generating the create script, will cause a drop script to be generated. The **Drop** option will cause only a drop script to be generated. The **Upgrade** option, if available, will generate neither a drop nor a create option but will generate a script with the appropriate upgrade SQL code.

> An important note about the upgrade option is that the target user must have certain extra privileges granted to him or her in the database to be able to perform an upgrade. If these privileges haven't been granted, an error will occur when trying to do a deployment with an Upgrade option:
>
> **RPE-02257: The following Oracle Roles have not been Granted to the Target User: 'SELECT_CATALOG_ROLE'**
>
> **RPE-02258: The following Oracle Privileges have not been Granted to the Target User: 'EXECUTE ANY PROCEDURE' 'EXECUTE ANY TYPE' 'SELECT ANY TABLE' 'SELECT ANY DICTIONARY'**
>
> **RPE-02259: Please run script <OWB-HOME>/owb/rtp/sql/grant_upgrade_privileges.sql**
>
> Simply run the script mentioned in the message as the system user to grant the privileges.

There are two buttons available in the Object Details window, **Default Actions** and **Reset Actions**. Every object created in the Design Center has a default deployment action associated with it, which is determined by the current design and deployment status. For example, a mapping that has not been deployed yet has a default status of **Create**. A table that was previously deployed but just changed will have a default action of **Upgrade**. The **Default Actions** button will change the displayed **Deploy Action** to show the default action for that object based on a comparison of its design status with its deploy status.

Now let's click on the **Default Actions** button and we'll notice that all the actions are updated to their default action. In our case, with just the POS_TRANS_STAGE table deployed and all others not deployed, all the objects except for POS_TRANS_STAGE have the **Deploy Action** changed to **Create** from **None**.

The other window in the Control Center Manager is the **Control Center Jobs** window. This is where we can monitor the status of any deployments and executions we've performed.

The Control Center Jobs window

Every time we do a deployment or execute a mapping, a **job** is created by the Control Center to perform the action. The job is run in the background while we can continue working on other things, and the status of the job is displayed in the Control Center Jobs window. Looking back at the previous image of the Control Center Manager, we can see the status of the POS_TRANS_STAGE table deployment that we performed. The green check mark indicates it was successful.

We can also see an ID column. This is the identification number that the warehouse builder has assigned to this job and it is the same number that appeared beside the table name in the Design Center log window results when we deployed the **POS_ TRANS_STAGE** table previously. If we want to see more details, especially if there were warnings or errors, we can double-click on the line in the **Control Center Jobs** window and it will pop up a dialog box displaying the details. An example of the dialog box is shown next:

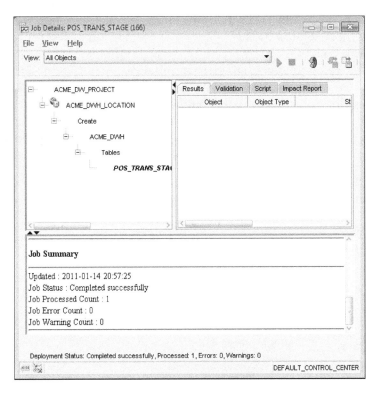

Clicking on the object in the tree view in the left window will update the right window to display the information in the tabs where we can see various items of information such as the result, the validation results, and the script generated. The **Impact Report** tab is applicable to upgrades and will display information about changes resulting from doing an upgrade. The window at the bottom contains a summary of the job execution including the messages that provide the details about the process. It is a scrollable window, and the previous image only shows the last part of the messages.

Scrolling back through that window we can see that the validation messages are also included because when the Warehouse Builder deploys an object, it automatically does actual validation and generation first. It is not necessary to perform a manual validation and then a generation before doing a deployment if we need to redeploy an object, as it will do that for us automatically.

If there were any errors in deployment, these errors would appear in the previous window also. For deployments, as we're dealing with actual scripts executing in the target database to create objects or mapping code, the deployment errors will be of the form of errors generated by the database. These will have an error code of the ORA-XXXXX format with ORA being a generic indicator that it is an Oracle database error, and XXXXX being the five-digit error number zero-padded on the left. More details about these errors can be found in the *Oracle Database Error Messages 11g Release 2(11.2)* guide, which is available online at http://download.oracle.com/docs/cd/E11882_01/server.112/e17766/toc.htm. We can look up the Oracle errors easily in this manual by referring to the error number in the table of contents, which is organized by ranges of error numbers in a sequential order.

The following example will illustrate errors and warnings that could be encountered when deploying a mapping, which in this case is the STORE_MAP mapping:

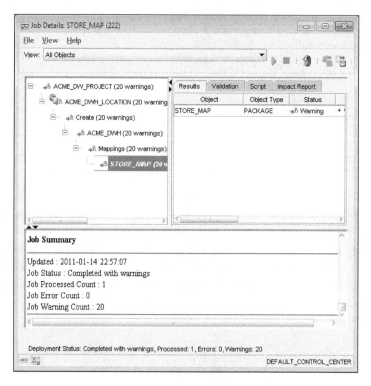

This dialog box indicates warnings occurred while trying to deploy the STORE_MAP mapping. To see the full error, we can view the contents of the scrolled window at the bottom that displays the full error message and scrolling up we see the following:

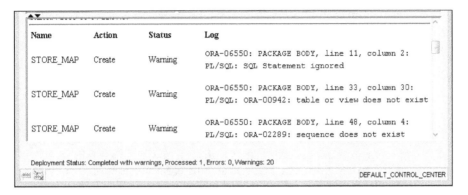

Name	Action	Status	Log
STORE_MAP	Create	Warning	ORA-06550: PACKAGE BODY, line 11, column 2: PL/SQL: SQL Statement ignored
STORE_MAP	Create	Warning	ORA-06550: PACKAGE BODY, line 33, column 30: PL/SQL: ORA-00942: table or view does not exist
STORE_MAP	Create	Warning	ORA-06550: PACKAGE BODY, line 48, column 4: PL/SQL: ORA-02289: sequence does not exist

Deployment Status: Completed with warnings, Processed: 1, Errors: 0, Warnings: 20

DEFAULT_CONTROL_CENTER

This screenshot is telling us that a table or view does not exist and also that a sequence does not exist. We can see the Oracle errors above that we referred to previously. Because we're deploying code into the database now, a PL/SQL package that references a database table or sequence will generate this error if the physical table or sequence does not exist yet in the database. As this mapping was deployed before deploying the tables and sequence that it references, these errors are generated. The Warehouse Builder for some reason thinks this is just worth a **Warning** status and not a full blown **Error** but whether you call it a warning or error, the mapping is not going to execute until those objects are deployed. In this case the Warehouse Builder is just saying the actual deployment was successful because the object was created in the database but it is warning us that there are errors in the code which will prevent a successful execution. The metadata in the Design Center was correct—the table definitions and sequence included in the STORE_MAP mapping were created in the Warehouse Builder—which is why the validation was successful, but they had not been deployed physically to the database yet.

Looking up the Oracle errors

Sometimes error numbers don't appear in the most recent edition of the Oracle Error Messages manual. The previous ORA-00942 error is an example of such an error. Looking in the table of contents in the Oracle Database 11g Rel.2 error messages guide referenced previously, the error numbers go up to ORA-00912 in Chapter 3 and then jump up to ORA-00953. In fact, we have to go all the way back to the Oracle 9i Database Error Messages Release. 2(9.2) guide at http://download.oracle.com/docs/cd/B10501_01/ server.920/a96525/e900.htm#ERRMG102 to find that error listed.

Some of these errors have been around for quite some time and many new error messages are created with each new database release, so some get left out. In that case, searching older versions of the Error Messages manuals or doing a simple Internet search on your favorite search engine for the ORA and 00942 strings (or whatever the error number is) will turn up some additional information.

With this illustration of the Control Center Manager and its windows, we need to discuss how to deploy objects from within the Control Center Manager.

Deploying in the Control Center Manager

The previous overview of the Control Center Manager windows showed us how it displays the results of our deployments, in particular the ones we initiated from the Design Center, but we can also deploy objects from within the Control Center Manager. This is one of its major functions, along with executing code and checking on the status of jobs.

All of the functions we can perform from the Control Center Manager are initiated from the tree view on the left. There are pop-up menus available on each object and also main menu entries that will perform the action on the currently selected object. The Control Center Manager also has a toolbar with a couple of icons that we can use to deploy and execute objects that have been selected. They are circled in the following image and will be grayed out if there are no objects selected that can be deployed or executed:

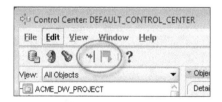

Let's deploy the STAGE_MAP stage mapping from the Control Center Manager by finding it in the tree view. We have to expand the ACME_DW_PROJECT project and the location for our ACME_DW_LOCATION target, and then the module for the ACME_DWH target database. As we want to deploy a mapping, we need to look under the **Mappings** node. So we expand that entry in the tree view, right-click on it, and select **Deploy** from the pop-up menu. We can also click on it and then select **File | Deploy | To Control Center** from the main menu.

The pop-up menu on an object, the main menu in the Control Center Manager and the icons in the toolbar will update depending on the deploy action currently set for the objects. If the current deploy action is **None**, the **Deploy** pop-up menu entry, the **File** menu **Deploy** submenus and the deploy icon will be grayed out, and will not be selectable. If we wish to deploy in that case, we can change the deploy action using the pop-up menu or change it in the **Object Details** window and the **Deploy** menu entry will become active. We can also just use the **Default Actions** button in the **Object Details** window to set a default deployment action. In this case, it defaults to **Create** as we saw previously and the **Deploy** menu option is now available.

A new entry will be created in the Control Center Jobs window and the status will update as the job progresses. It's possible we might be presented with another dialog box saying a location hasn't been registered yet and it will prompt for the connection information similar to what we mentioned earlier when deploying in the Design Center. The STAGE_MAP references the ACME_POS source SQL Server database using the ACME_POS_LOCATION location, which also needs to be registered. As before, we can just fill in the password for the **ACME_DW_USER** login, double-check the remaining information, and click the **OK** button. Now it will proceed with the deployment. Remember to enclose the password in double quotes as this is a SQL Server database location. When it is completed, we'll be presented with a pop-up window indicating success or failure if we've configured that option in **Preferences** as previously discussed.

We can close that pop-up window and the status will update to reflect the final result. If we haven't selected the option in preferences to display the completion pop-up window, we can check the status of the job in the Job window which updates to reflect the success or failure of the job. In either case, we can view details by double-clicking on the job if we need to. One final place we can check is back in the Log window of the Design Center which we'll see has been quietly logging all this deployment activity we've been accomplishing in the Control Center Manager in separate tabs like it did for our very first deployment of the **POS_TRANS_STAGE** table. We can close any of those deployment status tabs in the log window if we'd like to clean it up but it's not required.

Executing

Now we have our staging table deployed to the target database, the POS_TRANS_STAGE table, and have successfully deployed the STAGE_MAP mapping to load that table from our source database. This means we now have enough of our target database deployed to be able to execute the STAGE_MAP mapping to load the staging table. Let's do that now so that we will have progressed through the entire process once. Loading the staging table is the first step we have to take to load our database before we can proceed to load the actual target dimensions and cube. After we execute this mapping, we can go back and deploy the remaining objects, and execute them to load the dimensions and cube.

The process of executing a mapping can be performed from the Design Center as well as from the Control Center Manager. The process of executing is very similar to deploying. Results are displayed in the Control Center Jobs window, which is the same as that of the deployment results, but on a different tab, that is the **Execution** tab. We also get results displayed in the Log window in the Design Center.

To execute a mapping we might think to look for a menu entry that says **Execute**, but we will not find it. We need to select the menu entry that says **Start** to start the code running. This menu entry is available from the pop-up menu by right-clicking on an item in the tree view, and from the **File** menu when an item is selected in the tree view. These menu entries are available in both the Design Center and the Control Center Manager. We can also click the Start icon in the toolbar, the one on the right in the above image in the Control Center. If executing from the Design Center, the start icon will appear as a large green arrow.

Let's just go ahead and do that now. We'll find the STAGE_MAP entry under **Mappings**, which is in the ACME_DWH_LOCATION in the tree view. Right-click on it and select **Start**.

When executing code, it's always a good idea to make sure the most recent version of the code has been deployed successfully. Before selecting Start, it is good to just glance at the **Object Details** window in the **Control Center Manager** for the object, which appears when the object is right-clicked, and make sure that the deployment status shows **Success** and the design status shows **Unchanged**.

If we had a problem with the deployment and the status is other than **Success**, we will have issues running it. If the design status shows **Changed**, we don't have the most recent version of the object deployed. We can then fix any issues first, re-deploy, and then execute it.

Having determined that we have successfully deployed the most recent version, we continue and select **Start**. So the Control Center Manager begins executing the mapping code. As it executes, the first thing we'll notice is that the **Control Center Jobs** window will update to display the **Execution** tab with our newly submitted job as the first entry and the Design Center Log window has updated to add another tab to display the results from this execution. The tab name will be the mapping name followed by the job id in parentheses like it did for all the deployments. Upon completion, if we have checked the preference option to display deployment completion status (which applies to execution status also), we'll get the results pop-up window.

The important thing to notice about this dialog box is the success or failure message. The counts (at least for the processed count) are not accurate. This is a minor bug, as it did indeed process this mapping. This is verifiable by double-clicking on the status for our job in the **Control Center Jobs** window to display the details about this execution. When we do that, we get the following dialog box in which we can clearly see the mapping executed and can see the counts of rows that were processed:

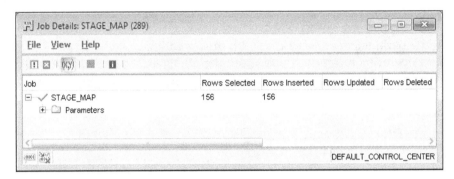

The contents of this dialog are also shown in the tab in the Design Center Log window. It displays more or less for the inserted count depending on how much sample data we actually have in the source database. As of this execution, there were **10026** records in the source POS_TRANSACTIONS table but we performed an aggregation on that data to sum it by day which resulted in **156** records actually being loaded.

The parameters entry in the above screenshot is for displaying the mapping input parameters if there are any defined in the mapping. We talked about mapping input parameters in Chapter 5 when discussing the various operators available to us when creating a mapping. They are for passing values into a mapping.

The input parameters are included with configuration options for running the mapping that involve the operating mode among others. We discussed the operating mode previously when talking about generating code and viewing the code for the various operating modes. We discussed accessing those parameters by selecting **Configure...** from the pop-up menu by right-clicking on a mapping in either the Design Center or the Control Center Manager and saw an example of the screen with the parameters.

> Instead of having to take that extra step to set the runtime parameters, there is an option that can be checked off to automatically display a dialog of those parameters, including mapping input parameters, when a mapping is started. That would allow us to set those parameters each time a mapping is run. To set that option access the **Preferences** menu entry from the **Tools** main menu in the **Design Center**. In the resulting dialog, expand the OWB entry on the left and click on the **Deployment** entry. There will be an option with a check box labeled **Prompt for Execution Parameters** on the right that can be checked to automatically display the parameters dialog when a mapping is run.

The runtime parameters are set along with the operating mode. We have covered the default operating mode previously, but the others are all more advanced than we'll have time or the need to cover here. There are good explanations of all the runtime parameters in the online help accessible by pressing the **Help** button. Select the **Configuring Mappings Reference** link and then the **Runtime Parameters** link from the resulting help dialog box to access detailed explanations of all the runtime parameters. For our purpose, the defaults will all be fine.

Deploying and executing remaining objects

This completes the process of loading our staging table. It's now ready to be used for loading our dimensions and our cube. We've now gone through every process we needed for creating our data warehouse. All that remains is for us to complete the deployment and execution of the remaining objects. The process is the same for all the objects.

At this point, the only issue we need to be concerned with is the order in which we deploy and execute the objects. We don't want to deploy and execute a mapping to load a dimension, for example, until we've deployed the dimension itself; otherwise we'll get errors. We can't deploy the dimension successfully until the underlying table has been deployed. We got a small taste of a possible error that can occur due to incorrectly timing our table and mapping deployments earlier in the chapter when we saw the errors that could occur when deploying a mapping before the underlying table was deployed.

Deployment order

With that in mind, let's talk about the order in which we should proceed to deploy and execute our objects. The group of objects we have to deploy consists of the following:

- Sequences
- Tables
- Dimensions
- A cube
- Mappings

We want to start with objects that do not rely upon any other objects, and then proceed from there. The only class of objects from the preceding list that doesn't rely upon any others would be sequences, so we'll do them first. Tables are likely the next candidate for deployment, but there could be foreign key dependencies between tables that will cause errors if the tables are deployed in the wrong order; so we need to watch out for that. In fact, the underlying table created for our SALES cube has foreign key dependencies upon the three dimension tables and so those must be done before the SALES table. The cube will rely upon the dimensions as well as its underlying table, and the dimensions need to have the underlying tables deployed first. So, it looks like the dimensions would be good to do next and then the cube. Finally, the mappings can be done since they depend on the cube, dimensions, and tables. Now that we have figured this out, here's the final list in order of the objects remaining to deploy:

- Sequences
    - DATE_DIM_SEQ
    - PRODUCT_SEQ
    - STORE_SEQ

- Tables
  - ° COUNTIES_LOOKUP
  - ° DATE_DIM
  - ° PRODUCT
  - ° STORE
  - ° SALES

- Dimensions
  - ° DATE_DIM
  - ° PRODUCT
  - ° STORE

- Cube
  - ° SALES

- External tables
  - ° COUNTIES

- Mappings
  - ° COUNTIES_LOOKUP_MAP
  - ° DATE_DIM_MAP
  - ° PRODUCT_MAP
  - ° STORE_MAP
  - ° SALES_MAP

We'll go through each of the objects in the order given in the Control Center Manager or the Design Center, and deploy them.

Rather than deploying each of the previous objects one at a time, we can make use of the Warehouse Builder's capacity to deploy more than one object at a time. We need to do the previous groupings in order, but within each group the order of the individual deployments is not critical. So, we can click on the node in the Control Center Manager corresponding to the previous groups, and then click on the **Default Actions** button in the **Object Details** window to set the default action. Then we can right-click on the node (**Sequences**, **Tables**, and so on), and select **Deploy** from the pop-up menu to deploy all objects under the node that have a current deployment action set or just click the deploy icon in the toolbar. This will start up a job in the Control Center Jobs window named for the project (**ACME_DW_PROJECT**), which will deploy all the objects under the node. When it completes, we can double-click on the job to display the details for each of the objects if needed.

When complete, we can check the status of everything in the Control Center Manager by clicking on the **ACME_DWH** database module to display all the objects. We can quickly scan down the list to verify that everything got deployed successfully.

You may encounter an error when deploying the COUNTIES external table. The error would look like the following as shown in the **Job Details** window upon completion of the deployment attempt on the COUNTIES external table:

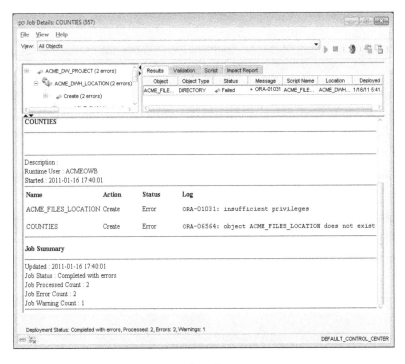

The problem that caused the above error is that the user being deployed to, the target data warehouse user, ACME_DWH, did not have the proper privilege assigned to create a directory object in the database. The Warehouse Builder utilizes a directory object in the database to access the directory indicated by the location associated with the external table and there is a special privilege required to be able to create that directory object. This is a new feature in this latest release of the Warehouse Builder that improves the security of the database by not automatically allowing a warehouse use to create any directory in the system. There are two options that can be taken to resolve this and we're just going to take the simplest option which assigns the CREATE ANY DIRECTORY system privilege to our target user. Since we're deploying, our target user is ACME_DWH and so that is the user we will assign the CREATE ANY DIRECTORY system privilege to.

To perform this action open a command prompt window and issue the following command to run the SQL*Plus command line utility and connect as the system database user:

```
sqlplus system
```

After entering the system password issue the following SQL command at the SQL*Plus command prompt:

```
SQL> grant create any directory to ACME_DWH;
```

Retry the deployment of the COUNTIES external table and it will complete successfully now.

This is the quick way to solve the problem but results in a potentially less secure system since the warehouse user now has the ability to create any directory in the system. The other option involves manually creating the SQL directory object in the database and assigning read/write permission to the target warehouse user. Then a connector must be manually created in the Warehouse Builder to be able to access it from there. This is discussed further in the OWB Sources and Targets Guide on DB Connectors and directories at the following URL:

```
http://download.oracle.com/docs/cd/E11882_01/owb.112/e10582/
importing_metadata.htm#WBDOD10524
```

When all the objects are deployed, we'll move on to the next section where we'll execute them.

Execution order

Now that we have all the remaining objects deployed, it's time to execute them to complete our data warehouse project. The execution only pertains to the code that is generated for the mappings. The execution of the code behind all the other objects was done previously when we deployed them to create the objects. For the mappings, the dependency will be determined by the foreign keys that exist in the tables that the mappings are loading. We can't run a mapping without errors to load a table that has foreign key dependencies on other tables before those other tables have been loaded. We know that our SALES table has foreign keys to the dimension tables, so we need to run them to load them before doing the SALES table. But we also know our STORE mapping needs to do a look up of county information from our COUNTIES_LOOKUP table, and so that mapping will need to be run before the STORE mapping. These are the known dependencies, and armed with this knowledge, we specify our order as follows for executing mappings:

1. COUNTIES_LOOKUP_MAP
2. DATE_DIM_MAP
3. PRODUCT_MAP
4. STORE_MAP
5. SALES_MAP

We'll execute these one by one as the individual order is important. After executing these mappings in the given order, our data warehouse is now complete and ready to be queried.

Summary

That's it! The data warehouse is now complete. We've now completed the work to develop our ACME Toys and Gizmos Company data warehouse. We covered quite a bit of information in this chapter about validating our objects, generating the code for them, deploying to the target environment, and finally executing the code. We were introduced for the first time to the Control Center Manager where we got to interact with the Control Center to deploy and execute objects in our target database environment.

We covered these topics together in this chapter as they are all related. But in actual projects, we will frequently find ourselves performing these steps in an iterative process as we work on the project. We don't have to necessarily wait until the end to perform all these tasks. We can perform some validation and generation as we design each object or mapping.

However, we still have a couple chapters remaining so don't quit yet because we are going to cover some more small details about what we've done so far and add a few minor topics that will help us maximize our use of the tool and then discuss a new feature of the 11gR2 release of the Warehouse Builder.

9
Extra Features

Congratulations on having made it this far and completing the data warehouse implementation! We've now covered all the Warehouse Builder basics that we need to begin building our data warehouses for our organizations. This chapter will deal with some extra topics that can help us get the most out of what we've learned so far and improve our use of the Warehouse Builder. The focus will be on those features that we will find useful as we create more complex data warehouses, and are faced with making changes and updates.

Metadata change management is an important practice we'll want to employ as we make more and more edits and changes to our data warehouse over time, and the Warehouse Builder includes a number of features that can help us with this. We'll look at the following features related to metadata change management:

- The **metadata loader** facility for making export files that can be saved to a file in a configuration management tool for backup or to transfer metadata
- The **recycle bin** for saving deleted objects
- **Copying** and **pasting** objects to make copies for backup or as the basis for new objects
- Taking **snapshots** of objects to save the state at a point in time

We'll also take a look at these additional features:

- How to keep objects synchronized between the object and its use in a mapping
- The binding of tables to dimensional objects
- A quick look at some online references for more information that will help us

We stepped through the process of building our data warehouse from start to finish in this book, but did not address having to go back and make changes to objects or mappings we've already completed. This presents some unique challenges so let's talk about the features the Warehouse Builder has that will help us with keeping a track of the various versions of our objects as we make changes.

Metadata change management

Metadata change management includes keeping a track of different versions of an object or mapping as we make changes to it, and comparing objects to see what has changed. It is always a good idea to save a working copy of objects and mappings when they are complete and function correctly. That way, if we need to make modifications later and something goes wrong, or we just want to reproduce a system from an earlier point in time, we have a ready-made copy available for use. We won't have to try to manually back out of any changes we might have made. We would also be able to make comparisons between that saved version of the object and the current version to see what has been changed.

Metadata Loader (MDL) exports and imports

One major change management-related tool that we'll look at in the Warehouse Builder is the ability to export workspace objects and save them to a file using the **Metadata Loader (MDL)** facility. With this feature we can export anything from an entire project down to a single data object or mapping. It will save it to a file that can be saved for backup or used to transport metadata definitions to another repository for loading, even if that repository is on a platform with a different operating system. Some other possible uses for the export and import of metadata are to quickly make copies of workspace objects in multiple workspaces for multiple developers, or to migrate to a newer product version. We would need to export from the old product version, upgrade the Warehouse Builder, and then import back to the new workspace version.

When exporting we can choose any project, node, module, or object in Design Center in either the Projects Navigator, Locations Navigator, or Globals Navigator windows. If we choose an entire project or a collection such as a node or module, it will export all objects contained within it. If we choose any subset, it will export the context of the objects so that it will remember where to put them on import. That means if we choose a table, for instance, it will include in the metadata the definition for the module in which it resides as well as the project the module is in. We can also choose to export any dependencies on the object being exported if they exist. So an export of tables with foreign key references to other tables, for example, will export these other tables as well to resolve the references.

Let's save an export file of our entire main ACME_DW_PROJECT to see how an export is done from the Design Center. We'll select the project by clicking on it and then select **File | Export | Warehouse Builder Metadata** from the main menu. If we have made any changes, we'll get a dialog box asking us to save the changes or revert the changes as we have seen previously. We'll click on **Save** in that case. The Metadata Export dialog box will be displayed, which will look similar to the following depending on the particular objects that are defined within the project:

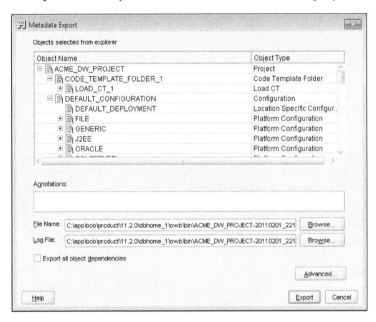

Every module, node, and object in our project is depicted in the list for reference, so we can see what will be exported. We also have the opportunity to annotate our export file with some notes. We can use the **Annotations** box to enter any information that we would like to save about the export. It is most often used to save a description of the contents of the export file for quick reference later. Below that we specify the file name of the export file and name for the log file it will create of the export. The dialog box will specify a default file name and location for each, but we are free to change that to any location that suits us.

In working with the Warehouse Builder there could be development, test, and production repositories on three different servers. So this feature would be very useful to copy metadata definitions from development to test, and then from test to production. A networked drive and folder that can be accessed from all three servers can be used to store the file, so the MDL file doesn't have to be copied from server to server after saving it.

There is also a checkbox on the dialog box for including any object dependencies. As previously mentioned, we can automatically export any objects our selected objects depend on. We might think that all the dependencies are included because we've chosen to export the entire project. But there are dependencies that can exist to objects outside our project such as the locations that are defined in the Locations Navigator or objects defined in the Globals Navigator. If we want to automatically include all of them, we can check this box.

> The Warehouse Builder automatically includes an internal project called **PUBLIC_PROJECT** that will contain any of the objects that are external to our individually named projects. These are the objects in the Locations and Globals Navigators that are accessible to any project defined in the workspace.

We'll not export any dependencies so will leave that checkbox unchecked. We'll accept the default file names and locations, and click on the **Export** button. This will start the export and display a progress dialog box with a slider, which will indicate the percent complete. When done, it will show 100% and a message indicating success. It will have a **Show Details** button, which will expand the dialog box to display the details of the export in a scrolling window, which shows step by step what it was doing, as well as a button labeled **Show Statistics**. If we click on **Show Statistics**, we get a dialog box loaded with counts of each individual object and attributes of the objects that were exported. This information is probably more than we'll ever need. But if we focus on the high-level objects such as mappings, tables, dimensions, cubes, and so on, this information can give us a quick validation that we exported what we thought we did—particularly if we've selected a subset of objects and want to make sure we have the correct count. It's just another way of verifying that our export was successful and includes everything we intended.

> The Metadata Loader log file that was created also contains those counts. If we want, we can save them for future reference along with other details about the export.

If we had checked the box for object dependencies on the Export dialog box earlier, we would have seen some additional objects that were exported.

That is where the **PUBLIC_PROJECT** we referred to previously would appear. It would show connectors, a control center, and locations that were included. Whether we want these included or not will depend on what we're going to do with the export file. For example, in the previous description about how export files can be used to transfer metadata from the development environment to test and then to production, location details are different for each server. In that case, we wouldn't want to include the location and connector information. As long as we use the same names for our locations and connectors on each server, the project metadata will import with no problems and will function in the same way on all three.

> The MDL file that is created is actually in a ZIP format and any application that can open a ZIP file can view the two files contained within it — a file with .mdx extension, which is the file containing the actual objects from the workspace that were exported, and a .xml file that contains the definitions of the exported objects.

Continuing our discussion of metadata change management-related features, the Warehouse Builder has a feature called the **recycle bin** for storing deleted objects and mappings for a later retrieval. After that we'll talk about a feature that allows us to make copies of objects by including a clipboard for copying and pasting to and from, which is similar to an operating-system clipboard, and then we'll talk about a feature called **Snapshots**, which allows us to make a copy (or snapshot) of our objects at any point during the cycle of developing our data warehouse that can later be used for comparisons.

Recycle bin

The recycle bin in OWB is the same concept as that which operating systems use to store deleted files. To try out the recycle bin, we need to have an object we can delete. So let's create a temporary mapping object named TEMP_MAP_FOR_DELETE. We'll launch the Design Center if it's not already running, and in our ACME_DWH module in ACME_DW_PROJECT we'll just right-click on the **Mappings** node and select **New Mapping**. We'll just close the resulting Mapping Editor that launches for this new mapping because we're just going to delete it next anyway, so it doesn't need to have anything created in it.

If we need to remove an object or mapping from our project, there are a number of ways to do that. In the Design Center, we can right-click on an object and select **Delete** from the pop-up menu, or we can click on an object and press the **Delete** key, or we can click on an object and select **Delete** from the **Edit** main menu. Let's perform one of these actions on this new mapping we just created and we'll immediately be presented with the following pop-up screen:

Notice the checkbox for the recycle bin. We have the option to delete the object and move it to the recycle bin where it would still be accessible later if needed, or just delete the object entirely so that it is never to be seen nor heard from again. In this case, we created a mapping just to delete, so it really wouldn't matter if it was not put in the recycle bin. But we'll leave the box checked and click on **OK**. This will cause some processing to be performed to actually save the object in the recycle bin.

> **Revert to Saved** can be used from the main **File** menu to restore the project back to the last saved state, which will cause objects deleted since the last save to be restored. That is another option besides the recycle bin and does not involve as much processing as it just reverses changes since the last save. If more than one change was done since the last save, they will all get reversed, even the ones that might have been valid, so use that feature wisely.

We could also click on the **Cancel** button and the dialog box would go away; nothing would happen further. So, leaving the **Put in Recycle Bin** box checked, we'll click on the **OK** button. Now we'll get a quick pop-up window titled **Snapshot Action** that actually mentions taking a snapshot. This is the method it uses to implement the recycle bin. That is why we're including both these discussions together here under metadata change management.

It is important to note that deleting objects in the Design Center, whether placing them in the recycle bin or not, does not affect the target database system to which we might have already deployed the object. The delete function in the Design Center affects only the metadata definition stored in the repository workspace of the object, and not the object itself in the target database. To remove that, normal database techniques for removing database objects must be employed.

Let's take a look at how to launch the recycle bin to recover a deleted object. The **recycle bin** is accessible from the main menu of the **Design Center** under the **Tools** menu entry as shown next:

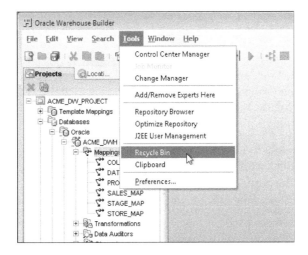

When we click on that menu entry, the recycle bin window will pop up as shown in the following screenshot:

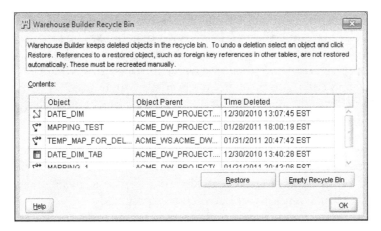

Let's do that now and take a closer look at it. There may be more objects listed and with different names depending on what has been deleted, but this is what the interface looks like. We can select the object with the left mouse button and click on the **Restore** button to cause that object to be placed back into our project in the same place it was deleted from, as shown by the **Object Parent** column. Of course, the **Time Deleted** is when we deleted the object. It is possible to have more than one entry in the recycle bin with the same name. For example, this can happen if we've deleted an object, created a new object using the same name, and then deleted it again. The time it was deleted can clue us into the correct one to restore if needed. The **Empty Recycle Bin** button will do just what it says—clear everything out of the recycle bin. However, this is an all or nothing procedure. We need to make sure we won't ever need anything in the recycle bin before clicking on that button because as soon as we click it, we end up with an empty recycle bin.

It would be nice if we could selectively remove objects from the recycle bin. However, the only way to selectively remove an object is by restoring it and then deleting it again, except this time un-checking the recycle bin checkbox so that it gets deleted permanently.

The recycle bin allows us to keep versions of deleted objects. However, if we don't want to delete the object, and instead want to save it before making changes to it, we can make use of the copy and paste feature of the Design Center. Let's close the **Recycle Bin** by clicking on the **OK** button and move on to discuss cut, copy, and paste.

Cut, copy, and paste

We mentioned the recycle bin as a concept borrowed from operating systems. Another concept the Warehouse Builder has borrowed from operating systems is the **clipboard**, and **cutting** or **copying** to and **pasting** from the clipboard. Anyone who has used a computer for any length of time has had recourse to the clipboard where objects and text can be copied between applications. The same concept applies here, but with objects in the Design Center. Even the key combinations that can be used to cut, copy, and paste are the same as for the operating system—*Ctrl+X* to cut, *Ctrl+C* to copy, and *Ctrl+V* to paste in addition to menu entries for copy and paste operations that are on the main **Edit** menu and on the object menus when right-clicking on an object.

We can use the cut, copy, and paste features to make a copy of an object in the current project, or to copy an object to another project we might have defined in the Design Center. Within mappings we can also now copy and paste operators, groups, and attributes within a mapping or between mappings.

The only difference between cutting and copying is whether the original object is left in place or not. When cutting, the original object is removed and placed on the clipboard; and when copying, a copy of the object is placed on the clipboard leaving the original intact.

Let's walk through a quick example to see this in action. We'll use the option to copy an object between projects by creating a new project just for copying an object there. It's quick and we can remove that project when we are done. To create a new project, we'll click on our ACME_DW_PROJECT in the Design Center and then select **File | New** from the main menu, or click the *Ctrl+N* key combination, or right-click on the project name and select **New**. It will present us with a dialog box labeled New Gallery. This is a new dialog in this latest release of the Warehouse Builder and is a general dialog for creating any of a large number of different types of objects. We have to scroll down the window on the right until we find the object type we want to create, which in this case is a Project. We'll click on that as shown in the following image and click the **OK** button.

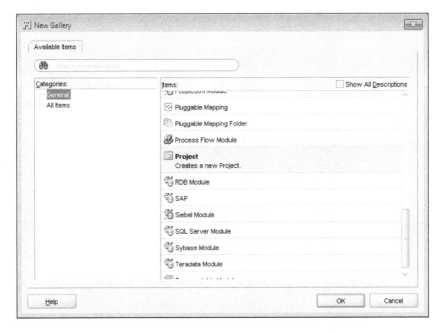

We may be presented with a dialog box at this point asking us to either save our work or revert back to the state the project was in when we last saved it. If there have been no changes detected since the last save, we won't see this dialog box. We'll click on the **Save** button to save our project and it will immediately present us the dialog box to enter a name for the new project. We'll name our project ACME_PROJ_FOR_COPYING and click on the **OK** button to create the new empty project.

We're going to copy a table—our staging table—to this new project, so we need to have a database module defined into which we can copy it. So let's create one now. We'll expand the new project by clicking on the plus sign next to it, and expand **Databases** by clicking on the plus sign next to it.

> Notice that our original project, ACME_DW_PROJECT, is closed and this new project is opened. We are not able to have more than one project open at a time in the Design Center.

We'll create an Oracle module by right-clicking on **Oracle** and selecting the **New Oracle Module** menu entry to launch the **Create Module Wizard**. We're not going to worry about any specific settings on the following screens and just accept the defaults. This is because we're just using this project to demonstrate some features for this chapter and want to get one created as quickly as possible.

However, on the step 1 screen, we do need to give this module a name. It doesn't matter what we call it, so we'll name it COPY_MODULE. We'll leave the other options set to their default and click on the **Next** button. The next screen is where we will specify the connection information. Because this is only a temporary module and we're not going to actually have to connect anywhere for real, we can leave the defaults on this screen as they are. The wizard will just create an empty location for us named after the module we just specified with _LOCATION1 on the end. We'll just click on the **Next** button and then on **Finish** to create the empty database module.

> This is a technique for creating a new project that we actually could employ for a real project if we did not have the connection details finalized yet. For example, the actual target database might not be available yet, or maybe we have multiple database servers available and we're not yet sure exactly which one would be used as the target. In that case, we can create a new project quickly just as we did here and leave the connection details unspecified. When the details are finalized, we can edit the connection to fill them in later. We would definitely need to have the connection details specified if we wanted to deploy any objects, but until that point we could create, validate, and generate objects as much as we wanted.

Let's click on the plus sign next to our newly created database module and we'll see that it has no objects defined in it yet. At this point our Design Center window will look similar to the following:

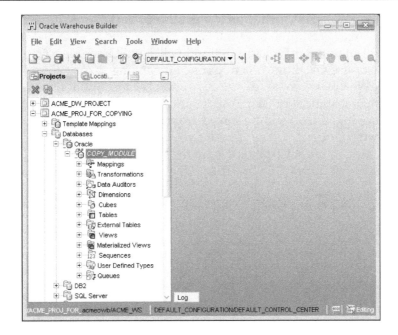

Now that we have a database module, we can copy our table. So let's go back to our real project, ACME_DW_PROJECT, that has some objects in it, by clicking on the plus sign next to it. If we have any unsaved changes that we've made to our project, we will see a dialog box pop up, about saving or reverting changes and which also refers to closing any open windows.

It is similar to the dialog box we just saw when creating a new project and had to save or revert changes. We cannot have more than one project open in the Design Center at the same time, so this is just warning us that it will have to close any open windows we might have for this project, such as an editor window to edit a mapping or other object, and that we will have to decide whether to save our changes or not. We have the choice to save the changes, revert back to the previously saved version of the project, or just cancel the project switch.

As we have an empty project, we won't have any windows open for it, but we have not saved what we've created so far. We'll need to be sure to click on the **Save** button. That will save the project we just created, close it, and open our original project.

So let's copy the POS_TRANS_STAGE table from this project over to our new project that we just created. We'll find it in the **Tables** node in our ACME_DWH database module under **Databases | Oracle**. We'll right-click on it and select **Copy** from the pop-up menu, or use one of the other options for copying to copy this table object to the clipboard. We don't want to use the cut option because we don't want to remove the object from our original project. A very quick pop-up window will appear and go away as it's copying. If the window stayed around long enough to read, it would tell us it was copying. Our POS_TRANS_STAGE table is now on the clipboard. If we want to verify that, we can select **Clipboard** from the **Tools** main menu to pop up the clipboard window to display the contents of the clipboard as shown next:

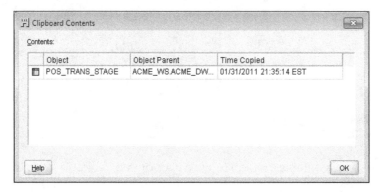

Note that the clipboard can contain only one object at a time. If we cut or copy another object to the clipboard, it will replace this one. So when we're copying multiple objects, we need to be sure to paste from the clipboard before copying another object to it.

Now that we have the POS_TRANS_STAGE table on the clipboard, we can paste it into the other project we just created. So let's click on the plus sign beside the new project we created to close our main project and open the new project. The objects that are placed on the clipboard using a cut or copy feature will only be pasted back to the node in the currently open project corresponding to the type of node they were originally cut or copied from. In our case this is a table, so it will be pasted back to the **Tables** node of the new project. Therefore, the **Paste** menu option will only appear on the menu for the **Tables** node. So let's navigate there in the project tree by right-clicking on **Tables** and selecting **Paste**. We can also click on the **Tables** node and type the *Ctrl+V* key combination, or select the **Paste** menu entry on the **Edit** main menu of the Design Center. The Warehouse Builder will now paste the contents of the clipboard into the project, creating a POS_TRANS_STAGE table in our new project. It will display the following pop-up window as it is pasting the object:

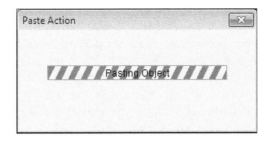

We could also have pasted the table back into the **Tables** node of our original ACME_
DW_PROJECT and it would have created a copy of the table with COPY_OF_ prefixed to
the table name.

This cut-and-paste technique is very useful for trying out different
things with a mapping to see how they will work. If we don't want
to risk making edits to our mapping, we can make a copy of it using
the copy and paste technique and then edit the copy. It's also possible
that we might need two mappings that are almost identical, except for
one or two operators. We can develop the mapping, copy and paste
it, and then make the edits to the copy to change those one or two
operators. We have the whole second mapping created without going
back through the entire create process. This can be done with tables and
other objects as well and is a very handy time saver.

The contents of the clipboard will not last forever. When we exit the Design Center,
the clipboard contents are emptied out. The next time we start Design Center, we start
with an empty clipboard. So, we must be very careful not to leave anything on the
clipboard that we might need to save. If we want to save an object to have it available
for future use without keeping it in our project, we can use the Snapshots feature.
Snapshots will also give us the ability to back up our objects and compare them to see
what has changed. Let's keep our new project open with the POS_TRANS_STAGE table
because we're going to make use of it for the next discussion about Snapshots.

Snapshots

A snapshot captures all the metadata information about an object at the time the snapshot is taken and stores it for later retrieval. It is a way to save a version of an object should we need to go back to a previous version or compare a current version with a previous one. We take a snapshot of an object from the Design Center by right-clicking on the object and selecting the **Snapshot** menu entry. This will give us three options to choose from as shown next:

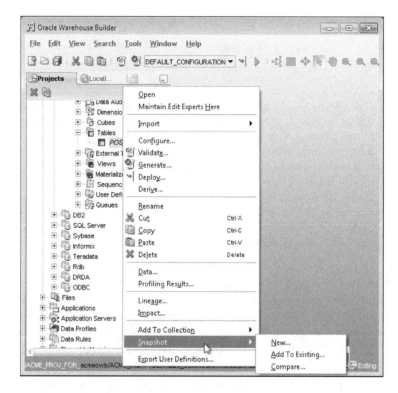

That same menu entry is available on the main menu of the Design Center under the **File** entry. We can create a new snapshot, add this object to an existing snapshot, or compare this object with an already saved snapshot. The last option is particularly useful for seeing what has changed since the snapshot was taken.

Let's first take a snapshot of our POS_TRANS_STAGE table in the new project we created in the last section. We'll right-click on the table name and select **Snapshot | New...** to create a new snapshot of it. This will launch the Snapshot Wizard to guide us through the three-step process as shown next:

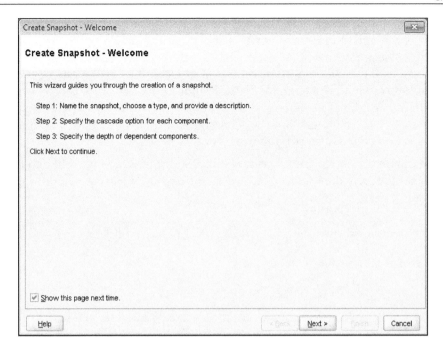

1. We'll click on the **Next** button to move to step 1 of the wizard where we'll give our snapshot a name. This name will be stored in the database as an object name, and so must conform to the Oracle Database requirement that identifiers be no more than 30 characters in length and also must be unique. The wizard will validate the name for us and pop up an error message if we've violated any of the naming conventions, including exceeding the 30-character limit or using invalid characters such as spaces. We'll call our snapshot POS_TRANS_STAGE_SNAP. If we like, we can enter a description also to further identify what is in the snapshot.

   There are two types of snapshots we can take: a **full** snapshot that captures all metadata and can be restored completely (suitable for making backups of objects) and a **signature** snapshot that only captures the signature or characteristics of an object just enough to be able to detect changes in an object. The reason for taking the snapshot will generally dictate which snapshot is more appropriate. We can click on the **Help** button on this screen to get a detailed description of the two options. In our case, we'll take a full snapshot this time. Full snapshots can be converted to signature snapshots later if needed, and can also be exported like regular workspace objects. Having selected **Full**, we click on the **Next** button to move to the next step.

2. This step displays a list of the objects we're capturing in this snapshot. We have the option on this screen to select **Cascade**, which applies to folder-type objects. We can take a snapshot of any workspace object, including nodes and even the entire project itself. We can then select **Cascade** to have it include every object contained within that folder object. This is an easy way to capture a large number of objects at once. In our case, we're only capturing the POS_TRANS_STAGE table, so **Cascade** would have no effect. We'll click on **Next** and move to step 3, the final step.

3. In the final step we are asked to select a depth to which we'd like to traverse to capture any dependent objects for this object. The screenshot of this step is shown next:

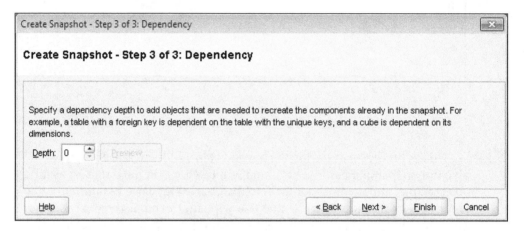

Since our POS_TRANS_STAGE table is a standalone table with no foreign key dependencies on any other tables, the default of zero is fine. Even if there were foreign key dependencies, we may not want to capture the additional tables and so would leave it at zero. If we set it to something higher, it will include any object this object depends on. If it is set to something higher than 1, it will proceed to objects that are dependent on those objects, and so on, until it reaches the depth we've specified.

So, leaving it at **0**, we'll click on **Next** and get the summary display showing us what options we chose. Then we'll click on the **Finish** button, which will actually take the snapshot. It will display a progress dialog box showing that it's working, as seen next:

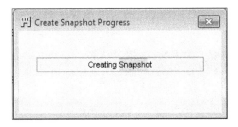

When it is done, it will present us with a completion message. If we want to see what snapshots we've created, there is an interface we can use, which is available on the **Tools** menu of the Design Center. It is called **Change Manager** and will launch the **Metadata Change Management** interface where we can manage our snapshots. It is shown next with our snapshot displayed:

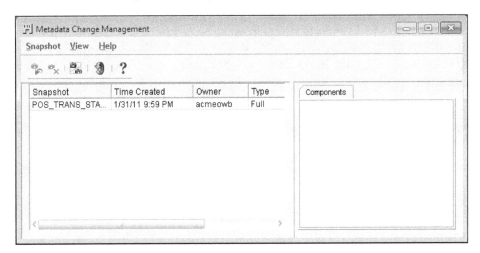

If there were more than one snapshot, each would appear in the list on the left. If we click on an entry on the left, the right **Components** window updates to display the objects that are contained within the snapshot. The following can be performed on the snapshots by clicking on them and then selecting the corresponding menu entry under the Snapshots main menu:

- **Restore**: We can restore a snapshot from here, which will copy the snapshot objects back to their place in the project, overwriting any changes that might have been made. It is a way to get back to a previously known good version of an object if, for example, some future change should break it for whatever reason.

- **Delete**: If we do not need a snapshot anymore, we can delete it. However, be careful as there is no recycle bin for deleted snapshots. Once it's deleted, it's gone forever. It will ask us if we are sure before actually deleting it.

- **Convert to Signature**: This option will convert a full snapshot to a signature snapshot.

- **Export**: We can export full snapshots like we can export regular workspace objects. This will save the metadata in a file on disk for backup or for importing later.

- **Compare**: This option will let us compare two snapshots to each other to see what the differences are.

Let's try the compare feature. We'll do a comparison between a workspace object in our Design Center project and a snapshot, rather than comparing two snapshots. This will make use of the third **Snapshot** menu entry we saw previously when right-clicking an object in the Design Center and selecting the **Snapshot** menu entry. We'll compare our POS_TRANS_STAGE table in our second project with the snapshot we just took. However, let's change something in the table first so that there will be a difference to be found. We could do the comparison now and it would just tell us that the objects are the same. We want to see what it tells us if any differences are found. So let's edit the table in the data object editor by double-clicking on it in the Design Center.

> We don't want to disturb our main project. So we'll make sure the POS_TRANS_STAGE table we double-click on is in the new project we just created, and not the main data warehouse project we just built.

Let's click on the **Columns** tab and scroll down to the end to change the size of the STORE_COUNTRY column to 100 from 50, and then close the editor.

> If we leave the editor open, we would have to click on another column or move the focus out of the length field we just changed for the change to actually be detected by the compare function.

At this point you may get an error popup saying the object cannot be edited in read-only mode. If you save the project, close it, and reopen it that error should clear up and you'll be able to edit the table. When we have made the change and closed the editor, or otherwise moved the focus from the STORE_COUNTRY column length field in the editor, we can go back to Design Center. There we can right-click on the POS_TRANS_STAGE table and select **Snapshot | Compare...** to compare this object with a snapshot. It will pop up a dialog box listing all the snapshots it found that contain the object we clicked on.

In our case it will display just the one snapshot we created as shown next:

If it did not find any snapshots containing the object we selected, it would tell this to us in a message dialog box. As it found one, we'll click on it to select it and then click on the **OK** button and it will do the comparison, giving us a progress dialog box similar to the previous one we saw when we were creating a snapshot. When the process is complete, it will pop up the results in a snapshot comparison window displaying a tree view on the left of the object with any changed elements in the object shown. On the right, it will display a window with tabs that we can select to view the information about the changes. It shows the STORE_COUNTRY column on the left. We'll click on that and the right window will update the tabs with information. The **General** tab will display an overview of the changed element as shown next:

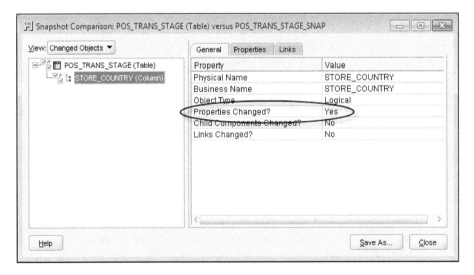

It clearly shows that a property (or properties) has (or have) changed. To see the actual change, we can click on the **Properties** tab and it reports that the length of the column has changed from **50** to **100** as shown next after we scroll the window down some:

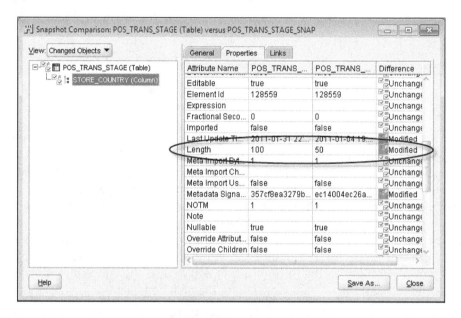

The image has been compressed slightly to better fit the page, but it can be expanded on the screen to display the full column headings. They will clearly show POS_ TRANS_STAGE for the left column with 100 as the length and POS_TRANS_STAGE_SNAP for the right column containing the length of 50 characters in the snapshot. There are also a couple of other modifications that it indicates but those are the date of last change and an internal signature assigned to the object, which we don't control.

This is a very powerful tool that we can use to manage our metadata changes and stay on top of the changes we've been making. So we'll definitely want to make full use of this feature as we build bigger and more involved data warehouses.

If we want to read information about snapshots, we can read the **Oracle Warehouse Builder Concepts Guide**, Chapter 7, **Dependency and Change Management**, which discusses snapshots along with other metadata management topics. It can be found at the following URL: http://download.oracle.com/docs/cd/E11882_01/owb.112/ e10581/metadatamgt.htm#WBCON4623

Before continuing, we'll make sure to edit the STORE_COUNTRY column length to change it back to 50 from 100. We'll then close the **Snapshot Comparison** dialog box by clicking on the **Close** button, and also close the **Metadata Change Management** window if it's still open.

That concludes our discussion about managing metadata changes. Now let's discuss an issue that can arise while we're actually making modifications to data objects and mappings, which is the issue of keeping things synchronized among all the objects we've defined.

Synchronizing objects

We created tables, dimensions, and a cube; and new tables were automatically created for each dimension and cube. We then created mappings to map data from tables to tables, dimensions, and a cube. What happens if, let's say for example, a table definition is updated after we've defined it and created a mapping or mappings that include it? What if a dimensional object is changed? In that case, what happens to the underlying table? This is what we are going to discuss in this section.

One set of changes that we'll frequently find ourselves making is changes to the data we've defined for our data warehouse. We may get some new requirements that lead us to capture a new data element that we have not captured yet. We'll need to update our staging table to store it and our staging mapping to load it. Our dimension mapping(s) will need to be updated to store the new data element along with the underlying table. We could make manual edits to all the affected objects in our project, but the Warehouse Builder provides us some features to make that easier.

Changes to tables

Let's start the discussion by looking at table updates. If we have a new data element that needs to be captured, it will mean finding out where that data resides in our source system and updating the associated table definition in our module for that source system.

Updating object definitions

There are a couple of ways to update table definitions. Our choice will depend on how the table was defined in the Warehouse Builder in the first place. The two options are:

- It could be a table in a source database system, in which case the table was physically created in the source database and we just imported the table definition into the Warehouse Builder.

- It could be a table we defined in our project in the Warehouse Builder and then deployed to the target database to create it. Our staging table would be an example of this second option.

In the first case, we can re-import the source table using the procedures we used in Chapter 2 for importing source metadata. When re-importing tables, the Warehouse Builder will do a reconciliation process to update the already imported table with any changes it detects in the source table. For the second case, we can manually edit the table definition in our project to reflect the new data element.

For a hands-on example here, let's turn to our new project that we created earlier while discussing snapshots. We copied our POS_TRANS_STAGE table over to this project, so let's use that table as an example of a changing table, as we defined the table structure manually in the Warehouse Builder Design Center and then deployed it to the target database to actually create it. For this example, we won't actually re-deploy it because we'll be using that second project we created. It doesn't have a valid location defined, but we can still edit the table definition and investigate how to reconcile that edit in the next section.

So, let's edit the POS_TRANS_STAGE table in the ACME_PROJ_FOR_COPYING project in the Design Center by double-clicking on it to launch it in the table editor. We'll just add a column called STORE_AREA_SIZE to the table for storing the size of the store in square feet or square meters. We'll click on the **Columns** tab, scroll it all the way to the end, enter the name of the column, then select **NUMBER** for the data type, and set the precision and scale to 0 for this example.

We can validate and generate the object without having a valid location defined, so we'll do that. The validation and generation should complete successfully; and if we look at the script, we'll see the new column included.

We now need a mapping that uses that table, which we have back in our original project. Let's use the copy and paste technique we used earlier to copy the STAGE_ MAP mapping over to this new project. We'll open the ACME_DW_PROJECT project, answering **Save** to the prompt to save or revert. Then on the STAGE_MAP mapping entry under **Databases | Oracle | ACME_DWH | Mappings**, we'll select **Copy** from the pop-up menu. We'll open the **ACME_PROJ_FOR_COPYING** project and then on the **Mappings** node, select **Paste** on the pop-up menu.

We ordinarily won't copy an object and paste it into a whole new project just for making changes. We're only doing it here so that we can make changes without worrying about interfering with a working project.

Synchronizing

Many operators we use in a mapping represent a corresponding workspace object. If the workspace object (for instance, a table) changes, then the operator also needs to change to be kept in sync. The process of synchronization is what accomplishes that, and it has to be invoked by us when changes are made.

Now that we have the updated table definition for the POS_TRANS_STAGE table, we have to turn our attention to any mappings that have included a table operator for the changed table because they will have to be synchronized to pick up the change. We saw in Chapter 6 how to create a mapping with a table operator that represents a table in the database. These operators are bound to an actual table using a table definition like we just edited. When the underlying table definition gets updated, we have to synchronize those changes with any mappings that include that table. We now have our STAGE_MAP mapping copied over to our new project. So let's open that in the mapping editor by double-clicking on it and investigate the process of synchronizing.

We'll double-check to make sure we've opened the mapping in the correct project as we now have the same mapping name defined in two separate projects. This is perfectly acceptable and any changes we make to one won't affect the other, but we need to make doubly sure that we're in the correct project. In this case we want to be in the ACME_PROJ_FOR_COPYING project, not in the original ACME_DW_PROJECT project. Another reason is that the operators in the mapping still point back to the original object, which we're going to fix by synchronizing; and we don't want to update the wrong mapping.

When we open the mapping, if we look at the POS_TRANS_STAGE mapping operator, we can scroll down the **INOUTGRP1** attribute group or maximize the operator to view all the attributes to see that the new STORE_AREA_SIZE column that we added to the table is not included.

To update the operator in the mapping to include the new column name, we must perform the task of synchronization, which reconciles the two and makes any changes to the operator to reflect the underlying table definition. We could just manually edit the properties for the operator to add the new column name, but that still wouldn't actually synchronize it with the actual table. Doing the synchronization will accomplish both—add the new column name and synchronize with the table. In this particular case there is another reason to synchronize, which is that we copied this mapping into the new project from another mapping where it was already synchronized with tables in that project. This synchronization information is not automatically updated when the mapping is copied.

To synchronize, we right-click on the header of the table operator in the mapping and select **Synchronize...** from the pop-up menu, or click on the table operator header and select **Synchronize...** from the main menu **Edit** entry. This will pop up the Synchronize dialog box as shown next:

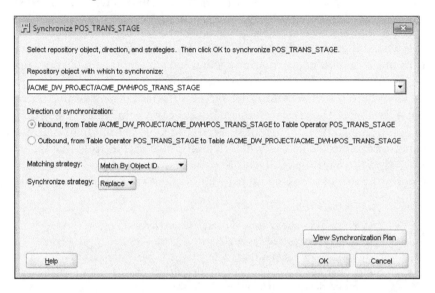

Now we can see why it's so important to make sure we're in the correct project. From the entry indicating the repository object from which it will synchronize, we can see that it's still set to point to the original POS_TRANS_STAGE table in the ACME_DW_PROJECT project and not the new one we just edited in this project. If we were to rely upon this, we would think we are in the wrong project. We need to click on the drop-down menu and select the POS_TRANS_STAGE table in our new COPY_MODULE. In fact, this new copy module is the only one we have available. This is good because we wouldn't want to select an object in another module. It's only set that way in this case because it was just copied from that other project. However, we can tell something is a little strange there because the path listed for the POS_TRANS_STAGE table stops at ACME_DW_PROJECT and no icon is displayed for the type of object. When we select the POS_TRANS_STAGE table in our new project, we get the correct display as shown next:

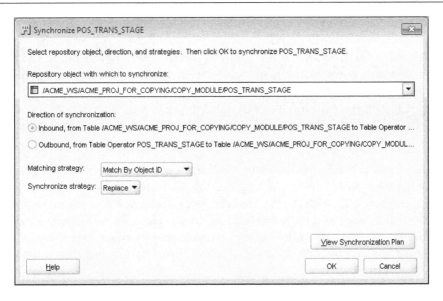

This looks much better. Notice how the path includes the workspace name now to fully place it in context. It knows what kind of object it is, a table, so it can display the correct icon. Now we can proceed with deciding whether this will be inbound or outbound.

Inbound or outbound

Now that we have the correct repository object specified to synchronize with, we have to select whether this is an **inbound** or **outbound** synchronization. Inbound is the one we want and is the default. It says to use the specified repository object to update the operator in our mapping for matching. If we were to select outbound, it would update the workspace object with the changes we've made to the operator in the mapping.

Matching and synchronizing strategy

Having decided on inbound, we now have to decide upon a matching strategy to use. The online help goes into good detail about what each of those strategies is, but in our case, we'll want to select **Match By Object Position** or **Match By Object Name**. The **Match by Object ID** option uses the underlying unique ID that is created for each attribute to do the matching with, and that unique ID is not guaranteed to match between projects. It is a uniquely created ID internal to the Warehouse Builder metadata, which uniquely identifies each attribute. The unique ID it stores in the operator for each attribute is the unique ID from the original table it was synchronized with. If we use that option, it will treat all the objects as new because it is not going to get a match on any of them due to using different unique IDs for the copied table.

If we select the **Replace** synchronize strategy, its side effect in the mapping is that all the connections we've made to the existing attributes in the table from the aggregator will be deleted. This is because it has removed all the existing attributes and replaced them with new attributes from the new table with all the new IDs. If we had selected the **Merge** synchronize strategy, it would have left all the existing attributes alone. However, it would have added in (or merged in) all the attributes from the new table, in effect duplicating them all in our operator, which is clearly not what we want.

Thankfully, there is a solution that will work fine and that is either of the other two **Matching Strategy** selections. By selecting **Match by Object Position**, we'd be telling it to match the operator with the repository object position-by-position, regardless of the unique IDs. So it will not wipe out any connections we've already made as long as there is an attribute in the same corresponding position in the workspace table object. The same holds true for **Match By Object Name**, but this option matches objects by the name of the object and not the position or ID. We know the operator will match all the names and positions of the existing columns, and that the new column has been added to the end. Therefore, we can use either of those two strategies to match and our mapping will remain intact with the existing connections.

With these two options, the **Synchronize Strategy** of merge or replace does not make any difference because all the attributes of the operator in the mapping will be matched in either case. They only indicate what to do with differences. And because the only difference is a new column in the table, regardless of whether we merge in the difference or replace the difference, the net effect is the addition of the new column in the operator.

Viewing the synchronization plan

Based on our selection of the matching and synchronization strategy, the dialog box gives us the option to view what it is going to do before we do it just to be sure we have made the proper selections. We can click on the **View Synchronization Plan** button to launch a dialog box, which will show us what it is going to do. It is nice because we can view the plan without having it actually do anything. So let's select **Match By Object ID** for the matching strategy and **Replace** for synchronization strategy, and click on the **View Synchronization Plan** button. This will launch the **Synchronization Plan** dialog box as shown next:

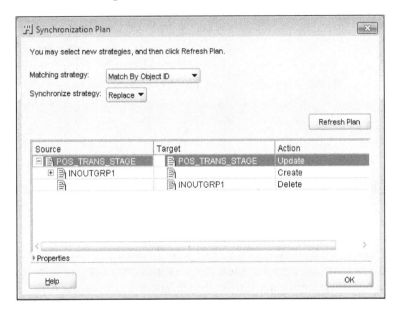

The source is the POS_TRANS_STAGE table definition in the workspace and the target is the table operator in the mapping for that table. When matching by object ID, nothing is going to match because the object IDs for the new table are all different from the original table. The **Replace** option says to replace all differences with the source definitions, so we'll see the INOUTGRP1 from the source will be created and the existing INOUTGRP1 in the target will be deleted. If we were to expand the INOUTGRP1 for the source, we'd see all the attributes listed. That is why all the connections would disappear from our mapping if we used this option.

Let's try the **Merge** synchronize strategy option with the object ID match by changing that drop-down in the dialog box to **Merge** and clicking on the **Refresh Plan** button. Remember that no actual changes are being made here; it is only telling us what it would do if we made those selections in the main dialog box and clicked on **OK** there. This option will display the following:

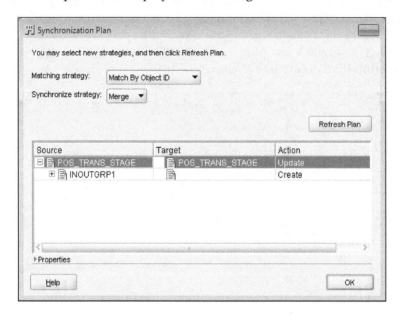

Here we can see that it is creating new entries in the target for the entire INOUTGRP1 attribute group from the source as it didn't find any matches. It is leaving all the existing target attributes alone, thus merging in the differences. The delete of the INOUTGRP1 in the target is gone. This is clearly not what we want because as indicated previously, it will add in duplicates of every attribute.

If we select either **Match By Object Position** or **Match By Object Name** and refresh the plan, we'll see that it lists one action of **Create** for the new column. There may be updates for existing columns that match, but there should be no other creates or deletes showing. This is what we want, so we'll click on the **OK** button to close the Synchronization Plan dialog box. Back in the main Synchronization dialog box, we'll select **Match By Object Name** as the matching strategy and **Replace** as the synchronization strategy.

If this had been an actual update that we had source data for, we would make sure the source data table definition in the workspace was updated to reflect the new data element. As this is related to the store, in our case it would probably have been the STORE source table in the ACME_POS module under **Databases | Non-Oracle | ODBC**. We would then perform the same synchronization operation we just performed on the STORES table operator. We would then have to map that new value through the joiner and to the new column in the POS_TRANS_STAGE table.

We will move along now and discuss one final change and the feature the Warehouse Builder provides for handling it. It is the changing of dimensions and their underlying tables, and keeping them properly bound.

Changes to dimensional objects and binding

When we created our dimensional objects (dimensional in this context being used to refer to both dimensions and cubes) back in Chapter 4, we saw how it automatically created a matching relational table for us. This would be used to hold the data for the object because we had selected ROLAP for the storage implementation. This table was then bound to the dimension with dimension attributes, and levels bound to columns in the table, which we can see on the **physical bindings** tab of the dimension editor.

If we carried our previous example one step further, we'd need to add an attribute to our STORE dimension to hold the new value for the size of the store. This would mean we would have to make sure the STORE dimension and the STORE table stayed properly synchronized. This is not quite the same concept as we just discussed. We are now talking about two data objects, and not a data object and an operator in a mapping. That is why the Warehouse Builder generally refers to this as binding instead of synchronizing.

Let's begin by setting up our ACME_PROJ_FOR_COPYING project with copies of the STORE dimension and STORE table for trying this out. We're going to copy the STORE dimension over to the new project and leave the STORE table behind because, as we'll see in a moment, it is going to get automatically generated.

Now that we have the dimension copied over, there is a bit of housekeeping we need to do first. As with the mapping having a reference back to the table in the original project, our STORE dimension will still be bound back to the STORE table in the ACME_DW_PROJECT, and we need to fix that first before continuing with our example. This will be good for us to get more practice working with objects in the data object editor. So let's open the STORE dimension in the editor by double-clicking on it.

If we click on the physical bindings tab it displays both the dimension and its underlying table; however, we never copied over the table. The dimension is still bound to the original table in our main project we just copied from. Clearly, that is not good and is most likely a bug in the software since you should not be referencing tables in other projects. It can be easily resolved. We need to sever the connection with that table and rebind it to a table in the current project. So let's right-click on the STORE entry in the Projects Navigator and select **UnBind** from the pop-up menu. This will remove all the connections to the STORE_TAB table in the physical bindings tab. Now we need a table to be bound to this dimension. This is where the **Bind** function comes in. With Bind, the Warehouse Builder automatically creates the table for us with all the dimension attributes properly bound.

There is no officially documented process or function for manually binding a dimension and an existing table together. However, it's possible to do it via a feature called **Experts**, which is one of the more advanced topics we can't cover in this introductory book. There is an Expert that has been specifically developed already to do just that. It can be found on the Oracle Technology website via a link to the sample code website: https://codesamples.samplecode.oracle.com/servlets/tracking/id/S604.

Scroll down until you see the Create_Dimension_From.zip file that has an **Expert** to manually bind a table and dimension. The version says 10gR2, but it will still work in 11gR2, which we're using for this book.

This is a site Oracle maintains for Warehouse Builder tips, features, code, utilities, and so on that are not found in the official release and are not officially supported. However, much of the content (including the previously referenced Expert) is developed by the Oracle developers themselves who actually work on the Warehouse Builder. We can find a lot of good stuff on that site, so need not fear the fact that Oracle says it's "unsupported".

Let's right-click on the STORE dimension in the Projects Navigator and select **Bind** from the pop-up menu. This will create a new STORE_TAB table for us, automatically bind the existing dimension attributes and levels to columns in the table, and update the physical bindings tab to show the new table connection. Now if we look in Projects Navigator under the **Tables** node, we can see the new table it created. We can now proceed with our previous example about adding a column. In this case, we'll want to add a column to the STORE dimension to save the size value, So let's go back to the dimension editor to do that.

> We could have saved ourselves a Bind step here by just editing the dimension before we did the first Bind. But the intent was to re-create the situation as it would be for real if we had to edit a dimension that was already bound to a table, which is a real-world situation we'll run into quite frequently. The first Bind was just to set up that scenario.

On the **Attributes** tab, scroll down to the end and enter a new attribute called AREA_ SIZE. Change the data type to **NUMBER** with the precision and scale set to zero. We'll make it an attribute of the STORE level. So click on the STORE level on the **Levels** tab and scroll down the attributes, and check the box beside the AREA_SIZE name.

Let's save our work and go back to the **physical bindings** tab to check the STORE_TAB table, and we'll see that there is no AREA_SIZE column. We need to perform the **Bind** again on the dimension, and that will update the table to include the new column. We do not need to do the **UnBind** this time because the correct table is bound; we just want it updated in place.

After the Bind, the table has been updated now to include the new column. We can verify this on the **physical bindings** tab by inspecting the table.

If this were a working project we had previously deployed, we would need to deploy this updated table and the dimension to actually update the database. We would also need to perform the synchronization (which we discussed in the previous section) in any mappings that included a dimension operator for the STORE dimension, so any mapping operators that referenced the dimension would be up to date.

> When making a change for real like this, make sure the deployment action for the table is set to **Upgrade** and not **Replace** if there is data in the table already, else the deployment will fail. It should default to **Upgrade**.
>
> However, watch out for the error that may occur when trying to do a deployment with an Upgrade status that we discussed in the last chapter.

This completes our discussion of some additional editing features that we can use as we develop and maintain increasingly complicated data warehouses. We are touching upon just the basics about the Warehouse Builder in this book that we need to know to be able to use it to construct a data warehouse. There is a wealth of more advanced features and capabilities we did not have time to cover in this book, so we just mentioned a few along the way. But this lays the groundwork and has equipped us with the ability to build a complete working data warehouse. There are a lot of resources on the Internet to help us further our education about the tool and to provide assistance if we have questions, much of which Oracle provides directly from its websites. We'll finish up the chapter with a brief discussion of some of these resources.

Warehouse Builder online resources

Oracle provides a number of resources to assist us with using the Warehouse Builder and with Data Warehousing in general. We saw one such resource earlier in this chapter when we talked about binding a table to a dimension. That download is just one of many that are available from that OWB Sample Code tips and tricks web site, which is available directly at the link provided previously or as a link off the much larger web page Oracle has that is devoted entirely to Oracle Warehouse Builder at `http://www.oracle.com/technology/products/warehouse/index.html`.

The link to it is under technical information at the bottom of the page.

The OWB developers maintain a blog that they frequently update with various news and notes about OWB—its future or features of interest. The blog is available via a link from the above OWB page or directly at `http://blogs.oracle.com/warehousebuilder/`.

This is an excellent source to get the latest information about OWB directly from the Oracle managers and senior developers who work on the Warehouse Builder. Recently, there is much talk around Oracle and the user community about Oracle's plans relating to their Data Integrator software and the Warehouse Builder software, and how they are moving toward combining the two. The blog has posts about how neither tool is going away and how investment in either tool right now is a good investment for years to come.

If we have questions, there is an Oracle Forum devoted specifically to the Warehouse Builder at `http://forums.oracle.com/forums/forum.jspa?forumID=57`.

Oracle developers as well as many from the user community who have been using OWB for a long time frequent the forum and are willing to answer questions.

The Warehouse Builder is just one tool in a large suite of applications that supports the area of business intelligence and data warehousing as a whole. Oracle's web page devoted to that topic, which includes OWB, is at `http://www.oracle.com/ technology/tech/bi/index.html`.

If we want more information about the larger topic of business intelligence and data warehousing in general, this is a good place to start.

Summary

In this chapter we've finished discussing some additional features of the tool. These are not necessarily essential to the initial development of a data warehouse, but are nevertheless valuable features to have available for further development and maintenance. These include features such as metadata change management, which become critical as more and more changes are required to a data warehouse. The Recycle Bin, the Cut, Copy, and Paste features, Snapshots, and the Metadata Loader all assist greatly in our efforts to control the changes we have to make and to keep a track of prior revisions.

Another valuable feature is the ability to keep the objects synchronized with the operators in the mappings that refer to those objects. Also, we can automatically update objects that are bound together, such as dimensions and the tables used to implement them. These features will assist greatly in the task of making changes to our data warehouse, which will inevitably need to be done in any data warehouse project we undertake as nothing stays static for very long and constant improvement should always be happening.

We have one more extra topic to discuss and that has been saved for a whole chapter at the end. In the final chapter next we'll discuss the new code template technology that's been added to OWB from Oracle Data Integrator (ODI) and making connections natively to heterogeneous databases using Java Database Connectivity (JDBC). These are brand new in this latest 11*g*R2 release of OWB and provide some great new functionality and are evidence of Oracle's strategy for combining features from both tools without leaving either tool behind.

10
Code Template Mappings

Up until now we've covered features in the Warehouse Builder that have been in the product for quite some time now. The 11gR2 release now takes the product a step further, adding new features that are starting to bring functionality in line with Oracle's other data integration product, **Oracle Data Integrator (ODI)**. Oracle's long-term data integration strategy is to combine both OWB and ODI eventually into a single product that serves all the data integration needs of their customers in a way that does not leave behind any work that may have been done by customers in each individual product. By adding features to OWB that are currently in ODI, Oracle is beginning to implement that strategy. To read more about Oracle's intent in this area the following URL contains a white paper that outlines their strategy—(`http://www.oracle.com/technetwork/middleware/data-integrator/overview/sod-1-134268.pdf`). It is available as a link from Oracle's main Oracle Data Integrator Enterprise Edition web page also (`http://www.oracle.com/us/products/middleware/data-integration/059305.html`). Look for the link that says "**Learn more about this strategy**".

The main new feature in the 11gR2 release of OWB that has been included from ODI is the **Code Template** feature otherwise known as **Knowledge Modules** in ODI along with support for **Java Database Connectivity (JDBC)** for extensive built-in support for natively connecting to heterogeneous database systems. This is in addition to the ODBC connectivity we made use of earlier in the book and the gateways that we mentioned as part of Oracle Heterogeneous Services With code templates and JDBC connectivity, OWB now has the capability of in database ETL (Extract, Transform, and Load) capability in non-Oracle databases that was lacking in earlier releases of the Warehouse Builder. In this chapter we're going to build a code template mapping and deploy and execute it. We'll use the existing STAGE_MAP regular mapping we built back in Chapter 6 and implement it as a code template mapping using JDBC.

To do that we'll perform the following tasks:

- Define a JDBC connection to an SQL Server database
- Import table objects from the SQL Server database using the JDBC connection
- Start the Control Center Agent
- Define a template mapping module
- Create a code template mapping by copying another regular mapping
- Deploy and execute a code template mapping

Let's begin with a closer look at the code template concept and discuss a little more exactly what the benefits and features are.

Code templates

The Oracle Warehouse Builder has always provided a rich set of SQL and PL/SQL code that is included for extracting data, transforming it and loading it: but that rich feature set was always centered around an Oracle database. There was, and still is, support for connecting to non-Oracle databases via an ODBC connection or via a gateway module specifically designed for connecting to a non-Oracle database as we discussed earlier in the book, but that feature does not provide any way to perform transformations of data or loading data directly in those other databases. There is also no support for alternative data sources other than flat files via SQL Loader and SAP Enterprise Resource Planning system.

Code template description

With the addition of code templates, which leverage the knowledge module feature of ODI, we now have the capability to perform complex transformations and data integration natively in non-Oracle databases and to access any number of alternative data sources, thus greatly expanding the ability of the Warehouse Builder to handle greater data integration needs. Code templates are a framework for coding support for various data sources. They contain connection information for various platforms as well as the platform-specific code and knowledge needed to perform tasks against those external platforms. A code template contains code written in languages that are specific to these other databases and data sources and greatly leverage the capabilities of those data sources for our use. Mappings can now be created in the Warehouse Builder that make use of the familiar flow-based OWB mapping paradigm using many of the same transformation operators that will now be able to take advantage of these code templates to execute directly in remote non-Oracle databases. These mappings are now known as **Code Template Mappings** and have a new module that is available in the Design Center Projects Navigator to hold them.

Types of code templates

There are various types of code templates that provide functionality for performing different tasks. More details about these types can be found in the *Oracle Warehouse Builder Sources and Targets Guide* in Chapter 12, *Using Code Templates to Load and Transfer Data* at the following URL — http://download.oracle.com/docs/cd/E11882_01/owb.112/e10582/code_templates.htm#WBDOD90618. The following is a list of the various types of code templates in OWB with the corresponding ODI knowledge module name and abbreviation in parentheses for reference along with a brief explanation of each.

- **Load Code Template** (Loading Knowledge Module (LKM)): This type contains code that is responsible for loading data into a staging area. It might better be thought of as an extract template because it extracts data from source databases.

- **Integration Code Template** (Integration Knowledge Module (IKM)): This type of template is responsible for the extraction of the data from the staging area, transforming it, and loading it into the target.

- **Control Code Template** (Check Knowledge Module (CKM)): A control code template handles error checking of data for data quality purposes.

- **Change Data Capture Code Template** (Journalizing Knowledge Module (JKM)): Change data capture is the process of determining what source data has changed so that new changes can be extracted.

- **Oracle Target Code Template** (No ODI equivalent): This code template is a wrapper for all existing OWB code generation capabilities in order to create a fusion of load code templates and OWB code generation for SQL or PL/SQL such that we can use arbitrary load code templates and the likes of match merge, dimension operators or OWB's code generation such as DML error logging. There is no corresponding ODI knowledge module for this one because it is for OWB specifically to allow all the features of OWB code generation to be used within the code template framework. .

- **Function Code Template** (No ODI equivalent): This type is for deploying user-defined functions, procedures, and packages of code.

There is a set of code templates in all these categories that has been supplied pre-defined for our use in OWB. In addition to that, we can also import any code templates (knowledge modules) that have been built in ODI to even further enhance the capabilities provided to us. We're going to construct a code template mapping in this chapter and will need the Design Center and some of those pre-defined code templates so let's go ahead and launch it now and take a look at where they are defined in the Design Center to see just what has been provided for us out of the box.

Pre-defined code templates

Pre-defined code templates are available to us in the **Globals Navigator**. We'll be making use of a load code template and an Oracle target code template in this chapter and we can see those in the following image of the **Globals Navigator**, along with the other categories of code templates.

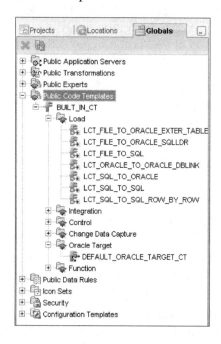

The names all start with an abbreviation that is based on the type of code template except for the **Oracle Target** one; so you have LCT for load code templates, ICT for integration code templates, so on. Following the initial abbreviation there is the name of the particular code template, which gives us some indication of the purpose. For load code templates, the name will indicate what database it extracts data from and then what database type it will load the staging table to. The first name we can see in the previous figure, **LCT_FILE_TO_ORACLE_EXTER_TABLE**, extracts data from a flat file and uses an external table in Oracle to load it. **LCT_FILE_TO_ORACLE_SQLLDR** extracts data from a flat file and loads it using the SQLLDR Oracle utility.

We're going to build a code template mapping that extracts data from an SQL Server database and loads it into an Oracle database so let's see which load code template we can use for that. If we scan the list we don't see any that say SQL Server specifically but we do see Oracle mentioned. We do see load code templates that mention just **SQL** all by itself—**LCT_FILE_TO_SQL, LCT_SQL_TO_ORACLE, LCT_SQL_TO_SQL,** so on. The SQL in this case refers to any heterogeneous database source that conforms to the SQL92 standard. That is any database that implements the standard SQL database language, which SQL Server does. So, one of those will be the one we need for our load code template. The name can give us clue about the source and target but to really verify the source and target platform we can click on the name and view the properties in the **Property Inspector** window. Since we're loading an Oracle database, the **LCT_SQL_TO_ORACLE** code template is the one we'll use, and if we click on it, we can see in the Property Inspector under the **Platforms** entry, that the platform is Oracle and source platform is Generic.

Now, what about a target code template to use? We said before that the integration code templates would be used to extract the data from the staging area, transform it, and load it to the target so wouldn't we want to use one of them? It was indicated above that we'd be using the Oracle Target code template—**DEFAULT_ORACLE_TARGET_CT** instead. Let's discuss briefly the difference and why we'll use the default Oracle target code template.

The integration code templates were all templates that were brought over to OWB from ODI and, as a result, are more generic in the code that they use for database access. They make use of the template-based code generator instead of the OWB regular mapping code generation and while the code that is generated is generally efficient set-based SQL code, it doesn't make use of the full range of set-based and row-based SQL code that OWB does, nor does it make use of PL/SQL like OWB does. For this reason, there are some operators in OWB that are not supported for use in integration code templates. If we're dealing with Oracle databases, and want to continue to make use of OWB's code generation for Oracle and all the available operators without restriction, the Oracle developers have provided us a separate code template called DEFAULT_ORACLE_TARGET_CT. It is really a wrapper around standard OWB mapping code and provides the capability to run regular OWB mappings with new code template mappings. We'll talk about this in more detail when we actually create a code template mapping later on in the chapter.

A discussion of all the pre-defined code templates can be found in the *Oracle Warehouse Builder Data Modeling, ETL, and Data Quality Guide,* *Chapter 7* at the following URL: http://download.oracle.com/docs/cd/E11882_01/owb.112/e10935/sap_km_mappings.htm#WBETL07001.

Before we can build a mapping to make use of these code templates we have to perform some preliminary steps to set up the environment so code templates can be created and connections can be made to the database using Java Database Connectivity (JDBC). Let's begin by defining a connection to our source SQL Server database using JDBC.

Connecting to SQL server using a JDBC database connection

A feature that the code templates bring to OWB is the ability now to make connections natively to other data sources. One of those connection options is the ability to make native connections to remote databases using **Java Database Connectivity**, or just **JDBC** for short.

 Code templates are a framework for using arbitrary APIs to connect to any number of alternative data sources. There is a knowledge module in ODI for making a connection to an Essbase database, which can be ported over to use in OWB, and some OWB users have even integrated PDF files into OWB using code templates.

By native connectivity, we mean being able to connect directly to the remote database without having to go through an external gateway and being able to run code directly in the remote database to perform extraction, transforming, and loading. Remember back to Chapter 2 where we went through all those steps to configure a remote connection to an SQL Server database using ODBC? That connection required that all code run in the Oracle database and just use a database link to connect to SQL Server remotely when data was needed from a table. Well JDBC is much simpler and is done completely from within the Warehouse Builder now and will allow us to now run code directly in the remote database as well.

Downloading the JDBC driver

A requirement to make a JDBC connection is that a JDBC driver is present first. A JDBC driver is specific to the database to be connected to and is supplied by the database vendor or by a third party for that particular database. The driver for SQL Server can be found on Microsoft's downloads site at http://www.microsoft.com/downloads/ and searching for "jdbc driver for sql server". On the resulting search results page, scroll down until you see **Microsoft SQL Server JDBC Driver 3.0** and click that to go to the download page.

If you don't mind typing, the complete URL to take you directly to the driver download page without searching is: `http://www.microsoft.com/downloads/en/details.aspx?FamilyID=a737000d-68d0-4531-b65d-da0f2a735707`.

Click the button beside the file **1033\sqljdbc_3.0.1301.101_enu.exe** to download it. Save the file to disk; the location doesn't really matter as long as we can remember where we saved it. Then we can run it to unpack the file contents. It doesn't matter much where we unpack the file contents to since we just need to get one file out of it, the `sqljdbc.jar` file in the root folder, which is the actual driver file we need. The remainder of the files in that downloaded file from Microsoft are not required for our purposes.

After unpacking the files, locate the `sqljdbc.jar`, file which should be in the root directory of the unpacked files, and copy it into the Warehouse Builder home folder in the following location:

`OWB_HOME/owb/lib/ext`

Substitute for `OWB_HOME` the actual drive and path to the home location where the OWB client software is installed, which will be under the main database home location. We can now proceed to creating a module to hold the tables imported from our SQL Server data source using this JDBC driver.

Creating a SQL server module

Back in Chapter 2, we used ODBC via the generic gateway to make a connection to the SQL Server database and created our module under the ODBC node under Databases in the Design Center. For JDBC, we will need to create our module directly under the SQL Server databases node. These steps are all provided in the OWB documentation, in the *OWB Sources and Targets Guide, Chapter 6 – Connecting to Data Sources Through JDBC*, which can be accessed at the following URL: `http://download.oracle.com/docs/cd/E11882_01/owb.112/e10582/jdbc_connection.htm#CHDHEGEK`.

Configuring SQL server TCP/IP port

The first thing we have to do, however, which is not mentioned in the documentation, is to get our SQL Server installation to listen on a TCP/IP port. SQL Server Express is not set up to listen on TCP/IP by default but it is easy to configure it to do that. These steps here are summarized from the SQL Server Books Online help documentation in the section about how to configure a Server to listen on a specific TCP Port.

- In SQL Server Configuration Manager (start menu under Configuration Tools in the Microsoft SQL Server 2008 group), in the console pane on the left, expand **SQL Server Network Configuration**, expand **Protocols for <instance name>**, and then double-click **TCP/IP** on the right.

- In the resulting **TCP/IP Properties** popup, on the **Protocol** tab, make sure **Enabled** is set to Yes.

- Click the **IP Addresses** tab and there will be entries for a number of IP addresses on the computer. At a minimum just make sure the localhost IP address, 127.0.0.1, is enabled and the local loopback address is enabled. The IP address for the local loopback adapter will be something like 10.10.10.10 or some other non-routable IP address. Check what address that is from a command-prompt window with the command ipconfig /all and just look for the one with the description **Microsoft Loopback Adapter**.

- There will be an entry at the end of the IP addresses called IPAll, which applies to all the IP addresses and it will list a TCP/IP port number labelled **TCP Dynamic Ports**. Remember this port number because that is the one we'll need to use in a moment when configuring connection details back in OWB.

- Restart the SQL Server instance. It can be done from within the **SQL Server Configuration Manager** by clicking the **SQL Server Services** entry on the left and then right-clicking the SQL Server service on the right and selecting **Restart**.

 To verify that our configuration settings actually took effect and SQL Server is now listening on a TCP/IP port we can check the SQL Server log file. The SQL Server database log file is accessible from the SQL Server Management Studio. Connect to your SQL Server database as your administrative user and access the database logs under the **Management...SQL Server Logs** entry. Double-click the current log and search for text similar to what is shown circled in the following image and be sure to note the port number since we'll need it in a moment:

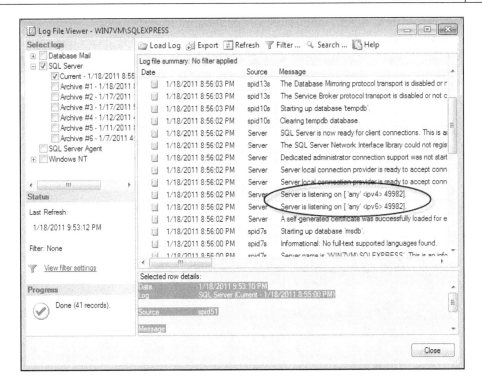

Now that we have SQL Server listening on a TCP/IP port and know what that port is, we can continue with creating a module to hold our SQL Server tables.

Creating SQL server module

We'll summarize the steps here to get our module set up complete with some screen shots that you won't get from the documentation to help visualize the steps. These steps are very similar to what we did back in Chapter 2 to set up the ODBC module but the connection information will be different since we're connecting via JDBC now and not ODBC.

1. In the **Design Center Projects Navigator** we'll right-click on the **Databases... SQL Server** node and select **New SQL Server Module** from the pop-up menu and then click the **Next** button to bypass the introductory screen if it displays.

2. The first step as shown below is to give the module a name, an optional description, and to choose the access method to use. We'll call our new module `SQL_Server_JDBC` to distinguish it from our ODBC module. The name can be anything we want as long as it is different from any other module names we've already used. This name is OK to indicate the source database and the connection type but if there is more than one database on the source system, we could use a variation of the database name instead. For the access method, we'll choose the **Native Database Connection** since we're using JDBC. After entering the name, we'll click **Next** to continue.

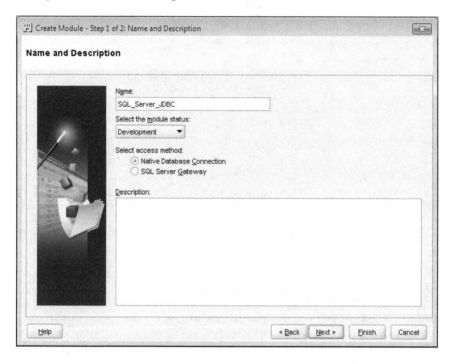

3. The next screen is where we choose our connection information. We've seen this kind of screen before for specifying connection information but the options are slightly different. We'll click the **Edit** button beside the name to open the SQL Server Location dialog box. It is shown next after being filled in.

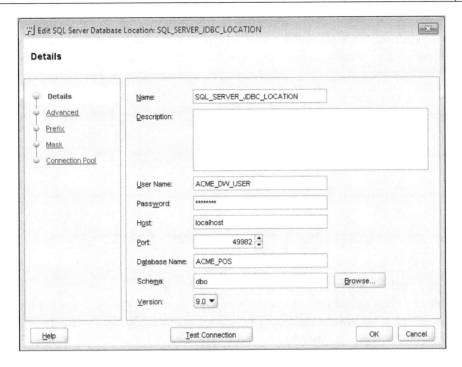

- ○ The name it suggests is fine except we'll remove the number one from the end.

- ○ For user name and password we'll be using the same user name and password we used for the ODBC connection. Notice, however, that unlike the ODBC connection, we do not have to enclose the name and password of our ACME_POS SQL Server database user in double quotes. That was required by the ODBC connection because the information was passed through the Oracle database first, where as this connection will be straight to SQL Server using JDBC.

- ○ The host name in this case is the host where the SQL Server database is actually located and the Port will be the port it is listening on that we configured and verified from the SQL Server log above.

- ○ The database name and schema are the same as we used for the ODBC connection but no double quotes are required here either.

- ○ The version in this case is different since it refers to the version of SQL Server and not the Oracle version. The highest version available to select is version 9.0 but SQL Server Express 2008 is actually version 10 of SQL Server. That turns out not to be a problem. It will still work as version 9.0 so we'll leave it set as that.

4. We can press the **Test Connection** button now to make sure we've specified everything correctly and we should get a success message pop up. If we have specified something incorrectly like the TCP/IP port, we'll see something like the following:

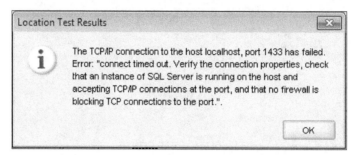

5. We'll click the **OK** button to close the **SQL Server Database Location** dialog box after the connection details have all been set.

6. Back on the Connection Information page there is a checkbox at the bottom to check if we want to import into our new module after we finish. We'll go ahead and click on that box to check it.

7. We'll click **Next** on the Connection Information page after checking the box to import after finishing and it will show us a summary of the configuration, which we can verify and go back and correct if needed. When we are happy with the configuration, we can click the **Finish** button on the **Summary** page to create the module.

Importing metadata

Since we checked the box to import after finishing we will be launched right into the Import Metadata Wizard. This a very similar process to that for the ODBC import, but there are a couple of additional database object types we can choose to import in addition to Tables and Views—Transformations and Sequences. We'll see that in a moment. At this point we should be seeing the Import Metadata Wizard introductory screen as shown next:

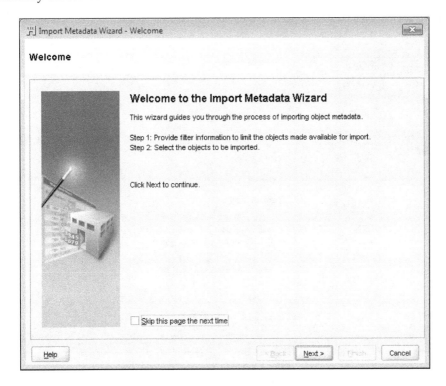

If we don't have the Import Metadata Wizard running if import after finish wasn't checked we can easily start it up manually by right-clicking on the newly created **SQL_Server_JDBC** module under **Databases...SQL Server** and clicking the **Import... Data Objects** menu entry. We will perform the following steps to import our source tables from SQL Server using our new module and JDBC connection.

1. The first step, Step 1 of 3, is to choose the type of objects we'd like to import. We can see on this screen, as shown next, that we can import tables, views, sequences or transformations. Transformations are functions and procedures. We only want tables so we'll check that box as shown below and click **Next** to continue.

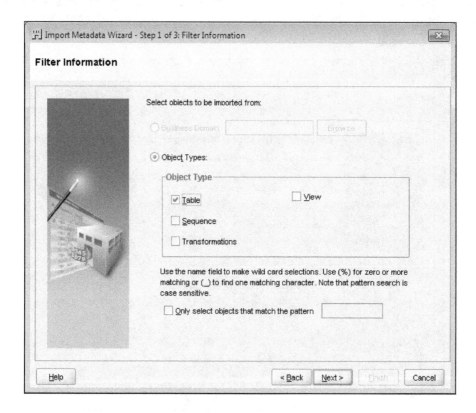

2. The next step is to select the actual objects that we want to import. We'll be presented with a screen that shows a tree view on the left of the object types we checked off from the previous screen and if we click the plus sign beside an object type, **Tables** in our case, we'll see a list of the tables that are defined in the SQL Server ACME_POS database, as shown next:

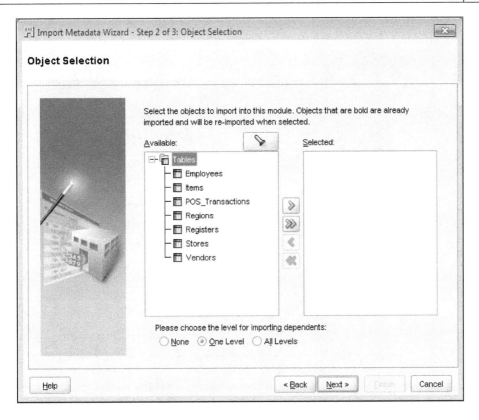

3. We can click on individual tables now and click the right arrow in the middle of the screen to move them over to the **Selected** side or we can just click the double right arrow to move them all over. If we change our minds after moving one or more over, we can always deselect them by clicking on a table on the right and then clicking the left arrow to move it back.

4. When we have made our selections our screen should now look like the following and we click the **Next** button to continue:

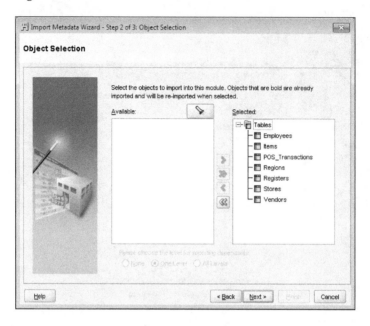

5. After clicking **Next** above, we'll be presented with the summary screen, which will show us what it is going to do based upon our selections as shown next:

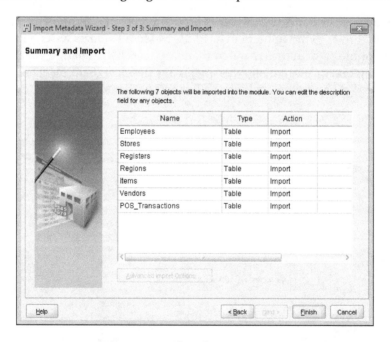

6. We'll click on the **Finish** button now to begin the import process. It will display a progress dialog box as it's importing so we can see how far along it is. When it completes it will pop up the **Import Results** Dialog box as shown next:

7. From here we can click the **OK** button to complete the import or if something does not look right we can click the **Undo** button to reverse all the changes we just made so they will not be saved.

Having clicked the **OK** button to close out the table import into our new SQL Server module we're now ready to build a mapping. We're going to build a mapping identical to the STAGE_MAP we built before except that this one will be a Code Template mapping. It will make use of the new code templates to execute its logic and load the staging table instead of the PL/SQL code and ODBC connection the regular mapping used.

Building a code template mapping

Code template mappings are not created under the **Mappings** node where we've created all our previous regular mappings because they are implemented differently than the regular mappings. To recall, regular mappings were created in the **Mappings** node, which fell under the **Oracle Database** node for our project. That is because mappings up until now were mostly only executed in an Oracle database. There are exceptions to that such as flat file loads using the SQL Loader utility or SAP mappings, but for the most part, existing mapping execute in Oracle databases. With the introduction of code template mappings, a single mapping can now be executed across two or more databases and so the node to hold code template mappings was added at the same level as the **Databases** node in the **Projects Navigator** hierarchy. It is just to hold all code template mappings, and so is called **Template Mappings** and it is highlighted in the image below for reference:

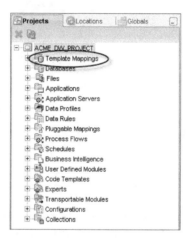

All objects created in the Warehouse Builder are contained within a module so, since the code template mappings are all stored here, separate from a database module, we need to create a template module first that will hold our code template mappings and that will define our connection information for the mappings.

The connection information for a template mapping module is different than for a database module. We're not going to specify a particular database connection like we did before because template mappings can execute in any database. They don't connect directly to a database but connect to a **Control Center Agent (CCA)**, which must be running on the database server containing the database or databases we want to connect to. The CCA will handle the JDBC connections to the database for executing the mappings. A CCA is required for any data source, not just databases. It can be hosted on any machine acting as a data source and there can be any number of them. For our purposes we're using just one.

When we create the module we need to specify the connection details, which means we need to have a CCA running somewhere to specify, so the first step we'll take in creating a mapping is to start up the CCA on our database server. Strictly speaking, we don't actually have to have the CCA running to be able to specify the module that points to it, but there is an optional test-connection step that we'll see in a moment that would be nice to have working, so we'll start up the CCA at this point.

Starting the Control Center Agent

Just as the Warehouse Builder has provided us a default control center location on our current server for use with our regular mappings, it provides a default control center agent also. We just need to make sure it is started up since it does not run automatically.

To start the CCA we need to open a command-prompt window and navigate to our Oracle home folder location and the folder `owb/bin/win32` under that. Execute the following command from the Windows command prompt in that folder:

```
ccastart.bat
```

If this is the very first time this has run, it will prompt us for a password to use to assign to the **oc4jadmin** user, which is the user it will use while running. Provide a suitable password and make sure to remember it since it will prompt for that password in the future if we try to stop the control center agent using the `ccastop.bat` script.

If you're running this on Windows 7 there may be some file permission issues that will cause the following error message to appear in the command-prompt window:

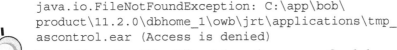

```
java.io.FileNotFoundException: C:\app\bob\
product\11.2.0\dbhome_1\owb\jrt\applications\tmp_
ascontrol.ear (Access is denied)
```

Your folder path will be different depending on your Oracle home location and the file name may be different but the gist of the error is that file permissions are not set so that the script can access the folder. To solve the problem, it is best to just set the permissions on the **owb** folder as a whole to prevent any further problems. In Windows Explorer, find the Oracle home folder, expand it, and right-click on the **owb** folder and select **Properties** from the pop-up menu that appears.

In the resulting dialog, click the **Security** tab and click the **Edit** button to edit the permissions for that folder. On the **Permissions** dialog that pops up make sure **Authenticated Users** is highlighted, which is for all Windows users who have been properly authenticated to Windows. Edit the permissions in the box below for Authenticated Users to check the box for **Modify** and the box for **Write** and leave the other boxes checked as is. The ccastart.bat processing needs to be able to write to folders and modify folders under the owb folder in Oracle home so these permissions are required for it to function properly.

After checking the required boxes, click the **OK** button to close the Permissions dialog and the **OK** button again to close the OWB properties dialog and run ccastart.bat again and it should run with no problem.

When the control center agent is fully running it will display a line in the output window indicating that it is initialized as shown next:

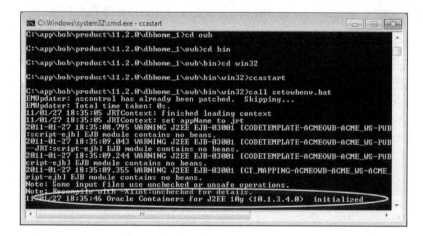

As soon as the initialized message appears, we're ready to begin the definition of our new template mapping module.

Defining a template mapping module

With the control center agent now running, we're ready to create a new module to hold our template mappings. We will create it under the Template Mappings node that we saw above, by right-clicking on it and selecting **New Mapping Module**. We'll run through the following steps, which will be familiar now from having created other modules previously:

1. The first screen is just the welcome screen that we'll click **Next** on to move to Step 1 where we'll give our new module a name and optional description. We're going to be lazy this time and just accept the default name it suggests, **MAPPING_MODULE_1**. Feel free to change if you would prefer something else. Clicking the **Next** button moves us on to Step 2 to provide connection information.

2. Step 2 is where we define the connection details. This is real easy because it has predefined a default agent location for us and all we have to do is provide the password we assigned above when we first started it up. So, we'll click the **Edit** button and it will display the **Edit Agent Location** dialog as shown below. All we have to do is type in the password. It has filled in the user name already and the remainder of the dialog is grayed out so we don't have to worry about setting anything else.

3. After entering the password, we can click the **Test Connection** button to make sure we can connect and since we started up the CCA prior to creating the module it should pop up a success message dialog. After closing that success dialog with the **OK** button, we'll close out of this one by pressing **OK** and we'll be back at the Step 2 screen, which is shown below with our password filled in and all the other connection details entered for us:

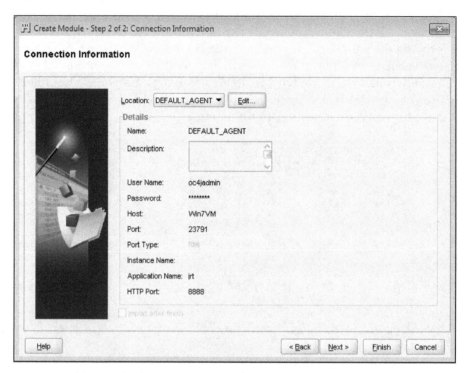

4. We'll click the **Next** button and we will get the summary screen shown next and we can just click **Finish** to complete the module creation.

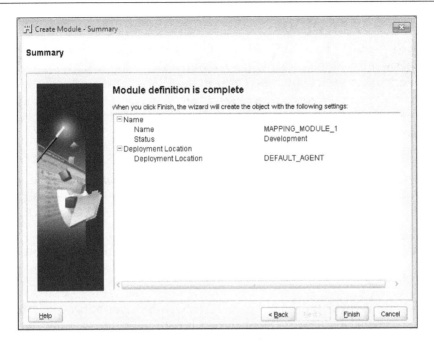

5. Upon completion, the new module will be available in the **Projects Navigator** window under the **Template Mappings** node.

Now that we have a module created we're ready to create a code template mapping in it so let's proceed directly to that step.

Creating a code template mapping

Code template mappings are created just like regular mappings; we can right-click on the **Template Mappings** node and select **New Code Template Mapping** and then begin defining our template on the canvas by dragging and dropping objects from the component palette. That is if we want to start out from the very beginning—but we've already built a map to load the staging table as a regular map—let's see about copying that and turning it into a code template mapping. That would save us a lot of work and it demonstrates some of the power of the Warehouse Builder to make use of existing features while adding new ones.

Copying a mapping

So, what we'll be doing is copying the **STAGE_MAP** regular mapping we've already built and pasting it into the code template module so we can make a few edits to it so it will work using code templates. Perform the following steps to copy and paste the mapping. We went over copying and pasting in the last chapter and this is very similar to that; however, we won't be pasting into a completely new project. We'll use the same project but just a different module.

1. The first step is to find our existing **STAGE_MAP** mapping in the **Databases | Oracle | ACME_DWH | Mappings** node. Right-click on it and select **Copy** from the pop-up menu or left-click on it to select it and then press the *Ctrl+C* key combination. We now have the **STAGE_MAP** in our clipboard.

2. Next we'll access the **MAPPING_MODULE_1** module in the **Template Mappings** node by expanding it in the Projects Navigator if it's not already expanded.

3. We'll right-click on the **MAPPING_MODULE_1** module and select **Paste** from the pop-up menu or just click on it with the left mouse button and press the *Ctrl+V* key combination to paste our copied map into the Template Mappings module. We will get the same Paste Action popup as we saw in Chapter 9 while it pastes the mapping.

We'll get a warning popup with the following message:

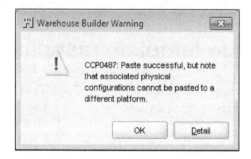

The physical configuration it is talking about refers to the Oracle database-specific configuration properties that were created for the mapping. As a code template mapping, the physical configuration now is a JDBC connection location and code template code instead of Oracle specific. All we have to do is make a few edits and it will be ready to go as a code template mapping, so this is not a problem.

Editing a code template mapping

We'll just click the **OK** button on the warning dialog to close it and we now have our **STAGE_MAP** mapping copied over to the code template module and it appears now under **MAPPING_MODULE_1**. Let's double-click on it to open it in the Template Mapping Editor window. When opened, it will look very similar to the mapping editor for a regular mapping. It will look similar to the following:

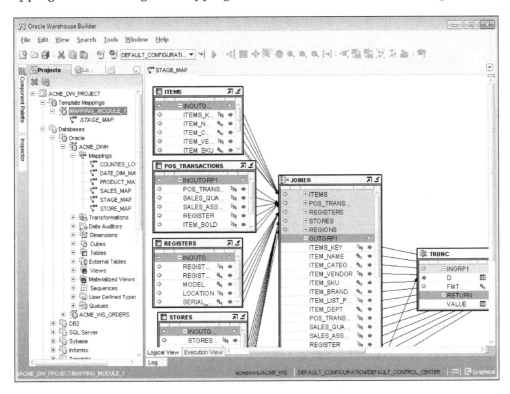

What is different is that we can see that there are two tabs available for this editor at the bottom of the screen, one for the Logical View, which it is showing in the above image, and one for the Execution View, which we'll get to in a moment and which is where we'll specify the code templates to use.

Working in the logical view

For now, however, we'll continue working in the logical view because we have a few minor modifications to make. Keep in mind while working in the logical view that it is exactly like working in the regular mapping editor. Operators can be moved around and joined together and they can be dragged and dropped from the Component Palette and Projects Navigator just like before.

When using code templates, not all the operators will work with all code templates. We have to be aware of that as we're building our logical view. We talked earlier in the chapter about how some operators are not available for use with Integration Code Templates for example. For a complete list of the operators that cannot be used with integration or load-code templates see the *Oracle Warehouse Builder Data Modeling, ETL, and Data Quality Guide, Chapter 7* section on *Mapping Operators Only Supported in Oracle Target CT Execution Units:*

```
http://download.oracle.com/docs/cd/E11882_01/
owb.112/e10935/sap_km_mappings.htm#WBETL07012
```

The main modification we're going to have to make here is to change the source table operators. Recalling back to when we built the STAGE_MAP mapping in Chapter 6 in the *Adding source tables* section under *Creating a Mapping* we dragged and dropped all the source tables from our ACME_POS module under the ODBC node. They are still bound to that module as we can see next when holding the mouse pointer over the title bar of the table operator:

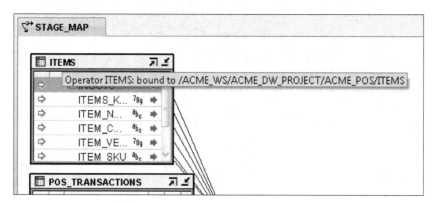

To fix this we can just delete all those existing source table operators and then drag and drop them from the **SQL Server JDBC** module under the **SQL Server node** instead of the **ODBC** node. Another option would be to select each existing table in turn and perform the **Synchronize inbound** procedure on it to select a different table object but we're going to see a new feature in a moment, connecting two attribute operator groups together, that we wouldn't see if we used the option to synchronize. We talked about the synchronize process in Chapter 9 in the *Synchronizing Objects* section so, rather than repeat that, we'll delete the tables and add them again to gain some exposure to additional features of OWB. So let's do that now.

We'll just click on each source table and press the *Delete* key and answer yes to the popup that appears asking for confirmation to make sure deleting them is really what we want to do. We can also right-click on the title bar of the table operator and select **Delete** from the pop-up menu. To recap, we're going to delete the following five table operators from our STAGE_MAP template mapping logical view:

- ITEMS
- POS_TRANSACTIONS
- REGISTERS
- STORES
- REGIONS

After they are all deleted, we'll open the **SQL_SERVER_JDBC** module under the **SQL Server** node in the Projects Navigator so we can drag the tables back into our mapping from there. We'll click on the above five tables one at a time under the **Tables** node of the **SQL_SERVER_JDBC** module and drag them onto the mapping, placing them where the table operators were that we deleted. We'll use the above ordering of table names so our connector lines will not cross over when we connect them up to the **JOINER** operator.

When we have our table operators all placed we can now connect them up to the **JOINER**. We'll make use of the feature of the mapping editor that allows us to drag an output group from one operator and drop it on an input group of another to connect all the attributes in that group. The difference now is that there are already attributes defined in the **JOINER** input groups for each table and so the Warehouse Builder is going to pop up a new screen we haven't seen yet that asks us how we want to handle the matching.

Let's do that now with the **ITEMS** table and drag a connector from the **INOUTGRP1** input/output group of the **ITEMS** table operator and drop it on the **ITEMS** input group of the **JOINER**. When we do that a dialog will pop up in which we can specify how to connect up the attributes as shown next:

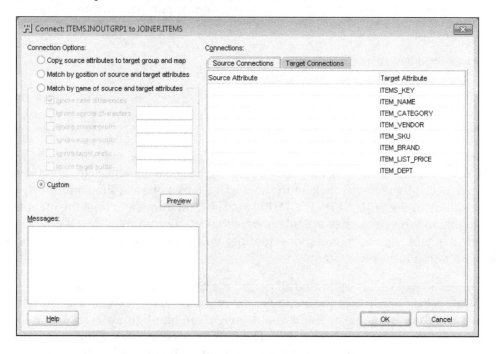

We can choose from four different options on the left. Each of them will be described next:

- **Copy source attributes to target group and map**: This option will just copy each source attribute to the target and create a new attribute in the target for it without matching anything. If an attribute with the same name exists in the target it will just rename it when it copies it so it doesn't conflict with an existing attribute. The **Preview** button is to have it display for us what it's going to do so we can verify that's the behavior we really want. If we choose that option right now and click **Preview** we'll see the following in the **Messages** box, which tells us we really don't want this option because we want to match the names:

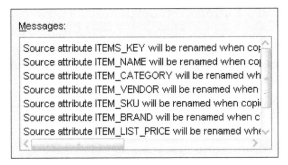

- **Match by position of source and target attributes**: This option will match up a source attribute to whatever target attribute is in the same position as it regardless of the name. This option looks like it could work for us. Let's click that option and then click the **Preview** button. It will fill in source attributes on the **Source Connections** tab on the right each lined up with the target attribute that it will connect to and we can see that they all line up perfectly. Let's discuss the other two options first before completing this dialog.

> The **Source Connections** tab is for specifying the source attributes that will be connected to the listed target attributes and the **Target Connectors** tab is for specifying the target attributes and will be connected to the listed source attributes. They both really provide the same information in the end but just offer a different perspective, either from source to target, or from target to source for specifying the connections. Those tabs are what get updated when we press the **Preview** button to tell us what it's going to do.

- **Match by name of source and target attributes**: This option will do just what it says, match up any matching names between source and target. If there are no matching names, it will create a target attribute to match. Let's select that option and press the preview button and see what our Source Connections and Target Connections tabs look like now. They look exactly like they did with the previous option that matched by position because, in this case, it just so happens that there are matching source and target names and that the matching names are also in the same position. When this option is selected there are a number of other options that become selectable to dictate some rules it will follow to do the match. We can check and uncheck any of them and click **Preview** to see the effect. We'll just leave the first one checked by default to not be case sensitive.

- The final option is **Custom**: This option will allow us to just type in an attribute name in either the **Source** or **Target Connections** tab depending on which one we'd like to specify. If we select that option and press **Preview**, it will clear out any previously filled in source attributes on the source tab and leave them all blank because we have to explicitly tell it what to match. If we select **Custom** and then click in the first source field on the **Source** tab and start typing one of the source attribute names, a pop-up menu of names will appear of all the source attributes as displayed below and we can just select the one we want and it will populate that field. If we type something that doesn't match the start of any source attributes it will just display **(no match found)**. We can then do the same on each subsequent field until they are all matched. This option would be good if names don't match and the positions are not the same either.

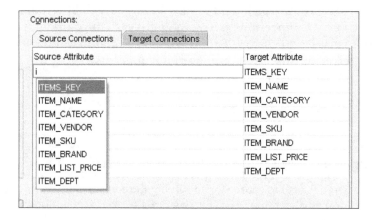

So, after all that discussion, we can see that either the match by position option or the match by name option will work so we'll choose one of those and click the **OK** button and it will draw all the connecting lines for us from **ITEMS** to the **JOINER ITEMS** input group. If the **OK** button is grayed out and not selectable, we need to just click the **Preview** button first and then we can click **OK**. That is a real time saver when doing mappings like this and saves us from having to draw individual lines from each attribute to remap them.

Let's continue now in like manner through the remainder of the table operators dragging each **INOUTGRP1** group to the appropriate input group of the **JOINER**, selecting the match by name option, clicking **Preview** and then **OK**. After we have done that. we'll save our work so far before continuing.

There is one final step we need to take while in the Logical View and that is to set the **Loading Type** property of the target **POS_TRANS_STAGE** table. Back in Chapter 6 when we originally built the mapping, we left it set to the default of INSERT, which means every running of the mapping will simply insert records into the table and leave any existing records there. We're now going to change that to TRUNCATE/INSERT so this code template mapping will first truncate the table (remove all existing records) and then insert the new records.

Let's click on the **POS_TRANS_STAGE** table operator in the logical view and in the **Property Inspector**, scroll down until we see the **General Section** and under that the **Loading Type** property. Click the dropdown and change it to TRUNCATE/INSERT. That way, since we've already populated that table using the regular mapping we won't get duplicate records in our staging table after running this mapping. We could also go back and change the original regular mapping to do that if we wanted to be able to run it more than once on the same set of data. The **Property Inspector** should look like the following after making that setting change:

Our logical view is now complete and back the way it was looking before, so we're ready to move on to define the **Execution** view. We don't need to do anything with any of the other operators since they will work as is, even the target table operator because our target hasn't changed. We're still writing to the Oracle database **ACME_DWH** target.

Working in the execution view

It is now time to configure our execution view for the mapping. A code template mapping gets broken up into **execution units**, which group various operators on the mapping for execution. There can be any number of execution units defined for the mapping depending on how complex it is and the processing that is needed. The execution units then get assigned code templates to use to execute them. That is how we will associate code templates with our mapping.

Knowing the different kinds of code templates that are available and the operators we have used in the logical view will help us decide how to break down our mapping into execution units. For instance, we've stated earlier in the chapter how we'll make use of a load code template for extracting data out of the source system. We can then look at our logical view of our mapping and decide what operators are involved in the extraction of data from the source system.

Let's get started with that now. We'll click the **Execution View** tab and we'll be presented with a completely new canvas type interface we've not seen yet. It is new in this latest release of the Warehouse Builder just to give us a view of our mapping for defining execution units and assigning code templates. When we first look at the Execution View, it will look like the following:

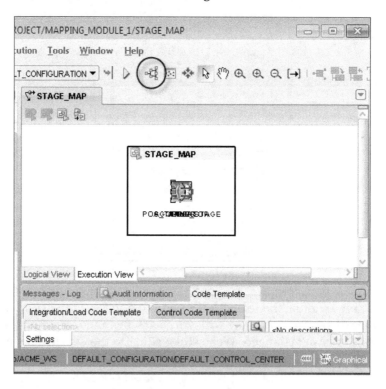

Well, that doesn't look very helpful, does it? When we copied the regular mapping into the templates module, it created a default execution unit for us named for the entire mapping and just put everything inside it on top of one another. Fortunately, we have a way to make it look a little better and that is the auto-layout button in the toolbar, which we've seen before. It's circled in the previous image. Just click that and the operators will all expand so we can see better what is going on. We now have something that looks like this:

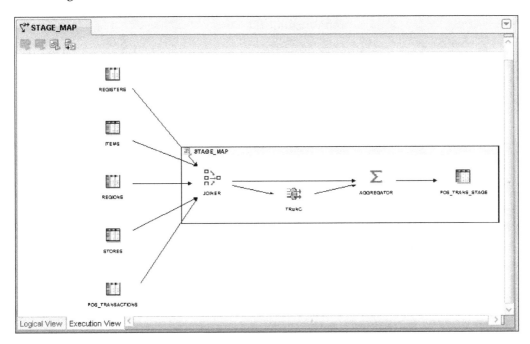

We can now see that not quite all the operators are inside that default execution unit called **STAGE_MAP**. The table operators we deleted and recreated are outside the execution unit. If we had looked at this view at the very start before making any edits, we would have seen them inside the execution unit also, but when we deleted them and recreated them, the assignment to an execution unit was deleted too because the table operators we dropped into the mapping to replace the original ones are from the JDBC module, which this default Oracle target mapping is not designed to handle. Remember we said earlier that the default target mapping is really just a wrapper around regular PL/SQL mapping code so any table operators would have to make use of regular modules, like ODBC or a gateway.

Let's take a look at that execution unit called **STAGE_MAP** that it created to see if we can use it or if we have to just delete it and create a new one. We'll click on it either on the top label bar or somewhere inside it but not on any of the operators defined in it. When we do that, we'll see that one of the tabs in the message window has updated. In fact it's a new tab that is added to the message window and viewable when working in the **Execution View**. It is the **Code Template** tab and currently displays the name of the execution unit we've selected as we can see in the following image:

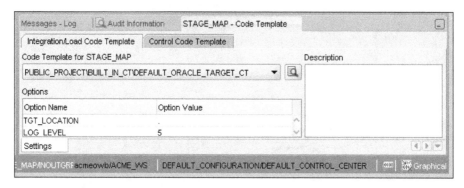

This tab is for assigning the code template that the execution unit will have and we can see that it has automatically assigned the **DEFAULT_ORACLE_TARGET_CT** code template. That is the one the Warehouse Builder will always automatically assign when a regular mapping is copied since it will allow all the regular operators to be used. In fact, we could run this mapping with every operator inside this one execution unit as it was first copied in before we replaced the source table operators and it would work. It would not have made use of our new JDBC native connection to SQL Server, so for that we have to use a separate code template.

We said earlier that we'd be using a load code template and the default Oracle target code template so we will be able to use this default one that has been assigned for us but we will make some changes to the operators that are in it and will add a new execution unit. We'll do that now.

Creating an execution unit

Let's start by creating a new execution unit around the five source table operators. To create an execution unit we have to first select the operators that we want in the execution unit so let's select the five source table operators by drawing a box around them to select them all at once. We'll just click on the canvas to the upper left of the operators and hold down the left mouse button while we drag the box down until it encompasses all five operators. We can now select **Create Execution Unit** from the **Execution** main menu or we can just click the **Create Execution Unit icon** that has now become active at the top left of the mapping canvas window as shown next:

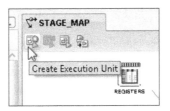

A new execution unit will now be created and we can see that it has assigned a default name, **EX_UNIT_1** (or some other number depending on how many other execution units were created this session). The first thing we'll do is rename the execution unit, so we'll right-click on it and select **Open Details** from the pop-up menu. We will change the name to SQL_SERVER_LOAD and click the **OK** button.

Let's now click on it and look at the **Code Template** tab of the messages window and we can see that no code template has been assigned to it. This execution unit will be for loading data from our SQL Server database and so we want to specify one of the load code templates to use. From our discussion earlier in the chapter we said we'd be using the **LCT_SQL_TO_ORACLE** code template to load from a generic SQL based database into Oracle so let's click on the dropdown on the **Integration/ Load Code Template** tab and select the **PUBLIC_PROJECT\BUILT_IN_CT\LCT_SQL_TO_ORACLE** entry and our Code Template window should now look like the following when the proper selection is made:

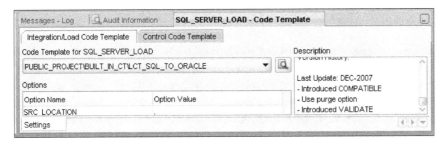

There are also several options we can specify in that window but we're going to leave them all set to the default as that will suffice for our purpose. A description of what all those options are can be found in the Oracle documentation in the *Warehouse Builder Data Modeling, ETL, and Data Quality Guide* at the following URL: http:// download.oracle.com/docs/cd/E11882_01/owb.112/e10935/sap_km_mappings. htm#BABJHFHI. This will take you right to the section entitled *Setting Options for Code Templates in Code Template Mappings*. We have one more step to take and that is to move an operator out of the **STAGE_MAP** execution unit into the **SQL_SERVER_ LOAD** unit.

Moving an operator between execution units

The use of code templates gives us some flexibility now in just what tasks we want to accomplish in what database. We're now able to do more using our source database than we could before with just regular mappings that all executed entirely in the Oracle database. We can add more operators to this new **SQL_SERVER_LOAD** execution unit other than just the source table operators. It would still work as it is now, but notice that the **JOINER** is defined over in the Oracle execution unit, which means the actual joining of the source tables would happen in the Oracle database once the tables have been copied over there by the load code template. That means the load code template would have to copy over five tables into the Oracle database and create five temporary work tables over there to hold them and then the Oracle code template would have to do the join. If we were to move that JOINER over into the SQL Server load code template, we could have the SQL Server database do the work of joining the tables and it would then have to copy over just one table to Oracle consisting of the results of applying the join to the five tables. That sounds like a good idea so let's move the **JOINER** over to the **SQL_SERVER_LOAD** execution unit.

To move an operator between units we have to first remove it from the unit it's in and then add it to the execution unit we want to move it to. So click on the **JOINER** in the **STAGE_MAP** execution unit and from the **Execution** main menu select **Remove Operator From Execution Unit**. That will cause the **JOINER** to be relocated outside the box for the **STAGE_MAP** execution unit. It is now no longer associated with any execution unit.

We now want to make it a part of the **SQL_SERVER_LOAD** execution unit, so make sure the **JOINER** is selected by clicking on it and also click on the **SQL_SERVER_ LOAD** execution unit by using the *Ctrl* key to select multiple objects, and then from the **Execution** main menu select **Add Operator to Execution Unit**. The **JOINER** will now appear inside the **SQL_SERVER_LOAD** execution unit box. We can rearrange the display in case objects are not displaying very well by clicking and dragging entire execution units or clicking and dragging individual operators inside execution units, which will resize the execution unit box accordingly. When neatened up, our Execution View should now look similar to the following:

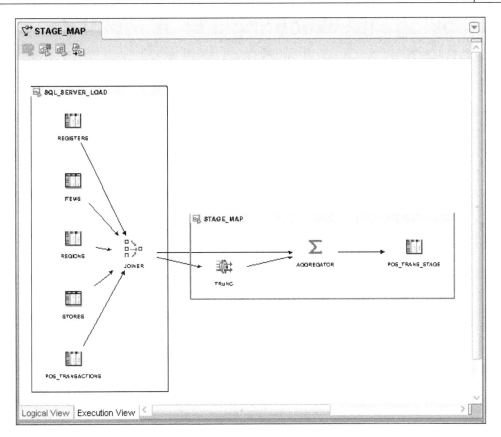

We can't move any more operators into the **SQL_SERVER_LOAD** execution unit because the next operator that we could move would be the **TRUNC** operator, representing the Oracle **TRUNC()** function on the date; however, **SQL Server Transact-SQL** (Microsoft's implementation of SQL) does not have a **TRUNC()** function. OWB 11*g*R2 has a heterogeneous transformation set defined in the **Globals Navigator** under **Public Transformations | Heterogeneous | Pre-Defined,** which has implementations per platform, which could be used here with no problem but we're going to stick with the Oracle specific function in this case.

That completes the configuration of our Execution View. Our code template mapping is now ready to deploy and execute. Let's save our work at this point and then continue to deploy and execute.

Deploying and executing a code template mapping

Now that we've completed building our code template mapping we're ready to deploy and execute it. The first step is to make sure our **Control Center Agent** process is running as we described earlier in the chapter. The process of deploying and executing a code template mapping is identical to the process for deploying and executing a regular mapping; however, the code template mapping will deploy to the **Control Center Agent**, not the **Control Center Service**.

To deploy, we'll right-click on the **STAGE_MAP** mapping under the **MAPPING_MODULE_1** module in **Template Mappings** and select **Deploy**. If this is not the first time we've deployed this mapping, we may see a popup like the following:

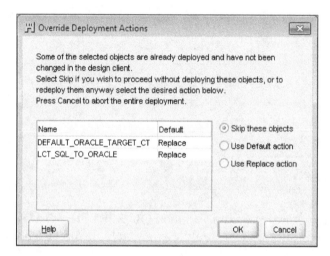

This will happen if some but not all objects have been deployed successfully previously and the Warehouse Builder will offer to skip them. We'll choose **Use Replace action** to force them to be deployed again and click the **OK** button if that dialog appears.

We'll then get the **Log** window popup showing us the progress of our deployment, which as with regular mappings will do a validate and generate first automatically and then deploy it. Our **Log** window should look like the following after a successful deployment:

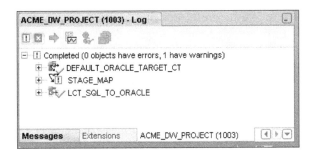

If we expand the **STAGE_MAP** entry we'll see some validation warnings, which can be safely ignored. If there is a red **X** appearing and a `CCA-1103` error ("Failed to check if CODETEMPLATE-xxxxx has been deployed") then the control center agent is most likely not running. Just go back and start it up and deploy again.

Now that we have the mapping deployed, it's time to execute it. We'll perform a similar process to deploying by right-clicking on the **STAGE_MAP** mapping under **MAPPING_MODULE_1** in **Template Mappings** and selecting **Start** from the pop-up menu this time.

The **Log** window will display the job steps as it executes each execution unit of the code template mapping. The steps it displays will depend upon the execution units and assigned code templates that were specified for the mapping. The final results should look similar to the following upon successful execution:

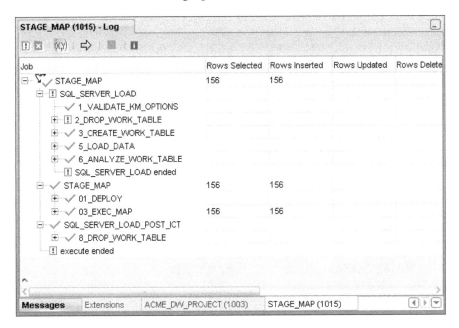

There are other columns of information in that log window to the right that will tell us how many errors and warnings there were in each step along with a start time and the elapsed time for each step.

We can see green check marks beside most of the steps, which is good. That is the signal that the step completed with no errors or warnings. However, there is one step, **DROP_WORK_TABLE** in the **SQL_SERVER_LOAD** execution unit, that has a yellow exclamation point appearing, meaning a warning was generated. If we expand that entry we can see there was an error generated under the JDBC step that the table or view does not exist. That is not a problem because this is just a temporary work table that the execution unit creates to perform its tasks, which it's going to recreate anyway, so it's not a problem if it doesn't exist to start with. In fact, we can see a step at the end that it added to drop the work table, which shows a green check mark. It's possible that the mapping may have had a fatal error during a previous execution that caused it not to drop the work table so this step is there just to make sure it starts with a clean slate.

We saw the record counts in the log window that showed it loaded the data successfully but if we want to see the data ourselves just to verify it we can use the Data Viewer by right-clicking on the **POS_TRANS_STAGE** table in the **Databases | Oracle | ACME_DWH | Tables** node and selecting **Data** from the popup. An error dialog may pop up warning that the connection failed and that the location is invalid and asking whether we want to edit the location details. Simply click **Yes** and the password can be set for the ACME_DWH_LOCATION location, which is usually the cause of that error. After entering the correct password on the Edit Oracle Database Location popup and clicking **OK**, we'll see the data that it has loaded as shown next in the Data Viewer window in the Design Center:

We have now completed implementing our first code template mapping. For connections to other databases, the native JDBC connection is much simpler to set up and can be done completely within OWB so code templates are definitely an excellent addition to the Warehouse Builder. With the default Oracle target code template and the ability to wrap existing OWB regular mappings, the power and utility of the Warehouse Builder has improved tremendously with this new release.

Summary

We have explored the 11gR2 code template technology that has been added to the Warehouse Builder in this chapter and have covered much of what we covered in earlier chapters for making connections to source databases, defining connections, importing data objects, defining mappings, and deploying and executing them all within the context of the new native JDBC connection capability and the code template feature added to OWB from ODI.

That is it. We have come to the end of our introductory journey through the Oracle Warehouse Builder. Hopefully, you have enjoyed it and will take what you've learned and put it to good use in the world of data warehousing with the Oracle Warehouse Builder.

Index

deduplication 186
default operating mode
  row-based 292
  row-based (target only) 292
  set-based 292
delete option, snapshots 337
de-normalized database structure 110
deployment order 315-318
design center
  deploying in 298-301
  object, generation 286, 287
  object, validating 281-283
Design Center Projects tab 55
Design Center screen
  about 54
  globals navigator 54, 55
  locations tab 54
  projects tab 54
Design Center search function 204
design center, Warehouse Builder
  about 51
  Connection details 52
  Databases node 54
  Design Center window 53
  locations tab 54
  Logon dialog box 52
  Logon screen 51
  Password 52
  projects tab 54
  Show Details >> button 52
  User Name 52
Design drop-down menu 56
dimensional design
  about 106
  cube and dimensions 107, 108
dimensional model
  implementing, in database 109
  multidimensional implementation (OLAP)
    112
  relational implementation (star schema)
    109-111
dimension operator 184
dimensions
  attributes 131
  characteristics 130
  creating 130
  identifying 113, 114

product dimension 141
store dimension 150
time dimension 130-132
dimensions, characteristics
  dimesnion attributes 130
  hierarchies 131
  level attributes 131
  levels 130
downloading
  Oracle software 11
DSN (Data Source Name) 66
Dynamic Host Configuration Protocol
    (DHCP) 14

E

Edit menu entry 56
editor window
  about 161
  attributes tab 162
  hierarchies tab 163
  levels tab 162
  name tab 161
  orphan tab 163
  SCD tab 163
  storage tab 162
effective date attribute 148
Entity-Relationship (ER) diagram 46
ETL (Extract, Transform, and Load)
  about 32, 167, 168
  manual processes 168
execution order 319
Exit button 27, 31
expiration date attribute 148
export option, snapshots 338
expression 186
Expression Builder 214
Expression operator
  mapping 272-274
external table 101
external table, lookup operator
  creating 245, 246
external table operator 184

F

fact table 110
Field Properties screen 104

uppercase, issues 237
UPPER() function 238
UPPER transformation 238
STORE_NAME field 271
STORE_NAME, STORE_NUMBER 234
STORE_REGION 234
structure view 176
structure window 202
SUBSTR transformation operator, lookup operator
adding 251-253
Surrogate Identifier 150
SYSDATE Oracle function 269
SYSDBA 33

T

table editor
about 86
attribute sets tab 200
data rules tab 200
indexes tab 199
keys tab 198, 199
partitions tab 199, 200
source metadata, defining manually 86-91
used, for building staging area table 194-197
table operator 184
tablespace 39
target module
creating 122, 124
target operator
adding 231-234
Target Schema 32
target table, mapping
adding 208
target user
creating 118-122
template mapping module
defining 374, 376, 377
template mappings
about 372
Test Connection button 59, 60
time dimension
about 107, 130, 131
creating, time dimension wizard used 132-140

time dimension wizard
used, for creating time dimension 132-140
TO_NUMBER transformation, lookup operator
adding 255
toolbar icon
in mapping editor, used for validating 283, 284, 285
transactional database 43, 48
transformation 55
transformation operators
about 234
adding 235, 236
NAME attribute 239
POS_TRANS_STAGE mapping table 240
POS_TRANS_STAGE mapping table operator 241
STORE dimension 237
STORE dimension operator 239
STORE_NUMBER attribute 241
TRIM() function 236
TRIM operator 239
TRIM output 242
UPPER() function 238, 241
UPPER transformation 238
VALUE output attribute 237
transformations (data flow operators)
about 186
aggregator 186
deduplication 186
expression 186
filter 187
joiner 187
lookup 187
pivot 187
set operation 188
splitter operator 188
transformation operator 188
triggering attributes 148
TRUNC() function 236

U

UML (Universal Modeling Language) notation 46
unique key constraint 198
UPPER operators 269

UPPER transformation 237
Use Above Values button 224
User Name 52

V

values, mapping to code attributes 269
varchar type 89
Vendors 48
Very Large Databases (VLDB) 200
view operator 184

W

Warehouse builder
  online resources 352
Warehouse Builder Enterprise ETL 38
Warehouse Builder ODBC module
  creating, for SQL server 73-78
website order management database 49, 50
Welcome screen 56
Workspace Management button 53
workstation
  versus server 14

Thank you for buying
Oracle Warehouse Builder 11gR2: Getting Started 2011

About Packt Publishing

Packt, pronounced 'packed', published its first book "Mastering phpMyAdmin for Effective MySQL Management" in April 2004 and subsequently continued to specialize in publishing highly focused books on specific technologies and solutions.

Our books and publications share the experiences of your fellow IT professionals in adapting and customizing today's systems, applications, and frameworks. Our solution based books give you the knowledge and power to customize the software and technologies you're using to get the job done. Packt books are more specific and less general than the IT books you have seen in the past. Our unique business model allows us to bring you more focused information, giving you more of what you need to know, and less of what you don't.

Packt is a modern, yet unique publishing company, which focuses on producing quality, cutting-edge books for communities of developers, administrators, and newbies alike. For more information, please visit our website: www.packtpub.com.

About Packt Enterprise

In 2010, Packt launched two new brands, Packt Enterprise and Packt Open Source, in order to continue its focus on specialization. This book is part of the Packt Enterprise brand, home to books published on enterprise software – software created by major vendors, including (but not limited to) IBM, Microsoft and Oracle, often for use in other corporations. Its titles will offer information relevant to a range of users of this software, including administrators, developers, architects, and end users.

Writing for Packt

We welcome all inquiries from people who are interested in authoring. Book proposals should be sent to author@packtpub.com. If your book idea is still at an early stage and you would like to discuss it first before writing a formal book proposal, contact us; one of our commissioning editors will get in touch with you.

We're not just looking for published authors; if you have strong technical skills but no writing experience, our experienced editors can help you develop a writing career, or simply get some additional reward for your expertise.

Oracle Database 11g—Underground
Advice for Database Administrators

Beyond the basics

A real-world DBA survival guide for Oracle 11g database
implementations

April C. Sims

PACKT

Oracle Database 11g – Underground Advice for Database Administrators

ISBN: 978-1-849680-00-4 Paperback: 348 pages

A real-world DBA survival guide for Oracle 11g
database implementations

1. A comprehensive handbook aimed at reducing
   the day-to-day struggle of Oracle 11g Database
   newcomers

2. Real-world reflections from an experienced
   DBA—what novice DBAs should really know

3. Implement Oracle's Maximum Availability
   Architecture with expert guidance

Oracle SQL Developer 2.1

Database design and development using this feature-rich,
powerful, user-extensible interface

Sue Harper

PACKT

Oracle SQL Developer 2.1

ISBN: 978-1-847196-26-2 Paperback: 496 pages

Database design and development using this feature-
rich, powerful user-extensible interface

1. Install, configure, customize, and manage your
   SQL Developer environment

2. Includes the latest features to enhance
   productivity and simplify database
   development

3. Covers reporting, testing, and debugging
   concepts

4. Meet the new powerful Data Modeling tool –
   Oracle SQL Developer Data Modeler

Please check **www.PacktPub.com** for information on our titles

Mastering Oracle Scheduler in Oracle 11g Databases

ISBN: 978-1-847195-98-2   Paperback: 240 pages

Schedule, manage, and execute jobs that automate your business processes

1. Automate jobs from within the Oracle database with the built-in Scheduler

2. Boost database performance by managing, monitoring, and controlling jobs more effectively

3. Contains easy-to-understand explanations, simple examples, debugging tips, and real-life scenarios

Oracle 10g/11g Data and Database Management Utilities

ISBN: 978-1-847196-28-6   Paperback: 432 pages

Master twelve must-use utilities to optimize the efficieny, management, and performance of your daily database tasks

1. Optimize time-consuming tasks efficiently using the Oracle database utilities

2. Perform data loads on the fly and replace the functionality of the old export and import utilities using Data Pump or SQL*Loader

3. Boost database defenses with Oracle Wallet Manager and Security

4. A handbook with lots of practical content with real-life scenarios

Please check **www.PacktPub.com** for information on our titles

CPSIA information can be obtained
at www.ICGtesting.com
Printed in the USA
LVHW101830110320
649747LV00005B/98